The
Secret
of
Chess

by Lyudmil Tsvetkov

The Secret of Chess

Table of Contents

In lieu of a foreword

This is a special book. You will not find many like this, or even a few ones. For the past 10 or so years, chess has changed tremendously, with the appearance of extremely strong chess programs, whose level is reputed to be way above that of the best humans. The existence of such programs, plus the availability of large knowledge databases allows us to look deeper into the game of chess. Gems of the past are now debunked, the widely acclaimed play of world champions like Capablanca, Alekhine, Kasparov and Carlsen appears to have lots of gaps, with a multitude of tactical mistakes throughout even their masterpieces.

Thus, we understand, there is something more to chess, something deeper, that should be investigated. On the other hand, chess computers do get improved on a regular scale, adding some 50 elo or so each and every year. This is yet another hint that we are still very far from perfection even with machines.

So, if machines play weak, and humans play weak, there should be certainly a lot of knowledge still undiscovered.

This books aims at doing precisely that: uncovering part of the secrets that still are not a general knowledge.

The book is split into 7 main chapters, covering material and major corrections to piece values, mobility, pawns, outposts, imbalances, king safety and general piece activity and coordination. Within these chapters, there are a lot of sub-sections allowing for better ordering of the text.

The book is provided with a table of contents and a complete alphabetical index of terms.

Each and every separate evaluation term is handled by giving its precise definition, an estimation of its relative value in centipawns, expanding on the properties of the term, and then finishing with establishing its frequency in game situations. In this way, it is easier to investigate the material.

One centipawn is one hundred of a full pawn. As very small terms, with values smaller than 10cps, are indeed very difficult to make sense, in the book I have included just terms with larger value than that one, though, there are also a few features with a bit lower value, just to spice things up.

When looking at the values of different terms one should bear 2 things in mind:
- those are just approximations, it is very difficult to come up with a precise number for each and every term, there are so many terms, so interdependent, and so prone to personal outlooks
- the values, although also having general significance, will be fully valid only within the current evaluation framework and its pool of existing features. In a different framework, with a smaller or larger pool of terms, the specific values might be different.

The values are split between mg and eg. We are following more or less the general accepted definition of the boundary between mg and eg, i.e. half of the available piece material, so called non-pawn material, taking account of the material of both sides. Any other approach, like using queen presence, etc., is much less relevant, obviously. So, middlegames will be positions with total available non-pawn material for both sides more than half of the starting non-pawn material, and endgames positions with non-pawn material lower than half of the starting material.

The centipawn estimation is, although seemingly a bit unusual, quite natural what concerns refined evaluation factors, especially in the age of computer chess. With the progress of computer chess, it is also believable, that our brain networks become more intricate too. If one centipawn is one hundredth of a full pawn, then 100cps will be equal to one pawn material, the winning or loss of a single pawn, 50cps will be the estimate of half a pawn material positional compensation, 25cps will be 1/4 of a pawn material positional compensation, and 10cps will be 1/10 of a full pawn.

As positional factors are so numerous and multi-faceted, it is only about natural that they have so different and refined scores. Not using such values will definitely miss quite a lot of the deeper essence of chess. Besides, on the chess board, one usually has tens of different evaluation factors worth multiple centipawns each, but less than a pawn, so adding all of those will certainly make more than a full pawn material compensation, something measurable by all means.

Positive terms will score positive values, in centipawns, while negative ones, negative values, again in centipawns, but with a minus sign before the estimate.

The general rule is that term definitions, more specifically the placement of pawns, are given from the point of view of white, but figuring out the respective black condition is very easy, bearing in mind that the chess board is vertically symmetrical, so white's 1st rank is black's 8th, white's 2nd rank is black's 7th, white's 3rd rank is black's 6th, white's 4th rank is black's 5th, white's 5th rank is black's 4th, white's 6th rank is black's 3rd, white's 7th rank is black's 2nd, and white's 8th rank is black's 1st. In this way, a white pawn or piece on e4 will be tantamount to a black pawn or piece on e5, a white pawn or piece on e6 will be tantamount to a black pawn or piece on e3, a white pawn or piece on a1 to a black pawn or piece on a8, and a white pawn or piece on g7 to a black pawn or piece on g2. Psqt tables are white-side only, with conversion following the same rules.

The book is based on pattern recognition, rather than vaguer reflections on the quality of certain chess positions. My claim would be that, by using pattern recognition, it is possible to learn the basics of chess, as well as perfectionise, at least 4 times faster. And this is not an overstatement, in no way. Remembering, even by heart, if necessary, some 1000 or so main evaluation features, is undoubtedly the much more preferable way to go than following the advice of an innumerable quantity of chess handbooks and masters. Without pattern recognition, in spite of all the invested hard work at playing and investigating different games, knowledge will more or less remain blurred, so less efficiently used in practice. When patterns are recognised, you might not need to play that many games and still be able to immediately see the properties of a position, indicating at the right move to make. Of course, there are no magical solutions to improving one's chess, no one would believe in a method preaching learning chess in a week or so, a lot of games should be played and positions analysed in order for a person to significantly improve one's tactical abilities, tactics is not perfectionised in a short time, but still, one can definitely significantly shorten one's way to the top by learning to recognise patterns.

Every chess position is basically a set of evaluation patterns. The best move is always available at the current ply, it is really not necessary to go deeper, doing any substantial search, all one has to do is to recognise all the relevant evaluation patterns making up a specific chess position. When you add up all available evaluation patterns, you should be able to come up with the solution what the best move is. Of course, in order to efficiently and flawlessly do that, one should be able to recognise all the subtleties of a position, and subtleties are hidden in the larger pool of non-standard, non-generally-recognised evaluation terms.

Someone might laugh at a range of terms I have enumerated, considering them as non-existing and the product of my ill imagination, but all of you would be surprised, if you knew how even the smallest of evaluation terms, worth some couple of centipawns or so, is capable of influencing the game. One more mobility square, added to one more square attacked of the enemy king shelter, and one more subtle pawn feature most persons would neglect already makes quite a lot and changes the course of the game as a whole.

In the book, there are over 500 diagrams and around 100 tables.

Concerning the diagrams, please bear in mind, that those are not simple fens, so do not check them with engines, they do not even have side to move. Rather, they are supposed to serve as an illustration accompanying specific features. Their purpose is just that: to illustrate the term.

What concerns psqt tables, well, those are meant just as indicative values, it is very difficult to have, of course, fully precise measurement of all 64 squares of a particular term, so take them with a grain of salt. Still, their usefulness is beyond any doubt, as an ad-hoc blanket value would be the much worse guess, sometimes even completely unrealistic and detrimental.

The target audience of the book are 4 categories of people:
- weak chess players
- intermediate chess players
- strong chess players
- chess engine programmers

Well, of course, weak chess players will be helped most, when following the approach of pattern recognition. In that way, they can cover couple of times faster the material they would otherwise take years to fully grasp and memorise. Memorising some 1000 feature patterns is definitely a lot less work than memorising many thousands of typical tactical positions and

positional approaches, not to mention the opening preparation.

Of course, one might do without any opening preparation at all, by just learning the successful opening feature patterns. That saves time, saves memorising a lot of theoretical stuff, but more importantly, lays a very sound theoretical opening foundation irrespective of the changing opening vogue, as the best opening moves are always one and the same, following the same patterns, and those will concentrate on just a few openings.

For the very same reasons, chess players of intermediate strength will find this book interesting. Although they are already supposed to know quite some stuff, no doubt these pages will still offer some useful additions to their knowledge, in the form of patterns they have never read about anywhere else.

I would be very much flattered, if some of the stronger players pay some modest attention to this handbook, too. Their first thought might be to totally dismiss a work of a relatively insignificant player with no track record at all, but here is where they might possibly be wrong. Because, on the pages of this work, there are terms and patterns I have never encountered in any other textbook previously. And the number of those is far from being negligeable. So, I would be very happy for a quick browse and possible massive criticism.

Chess programmers will also find these pages useful, as within there are terms no one has ever published before. Psqt tables will also come in quite handy, as engines are very much accustomed to those. If anything, my approach is to only further stress the importance and ubiquity of psqt tables. The wider they are used, the better, but of course, the tuning challenge will be enormous. I very much hope, that this handbook will contribute to the future development of a range of chess engines, and with this, to the advancement of the overall cause of chess, as chess enthusiasts all over the world will be using the very same engines the programmers prepare for daily game play and analysis.

This book is the product of 5 years of almost incessant concentration on chess. Whenever possible, I have been playing and investigating chess for 12 hours daily and more. Playing chess games with Stockfish and Komodo. Browsing Stockfish and Komodo games, investigating different databases. Then, playing more games with Stockfish and Komodo, and browsing and analysing more and more of their games. Of course, I have also looked at least twice at most of the chess collections of all world champions. Without knowing the past, one can not concentrate on the future, of course.

My chess rating, 2100+ FIDE elo, 2200+ Bulgarian rating(Bulgarian candidate master since 1998), is indeed very negligeable to suppose a person with such a strength to be able to write a book about chess, but the truth is, that it dates back 12 years. For almost 12 complete years, I have not been playing chess officially, so my rating stayed as it is, low, however, my actual strength has increased at least 4-fold. It is only after I finished playing tournament chess that much stronger engines, allowing to better train your skills, appeared, and in the last 5 or so years, engine strength reached its peak. So, I trained a lot my chess during the time I was an inactive player, and, in the last 5 years, I almost entirely devoted my time to chess. It is possible that I am a very strong chess player indeed, but currently, my abilities still have not been measured in any official way.

Since the appearance of the Stockfish framework, I have contributed a lot with ideas to it. At least 20 evaluation patches, based on my ideas, have been integrated in Stockfish code, and a lot more have been

useful in generating food for thought for alternative implementations.

July 2017

Basic definitions and abbreviations

Basic definitions

open file file with no own and enemy pawns on it

semi-open file (possible just from the perspective of a specific side) file with no own pawns and one enemy pawn on it

closed file file with one own and one enemy pawn on it

semi-closed file (possible just from the perspective of a particular side) file with one own pawn and no enemy pawns on it; the reverse of a semi-open file

blocked file closed file with the own and enemy pawns blocked

opposed pawn pawn that has an enemy pawn on the same file

unopposed pawn pawn with no enemy pawns on the same file

centipawn an evaluation measurement unit, one hundredth of a pawn

piece square table a table with values for the 64 board squares, sometimes just some of them, for particular evaluation features. Such tables are extremely useful and productive, as just about any chess term could be beneficially assigned different values for all 64 squares. This would actually be the right scientific approach, but I understand the problems of engine developers, having to tune their numbers, and also those of humans, who would need to memorise some dozen-fold stuff. Memorisation is not necessary, however, as most tables follow more or less a similar approach, with bigger bonuses for more advanced ranks, as well as more central files, for the strong features, and bigger penalties for less advanced ranks and more central files, for the weak features. This is not true in all cases, there are idyosyncracies, but the basic rule should hold.

psqtise assign psqt values for a specific term

Abbreviations

cp centipawn
cps centipawns
mg middlegame
eg endgame
psqt piece square table

20

Chapter I

Material and major corrections of piece values

The piece values

Well, the piece values are certainly the single most important evaluation feature on the chess board. Without having material piece values, it is difficult to evaluate anything at all, as they constitute a very large portion of overall evaluation assessment. Of course, when you lose your queen, the game is more or less over, but losing even a single pawn without proper compensation is also completely disastrous with perfect play. So, having correct piece values is quite essential to good play of chess engines, as well as to satisfactory human assessment of each and every chess position.

In the course of time, different handbooks have given different assessments of the values of the pieces, which more or less agree in the general terms, while sometimes disagreeing on the details. Mine assessment will not be very much different from previous ones, though I will have my points of emphasis too. First of all, one should mention, that all piece values within any framework are necessarily completely dependent on the rest of the evaluation factors in the framework, before all those concerning imbalances, various additional corrections of the values based on the presence of specific board conditions, etc. Thus, when one looks at the concrete numbers for the specific pieces, one should also look at those additional correcting factors.

Within my evaluation framework, the different pieces have the following mg and eg values(kings are excluded from the equation, as kings are uncapturable and do not have a specific value, as everyone knows):

pawn: 95cps in the mg, 105cps in the eg

knight: 310cps in the mg, 300cps in the eg

bishop: 320cps in the mg, 330cps in the eg

rook: 460cps in the mg, 490cps in the eg

queen: 900cps in the mg, 950cps in the eg

General remarks concerning the piece values

pawn: in distinction to what most authors of top chess engines believe, my understanding is that the value of the pawn is almost the same for the mg and eg, with the eg value being a bit higher, as in the eg the presence of passed pawns increases the probability of promotion with material increment. Giving a much bigger number for the eg is wrong, according to me, as the side with less pawns will usually have more pieces, and having a greater number of pieces is the better choice in the mg and eg alike.

knight: well, the knight is the second-weakest piece after the pawn, and the weakest non-pawn piece. The general rule is that the knight value is bigger in the mg and lower in the eg, as the knight is a much slower piece than the bishop or rook, for example, and its slowness is hidden in the mg by the presence of more pawns that will deter in their movements also the rest of the pieces, but quite evident in the eg. In the present evaluation framework, however, the availability of additional correcting factors, like the distinction between a bishop and a knight with pawns on both wings of the board, renders the difference between the mg and eg numbers quite small.

bishop: it is a general misconception, frequently repeated in various handbooks, that the values of the bishop and knight are almost equal. Of course, this is not the case at all. There is a, quite substantial, distinction between the strength of the bishop and that of the knight. In fact, the bishop is a much stronger piece, both in the mg and eg. Although in the mg the values are close, the bishop always remains stronger, as otherwise not keeping one's bishop in the mg will also result in not having it in the eg. The difference in strength increases in the eg, where the bishop moves around much faster.

rook: in my understanding, the rook value measures around one and a half times the average value of the 2 minor pieces. The basic rule is that the rook value increases measurably in the eg, on a par with its increased mobility. In the mg, the rook movements are thwarted by the presence of more pawns.

queen: here again, I will agree with most writers, that the queen value roughly equals 2 rooks. Most recognisable queen value rule is that the queen value gets significantly higher in the eg, where its movements are freer in comparison to earlier stages of the game. Different imbalances significantly correct the ad-hoc value.

Note: please, bear in mind, that above-cited piece values are only meant as a general assessment rule for human consumption. What concerns engines, the above values, in significant agreement with numbers found by a range of leading engines through exhaustive testing, should be adjusted accordingly, basically meaning that, due to the presence within any elaborated evaluation framework of a whole lot of particular pawn and minor piece features, the values of the minor pieces should be increased by some 30% over the above-cited ad-hoc values, while those of the major pieces by some 50%.

Piece square tables

Piece square tables(psqt), as widely implemented in most chess engines, and mentally used to much benefit by all strong chess players, represent the most obvious and significant correction of the plain piece values, based on the easy-to-make observation that the relative strength of each and every piece changes depending on the specific square that piece resides on.

The self-evident chess knowledge principles mirrored in the particular psqts largely reflect 3 basic and very valid observations:
- pieces in general do gain in value closer to the center of the board
- pieces in general do gain in value on more advanced ranks
- concerning only the king, kings do gain value closer to the edges of the board on less advanced ranks in the mg, and do gain in value, quite the opposite, in the center and on more advanced ranks in the eg

Below we will take a brief look at the separate psqts.

king psqt: as said, the king gains value closer to the edges of the board, especially the 2 corners, on less advanced ranks, in the mg, and gains value in the center of the board and on more advanced ranks in the eg. The reason for this is simple:
- king should be kept in the edges and corners on lower ranks in the mg, as there enemy pieces' attacks are significantly less frequent than in the center and on higher ranks, already in the lion's den
- king should go towards the center of the board and on higher ranks in the eg, as in the eg enemy piece attacks are significantly less dangerous, due to the smaller number of pieces, while the king itself is able to provide assistance to own passers in their march to promotion, successfully attack enemy pawns, restrict the enemy king activity, as well as quickly switch from one side of the board to

another on such squares, which is important, especially for such a very-slow-moving piece, as the king

As both above-mentioned reasons are very weighty, the king psqt values should be very significant too.

8	-170	-180	-190	-200	-200	-190	-180	-170
7	-130	-140	-150	-170	-170	-150	-140	-130
6	-120	-130	-140	-150	-150	-140	-130	-120
5	-80	-90	-100	-120	-120	-100	-90	-80
4	-30	-40	-60	-80	-80	-60	-40	-30
3	30	10	0	-20	-20	0	10	30
2	90	100	70	50	50	70	100	90
1	100	120	80	60	60	80	120	100
	a	b	c	d	e	f	g	h

king psqt(mg)

8	0	10	20	30	30	20	10	0
7	20	40	60	80	80	60	40	20
6	40	60	90	100	100	90	60	40
5	20	40	60	80	80	60	40	20
4	-20	20	50	70	70	50	20	-20
3	-35	0	20	40	40	20	0	-35
2	-40	-30	-10	0	0	-10	-30	-40
1	-50	-40	-30	-20	-20	-30	-40	-50
	a	b	c	d	e	f	g	h

king psqt(eg)

pawn psqt: pawn psqt is essential, though it is to be remarked that pawn psqt is probably the most unreliable table one can find out there, as it is dependent on the factoring in of so many other possible pawn features, that should also ideally have their psqts, that its numbers get to a big extent a matter of pure convention. One should never look at the pawn psqt table without also looking at the rest of the available pawn features within a particular evaluation framework.

Main rule of thumb is that central files and advanced ranks are bonised, but go figuring out the precise values, even with the help of a computer, given that an advanced pawn on e5, for example, can simultaneously be a storming pawn, a passed pawn, a defended pawn, an undefended pawn, an isolated pawn, etc., etc., etc. Similarly, a g2 pawn, for example, can also be most of the above, plus a valuable king shelter pawn.

8	0	0	0	0	0	0	0	0
7	0	0	0	0	0	0	0	0
6	25	35	45	55	55	45	35	25
5	17	25	33	50	50	33	25	17
4	13	17	30	45	45	30	17	13
3	7	10	13	20	20	13	10	7
2	5	7	10	13	13	10	7	5
1	0	0	0	0	0	0	0	0
	a	b	c	d	e	f	g	h

pawn psqt(mg)

8	0	0	0	0	0	0	0	0
7	0	0	0	0	0	0	0	0
6	35	45	55	65	65	55	45	35
5	25	33	42	60	60	42	33	25
4	20	25	40	55	55	40	25	20
3	10	15	20	30	30	20	15	10
2	7	10	15	20	20	15	10	7
1	0	0	0	0	0	0	0	0
	a	b	c	d	e	f	g	h

pawn psqt(eg)

knight psqt: knight psqt is doubtless the second most important psqt after king psqt. Reason for this is that the knight is a slow-moving piece, it takes time to go from one square to another, so the particular square the knight currently resides upon takes much greater significance. Hence, the values for the knight psqt should necessarily be quite big.

Main knight psqt features:

- it is extremely important for the knight to take the central squares of the board, much more so than for any other non-king and non-pawn piece
- taking edge squares, and especially corner squares, is extremely detrimental, as the slow-mover will need quite some moves until it reaches a better position
- taking advanced ranks is always a good choice, as it takes time to go there, and a

retreat will only partially worsen the present knight condition

An important remark is that knight psqt is redundant too, at least to knight outpost features, so one must very carefully check both feature numbers.

8	10	20	30	40	40	30	20	10
7	20	30	40	50	50	40	30	20
6	27	55	68	80	80	68	55	27
5	20	30	40	50	50	40	30	20
4	7	20	35	40	40	35	20	7
3	-7	7	20	27	27	20	7	-7
2	-13	-7	0	7	7	0	-7	-13
1	-30	-20	-13	-7	-7	-13	-20	-30
	a	b	c	d	e	f	g	h

knight psqt(mg)

8	-10	0	10	20	20	10	0	-10
7	10	18	25	33	33	25	18	10
6	27	55	100	120	120	100	55	27
5	20	30	60	70	70	60	30	20
4	10	30	50	60	60	50	30	10
3	-10	10	30	40	40	30	10	-10
2	-20	-10	0	10	10	0	-10	-20
1	-40	-30	-20	-10	-10	-20	-30	-40
	a	b	c	d	e	f	g	h

knight psqt(eg)

bishop psqt: bishop psqt is less important than knight psqt, but still an important one. The rules for assigning values for particular squares pretty much follow those for the knight, with the major distinction being that the bishop feels less awkward on edge files and ranks, because it can leave them much quicker than the knight, and besides, while being a sliding, long-range piece, the bishop is able to exert considerable pressure, attack particular squares on the board, the enemy king shelter, etc., even from squares far removed from the focal point. So, for example, a white bishop on c1, while sticking to its home edge square, can very successfully attack the h6 square of the black king shelter. Still, central and more advanced squares are preferable for the bishop too.

Bishop psqt is also redundant, at least to some bishop outpost features.

8	-10	-5	0	5	5	0	-5	-10
7	0	20	25	30	30	25	20	0
6	25	28	45	55	55	45	28	25
5	20	30	40	50	50	40	30	20
4	7	20	25	40	40	25	20	7
3	0	13	20	25	25	20	13	0
2	-7	0	7	13	13	7	0	-7
1	-13	-7	0	7	7	0	-7	-13
	a	b	c	d	e	f	g	h

bishop psqt(mg)

8	-15	-10	-5	0	0	-5	-10	-15
7	0	13	17	22	22	17	13	0
6	25	28	70	80	80	70	28	25
5	20	30	60	70	70	60	30	20
4	10	30	40	60	60	40	30	10
3	0	20	30	40	40	30	20	0
2	-10	0	10	20	20	10	0	-10
1	-20	-10	0	10	10	0	-10	-20
	a	b	c	d	e	f	g	h

bishop psqt(eg)

rook psqt: rook psqt is far less important than psqts for the minor pieces, reason being the fast-moving nature of the rook, which makes the current square, occupied by the rook, far less significant. Another reason is that rooks are much easier to evict from a particular square than minors, by pawn and minor threats alike, relativising thus residence.

Main rules:

- central files are important, it is easier to move around from the center, but this is further associated with attacks upon enemy objects in the center, as well as the center itself

- more advanced ranks are important, but only relatively, under a lot of caveats, as on more advanced ranks the enemy pieces usually have better control; on more advanced ranks the rooks can swing from

one wing of the board to the other to take aim at enemy objects, which is rarely possible on the 1st and 2nd ranks, with the presence of lots of own pawns
- the 7th rank is particularly important, as the rook is able to attack from there many enemy pawns, residing on their home rank, the enemy king shelter and, in the eg and mg alike, on occasion restrict the enemy king to its back rank

Rook psqt is redundant with different rook attacking features, possible rook outposts, etc.

8	5	15	35	45	45	35	15	5
7	25	35	40	50	50	40	35	25
6	5	15	35	45	45	35	15	5
5	0	10	30	40	40	30	10	0
4	-5	5	25	35	35	25	5	-5
3	-10	0	20	30	30	20	0	-10
2	-15	-5	15	25	25	15	-5	-15
1	-20	-10	10	20	20	10	-10	-20
	a	b	c	d	e	f	g	h

rook psqt(mg)

8	3	10	22	27	27	22	10	3
7	17	22	25	30	30	25	22	17
6	3	10	22	27	27	22	10	3
5	0	7	20	25	25	20	7	0
4	-3	3	17	22	22	17	3	-3
3	-7	0	13	20	20	13	0	-7
2	-10	-3	10	17	17	10	-3	-10
1	-13	-7	7	13	13	7	-7	-13
	a	b	c	d	e	f	g	h

rook psqt(eg)

queen psqt: queen psqt is the least significant psqt. Reason: queen is able to move around very fast, attack enemy objects from afar, which pretty much relativises its place on the board, but also for the fact that on more advanced squares, as well in the center, the queen is easier to evict by practically all enemy non-queen pieces than any other piece.

For queen psqt, occupying central squares is justified, as from there the queen is able

to more or less control all the board, though on such squares enemy attacks are also more likely. Whether the 7th rank, possibly other, non-central files, are bonised, will depend pretty much on other existing evaluation factors, as enemy king shelter attacks, queen on open/semi-open file bonus, the particular queen mobility definition, etc.

8	0	0	0	0	0	0	0	0
7	0	0	0	0	0	0	0	0
6	0	0	13	20	20	13	0	0
5	0	0	20	25	25	20	0	0
4	0	0	20	25	25	20	0	0
3	0	0	13	20	20	13	0	0
2	0	0	0	0	0	0	0	0
1	0	0	0	0	0	0	0	0
	a	b	c	d	e	f	g	h

queen psqt(mg)

8	0	0	0	0	0	0	0	0
7	0	0	0	0	0	0	0	0
6	0	0	20	30	30	20	0	0
5	0	0	30	40	40	30	0	0
4	0	0	30	40	40	30	0	0
3	0	0	20	30	30	20	0	0
2	0	0	0	0	0	0	0	0
1	0	0	0	0	0	0	0	0
	a	b	c	d	e	f	g	h

queen psqt(eg)

Pawns on squares the colour of the own bishop

Definition: any pawn placed on a square the colour of an existing own bishop

Note: the term will be considered even when one side has more than one bishop

Value: penalty, -8cps in the mg, -15cps in the eg, for any such pawn

Additional information: this is one of the most valid chess terms. The penalty is obviously due for a variety of reasons:

- with own pawns on squares the colour of the bishop, the chance that enemy pawns are on squares of opposite colour, not the colour of the bishop, increases, meaning that the enemy, whether it has bishop or knight for the imbalance, will be able to effectively target and attack those pawns, while the own bishop itself will not be able to do so

- as there is nothing to potentially compensate for the above-mentioned severe condition, it will usually be long-term and acquire much more positional outlines

- having a single non-compensatable liability will certainly render more awkward the rest of the own forces, while boost the performance of enemy forces, for the simple fact that such pawns should be defended somehow

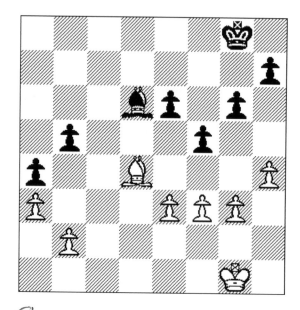

 almost all white pawns are on squares the colour of the own bishop, except for the f3 pawn. In this way, the g3 pawn is already directly attacked, while the h4,e3,a3 and b2 pawns potentially attackable.
None of the black pawns are on squares the colour of the d6 black bishop, so not directly attacked or potentially attackable by the opponent bishop.
Above condition will also tie other white pieces to the defence of the pawns, and naturally give more freedom to the rest of the black army.

The eg penalties are much bigger for the simple fact that, with decreasing board material, the weakness will severely grow, as other factors, giving variety to the game, will start disappearing, and the attackable pawns become more salient.

Frequency: very frequent

Specific conditions amplifying or changing the weakness

Those are plentiful and very important.

Blocked pawns on squares the colour of the bishop

Definition: pawns, blocked by enemy pawns on squares the colour of the bishop

Value: additional penalty, -10cps, both for the mg and eg

Additional information: the over-penalty is due because:
- the condition of being blocked makes the pawns fixed targets, unable to move; fixed targets are easier to attack and destroy
- blocked in general represents a more durable condition, further highlighting the weakness

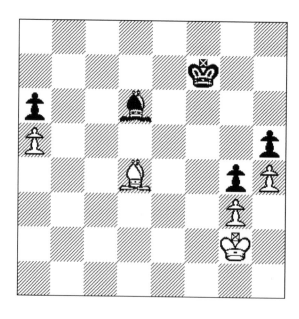

with only weakness being the presence of own blocked pawns on squares the colour of the bishop, white feels very awkward and black has big, winning advantage.

Thus, a single factor turns the game around.

Frequency: very frequent

Central and semi-central blocked pawns on squares the colour of the bishop

Definition: pawns on files c through f on ranks 3 through 5 that are blocked by enemy pawns on squares the colour of the own bishop

Value: additional penalties, specific for the different squares:

d4 or e4 square: -20cps, both for the mg and eg

d5 or e5 square: -10cps, both for the mg and eg

c4 or f4 square: -8cps, both for the mg and eg

c5 or f5 square: -5cps, both for the mg and eg

d3 or e3 square: -6cps, both for the mg and eg

c3 or f3 square: -3cps, both for the mg and eg

Additional information: the more central the blocked pawn is, the higher the over-penalty, because:
- a more central pawn will have bigger influence on events on different parts of the board
- a more central pawn is an easier target, more open to attacks
- critically, on a range of occasions, the more centrally-placed pawn will largely paralyse the movements of the own bishop, as most of the traffic naturally goes through the center, and compromise the activity of other friendly pieces

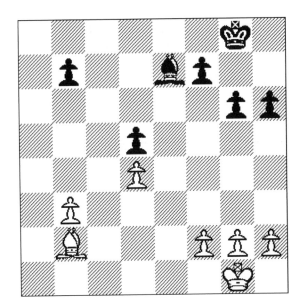

because of the central blocked d4 pawn, the white dark-square bishop has almost nowhere to go. His black counterpart, on the other hand, enjoys excellent activity.

less central blocked pawns are way less negative, but also represent a significant liability. The d5 and c4 blocked white pawns render the white light-square bishop extremely awkward.

Frequency: frequent

27

Central d4/e4 isolated pawn, blocked by an enemy minor outpost

Definition: central d4 or e4 pawn, that is isolated and blocked by an enemy minor piece outpost, knight or bishop, on square the colour of the own bishop

Value: additional penalty, -15cps, both for the mg and eg

Additional information: the over-penalty is due because:
- this very much simulates the condition of a blocked central d4/e4 pawn, reining in the own bishop's activity
- the pawn is still fixed and easier target
- the enemy minor piece outpost will be excellently placed, combining a range of functions
- finally, the blocker itself is not static, which allows for other enemy pieces to take its place, simultaneously blocking and attacking the pawn

d3/e3 twice backward pawn on square the colour of the bishop

Definition: twice backward pawn on d3 or e3, whether opposed or unopposed one, on square the colour of the bishop

Value: additional penalty, -12cps, both for the mg and eg

Additional information: the over-penalty is due because:
- this will severely paralyse the own bishop, with the twice backward pawn taking a very central place
- as the twice backward pawn will presume the presence of 2 other own pawns, blocked on same colour squares, central at that, the negative effect will spread over the entire board, often deactivating additional own pieces apart from the bishop

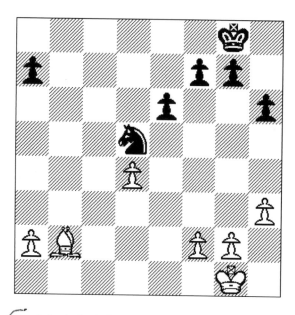

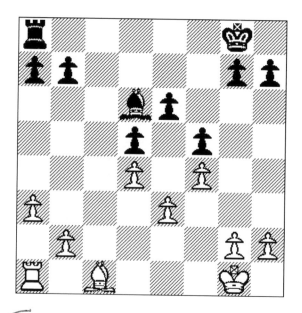

the black knight on d5 effectively blocks the white d4 pawn on square the colour of the white dark-square bishop. The white bishop has severe movement restrictions, looking pitiful, the d4 pawn is immobile and, additionally, the place of the knight can be taken successfully, after a walk to the center, by the black king, which will start attacking the pawn.

as easily seen, the white e3 twice backward pawn, blocked on square the colour of the bishop, represents a major liability. Apart from very successfully simulating blocked condition, full immobilisation, it also reins in not only the white dark-square bishop, but the rook on a1 too.

Frequency: infrequent

Special rule for the imbalance knight vs bishop

Definition: one side having just a single knight, and the other just a single bishop

Value: additional penalty, -7cps, both for the mg and eg, for each pawn, blocked by an enemy pawn on square the colour of the bishop

Additional information: this represents a very peculiar case.
The over-penalty is due because:
- in distinction to an own bishop, the knight will also be able to attack enemy pawns on squares of both colours
- the knight itself, when placed on squares opposite the colour of the enemy bishop, will remain invulnerable
- the possibility of exchanging bishop and getting rid of the weakness is much lower, as this could happen only on squares the colour of the bishop, and, as a general rule, statistically it is more difficult to trade pieces of different power
- occasionally, the knight could become a good blocker of enemy pawns, highlighting their weakness

well, this is a much more severe condition than otherwise. Black will be able to win the game with far less effort than if it had a dark-square bishop instead of the knight.

Frequency: infrequent

Special rule with bishop on more advanced ranks

Definition: bishop on ranks 5 through 8 in the enemy half of the board

Value: in case the bishop is on ranks 5 through 8 in the enemy half of the board, all associated penalties for the presence of own pawns on squares the colour of the bishop will be considered in half.
The rule will be valid just for the mg.

Additional information: the halving of the penalties is due to the fact that an advanced bishop will:
- either frequently be easier to exchange, so the penalties will become irrelevant
- or, sufficiently well-placed, maybe outposted or even attacking the enemy king shelter, so that the own pawns on same colour will mostly influence its play in no way at all

Still, some penalisation should remain, as returning to less advanced ranks within the limits of the larger structures of own pawns is a possibility to be reckoned with under specific circumstances.

what should the g5 bishop be penalised for, when it is easy to exchange it?

or, the nicely posted bishop on h6, attacking the black king shelter? The pawns on same colour have almost no influence on its play.

This condition is a bit difficult to understand for engines, which frequently underestimate it.

The eg penalty should remain in full force, due to the fact that endgame exchanges are far less common, bishops would rarely be gorgeously placed on advanced ranks in the eg, and besides, crossing the entire board, spanning own and enemy halves, is

the rule, rather than exception, in that stage of the game.

Frequency: frequent

Knight with blocked pawns

Definition: bonus for each knight for the number of blocked pawns on the board

the knight will get bonus for the a5,c6,e4,f5 and h4 blocked pawns

Value: bonus, equal for mg and eg, specific for the different files in terms of centralisation:

central e or d files: 10cps
semi-central f or c files: 7cps
g or b files: 4cps
h or a edge files: 2cps

Additional information: the bonus is due for the better relative performance of knights in positions with blocked pawns. Positions with blocked pawns are actually closed positions, contrary to the belief that closed positions are positions with large number of pawns, no matter their essence, present.

A position starts being closed, only when a bigger number of pawns get blocked by enemy pawns. Until that time, regardless of the quantity of pawns, a position is still not a closed one.

this one is not a closed one, although all pawns are present. It might be closed later though.

that one, quite the contrary, is already closed. Pawns blocking each other ensure closedness.

Knights perform better relative to, for example, bishops, as that will be the most common imbalance, for the simple reason that bishops, as sliding, long-range pieces, accustomed to quickly moving around the entire board with single long moves, will be severely thwarted by the closed condition of more blocked pawns present, so that knights will gain in value relatively to them.

It is not that much that the knights get stronger, rather that the bishops get weaker.

For the closedness of the position, central blocked pawns play a bigger role, of course, and that is why they get the larger bonus.

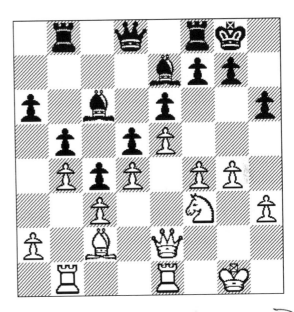

knights feel much more comfortable with larger number of blocked pawns present, especially central ones. As easily seen above, both black bishops feel very awkward, stopped in their movements by own and enemy pawns alike. The bishop on c6 is stopped by the own d5 and b5 blocked pawns, so it can move only on less advanced ranks. His counterpart on e7 is completely stopped by the enemy blocked pawns on b4,d4,e5, plus the pawn on f4. The white bishop is also stopped in its movements by the enemy blocked pawns on b5,c4,d5 and e6. That is certainly not true for the white knight on f3, though. Although it can not currently do a very useful job, with own d4 and e5 blocked pawns in its way, it can slow-jump its way around to a better position, after for example, Nf3-d2-f1-g3-h5. That manoeuvre takes time, but is certainly doable. It is very difficult for the bishops, on the other hand, to improve, so that for them that is more or less a permanent condition.

That is why knights always prefer positions of a more closed nature.

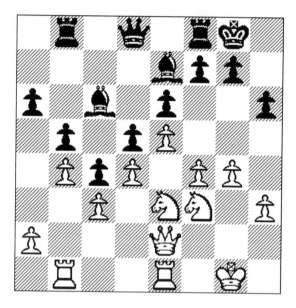

with more knights present, of course, both of them will get the bonus

Frequency: frequent

Bishop vs knight with pawns on both wings

Definition: one side having exactly one bishop, and the other side exactly one knight, with the bishop side having at least one pawn on the queen wing, a or b files, and at least one pawn on the king wing, h or g files, and no either own or enemy pawns present on central e and d files

well, we have this condition now: no pawns on the central e and d files, at least one white pawn on the queen wing, and at least one white pawn on the king wing

Value: bonus, 30cps in the mg, 50cps in the eg

Additional information: The bonus is due for the obvious reason the bishop will be able to perform better than the knight with play on both wings of the board and no central pawns thwarting its movements.

More specifically, the bonus is dispensed because:

- the bishop takes just one move to go from one flank to the other, the knight in comparison will need 2 or 3 for the same feat
- the bishop is able to simultaneously attack enemy pawns on one wing, and defend own pawns on the other, something the knight certainly can not do
- with passed pawns present, the bishop will be able to simultaneously support the advance of the own passers on one wing, and stop the advance of enemy passers on the other wing, by just taking, for example, a comfortable long diagonal; such tasks are far from feasible for the slow-moving knight

Chapter II

Mobility

the white bishop simultaneously attacks the enemy b6 pawn and defends the friendly g3 one, ensuring white big advantage.
The black knight can do nothing similar.

the white bishop on c6 simultaneously supports the advance of the friendly passer on a5 and stops the advance of the enemy passer on g3.
The slow-moving black knight can only do one task at a time.

The eg bonus is much larger, as in the eg the bishop movements are likely to be less burdensome because of the lower number of pawns.

Mobility is one of the most important evaluation elements in chess. Actually, the power of the different pieces themselves is derived from their mobility on an empty board. On a non-empty board, mobility will define the real power of chess pieces within the existing specific circumstances. Sometimes, high mobility pieces of lower power may prove stronger than low mobility pieces of higher power. A low mobility queen might be weaker than even a well-placed, high mobility knight or bishop.

Mobility is equally important for all pieces, but different pieces have separate mobility definitions, as well as mobility values. The lower the power of the piece, the less squares usually it has access to and consequently the more important their relative value is. Thus, the knight enjoys biggest mobility numbers, followed by the bishop, rook and queen.

King and pawn mobility stand apart and will be discussed separately.

Within our framework, accessible mobile squares will be psqtised for the entire board. I guess this is necessary to do, as different squares of the board have different importance for each specific piece. For example, the knight will strive towards the center of the board and advanced ranks, where it could be outposted, same more or less goes true for the bishop, the rook will find central files and advanced ranks, the 7th rank, etc. more suitable, while the queen will prefer the center of the board, as well as more advanced ranks.

Knight mobility

Definition: any empty square on the board that is not attacked by an enemy pawn, plus any board square occupied by an enemy piece or pawn which are not defended by another enemy pawn or piece, plus any board square occupied by an enemy bishop, rook or queen, which are defended by an enemy pawn or piece

c2,e2,f3 and e6 are mobile squares for the knight, as they are empty and not attacked by an enemy pawn. c6 is also a mobile square, as it is taken by an enemy pawn which is not defended by any enemy pawn or piece. f5 is a mobile square, too, as, although it is attacked by an enemy pawn, it is taken by an enemy rook. b3, on the other hand, is not a mobile square for the knight, as it is attacked by the a4 enemy pawn.

Value: bonus, valid in terms of psqt

8	12	13	14	15	15	14	13	12
7	16	17	18	19	19	18	17	16
6	20	28	30	32	32	30	28	20
5	18	26	28	30	30	28	26	18
4	16	24	26	28	28	26	24	16
3	14	20	22	24	24	22	20	14
2	12	13	14	15	15	14	13	12
1	10	11	12	13	13	12	11	10
	a	b	c	d	e	f	g	h

knight mobility psqt(mg)

8	10	11	12	13	13	12	11	10
7	12	13	14	15	15	14	13	12
6	12	17	22	24	24	22	17	12
5	16	24	28	30	30	28	24	16
4	16	24	28	30	30	28	24	16
3	14	20	22	24	24	22	20	14
2	12	13	14	15	15	14	13	12
1	10	11	12	13	13	12	11	10
	a	b	c	d	e	f	g	h

knight mobility psqt(eg)

Additional information: knight mobility is due the highest values of all pieces, because the knight by its nature usually accesses the smallest number of squares. Its values tend to somewhat increase for specific central squares in the eg, where the knight should be excellently placed, and decrease for more advanced ranks, due to the declining importance of outposts.

Frequency: an all-frequent factor, there is not a piece on the board lacking mobility, even if it is zero

Bishop mobility

Definition: any empty square on the board that is not attacked by an enemy pawn, plus any board square occupied by an enemy piece or pawn which are not defended by another enemy pawn or piece, plus any board square occupied by an enemy knight, rook or queen, which are defended by an enemy pawn or piece

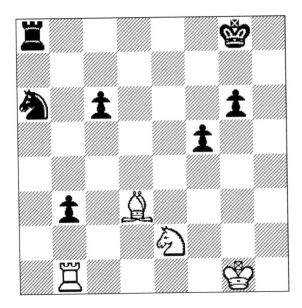

c4 is a mobile square for the white bishop, as it is empty and not attacked by an enemy pawn. a6 is also a mobile square, as there is an enemy knight, albeit defended by an enemy rook. e4,b5 and c2 are not mobile squares, as they are empty and attacked by enemy pawns. f5 is not a mobile square, as it is not empty and attacked by an enemy pawn. Finally, e2 and b1 are also not mobile squares for the bishop, as being occupied by own pieces.

Value: bonus, valid in terms of psqt

8	10	11	12	13	13	12	11	10
7	14	15	16	17	17	16	15	14
6	17	25	27	28	28	27	25	17
5	16	23	25	26	26	25	23	16
4	14	21	23	25	25	23	21	14
3	12	17	18	21	21	18	17	12
2	10	11	12	13	13	12	11	10
1	8	9	10	11	11	10	9	8
	a	b	c	d	e	f	g	h

bishop mobility psqt(mg)

8	8	9	10	11	11	10	9	8
7	10	11	12	13	13	12	11	10
6	12	17	18	21	21	18	17	12
5	15	22	25	26	26	25	22	15
4	14	21	25	26	26	25	21	14
3	12	17	18	21	21	18	17	12
2	10	11	12	13	13	12	11	10
1	8	9	10	11	11	10	9	8
	a	b	c	d	e	f	g	h

bishop mobility psqt(eg)

Additional information: bishop mobility deserves lower values than knight mobility, though relatively high ones in comparison to other pieces. Its values, similarly to the knight, tend to increase for certain central squares in the eg, while decreasing for more advanced ranks, due to the smaller importance of outposts.

Frequency: again, as with the knight, all-frequent

Rook mobility

Definition: any empty square on the board that is not attacked by an enemy pawn, plus any board square occupied by an enemy piece or pawn which are not defended by another enemy pawn or piece, plus any board square occupied by an enemy rook or queen, which are defended by an enemy pawn or piece

35

c4,c5 and e3 are mobile squares for the white rook, as they are empty and not attacked by enemy pawns. g3 is also a mobile square, as there is an enemy piece which is undefended. c6 is another mobile square, as, although attacked by an enemy pawn, it is occupied by an enemy rook. d3 and f3 are not mobile squares, because they are under attack of the enemy e4 pawn. c2 and b3 are not mobile squares for the white rook, too, as occupied by own knight and pawn

Value: bonus, valid in terms of psqt

8	11	12	13	14	14	13	12	11
7	15	16	17	18	18	17	16	15
6	13	14	15	16	16	15	14	13
5	11	12	13	14	14	13	12	11
4	9	10	11	12	12	11	10	9
3	7	8	9	10	10	9	8	7
2	5	6	7	8	8	7	6	5
1	4	5	6	7	7	6	5	4
	a	b	c	d	e	f	g	h

rook mobility psqt(mg)

8	6	7	8	9	9	8	7	6
7	10	11	12	13	13	12	11	10
6	9	10	11	12	12	11	10	9
5	11	12	13	14	14	13	12	11
4	9	10	11	12	12	11	10	9
3	7	8	9	10	10	9	8	7
2	5	6	7	8	8	7	6	5
1	4	5	6	7	7	6	5	4
	a	b	c	d	e	f	g	h

rook mobility psqt(eg)

Additional information: rook mobility deserves far lower values than mobility for minor pieces. Its values tend to decrease for advanced ranks in the eg, due to the fact that attackable enemy objects on those ranks are less frequent in the eg.

Frequency: all-frequent

Queen mobility

Definition: any empty square on the board that is not attacked by an enemy pawn, knight, bishop or rook, plus any board square occupied by an enemy piece or pawn which are not defended by another enemy pawn or piece, plus any board square occupied by an enemy queen, which is defended by an enemy pawn or piece

a1,b1,c1,c2,c3 and b5 are mobile squares for the white queen, as they are empty and not attacked by enemy pawns. b6 is also a mobile square, as there is an enemy undefended pawn. b4,d4 and e5 are not mobile squares, as they are empty and attacked by enemy pawns. f6 is not a mobile square, as it is occupied by an enemy pawn which is defended by an enemy knight. a2 is not mobile square, as under attack by the black bishop on f7. b3 is not mobile square, as under attack by the black bishop and knight. d2 is also not mobile, as the black rook on d8 attacks it. Finally, a3 and e2 are not mobile squares, as occupied by own pawn and bishop.

Value: bonus, valid in terms of psqt

8	3	3	3	4	4	3	3	3
7	5	5	5	6	6	5	5	5
6	6	7	7	8	8	7	7	6
5	5	6	6	7	7	6	6	5
4	4	5	5	6	6	5	5	4
3	3	4	5	5	5	5	4	3
2	2	3	3	4	4	3	3	2
1	2	3	3	4	4	3	3	2
	a	b	c	d	e	f	g	h

queen mobility psqt(mg)

8	2	3	3	4	4	3	3	2
7	3	3	3	4	4	3	3	3
6	6	6	6	7	7	6	6	6
5	5	6	6	7	7	6	6	5
4	4	5	5	6	6	5	5	4
3	3	4	5	5	5	5	4	3
2	2	3	3	4	4	3	3	2
1	2	3	3	4	4	3	3	2
	a	b	c	d	e	f	g	h

queen mobility psqt(eg)

Additional information: queen mobility has the lowest values of all pieces, which slightly decrease for certain squares on more advanced ranks in the eg, due to lesser importance of attacks upon enemy objects

Frequency: all-frequent

King mobility

Definition: any board square, be it free or occupied by an enemy pawn or piece, if not attacked by any enemy pawn or piece, including the king

h1 is a mobile square for the white king, as well as f1, one is free and the second one taken by an enemy piece, though both squares are not attacked by enemy pieces. h2 is not mobile for the king, as it is under attack by enemy knight on f1 and bishop on e5. f2 and g2 are also not mobile, as taken by own pawn and bishop.

Value: small bonus, 2cps in the mg, 5cps in the eg

Additional information: king mobility is relatively unimportant in the mg. Reason for this is that it is actually very difficult to make sense when it is good to have more free available squares, and when not. For example, having a lot of free squares around the king might simply mean that the king has no or very limited pawn shelter. On the other hand, even if it has no or just a single available mobile square, it might be still very well sheltered by own minor and other pieces. Sometimes, it is good to have more square freedom, at other times not, and at still other times this is pretty much irrelevant. Still, a bit of freedom is always appreciated.
In the eg, quite the opposite, more king mobility frequently means more active king, so it is only to be encouraged there.

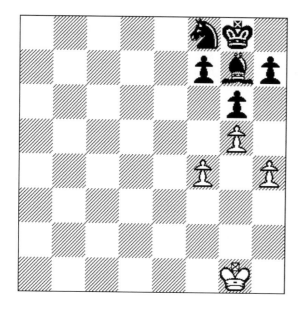

the white king has a lot of available mobile squares, but is unsheltered. The black king almost has no free mobile squares, but is very well sheltered.

in the eg, higher mobility is often synonymous with improved activity. As easily recognised above, the black king on the edge has just 2 available mobile squares, while its white counterpart enjoys the proximity of 5 such.

Frequency: all-frequent, as with other pieces

Pawn mobility

Pawn mobility stands quite apart from the rest of mobility definitions and that follows from the nature of the pawn. Generally, pawns are mobile, able to do a legal move, whenever they are able to either capture diagonally any enemy pawn or piece, or advance one or 2 squares vertically. As diagonal pawn captures are identical with levering, while diagonal non-pawn captures with existing threats upon enemy pieces, here we will be concerned with just possible vertical pawn advances. It is to be acknowledged that not all available pawn pushes are equally significant. Pushes to the 3rd and 4th ranks are mostly lacking any real value, unless done under special conditions, for example when done to attack an enemy piece, or when such a push would be a double pawn push from the 2nd to the 4th rank. Thus, within our evaluation framework, we will concentrate on just available pawn pushes on advanced ranks, starting from the 5th and ending with the 8th rank.

Pawn mobility here will include mobility of just about any pawn, be it a passer, a storming pawn, or any other featurable pawn. This will be a bit redundant, at least to unblocked storming pawns, but very consistent at the same time, as most pawn pushes, no matter the specific nature of the pawn, do enjoy quite similar values.

Value: bonus, valid in terms of psqt

8	23	28	30	35	35	30	28	23
7	14	17	19	22	22	19	17	14
6	5	8	10	12	12	10	8	5
5	2	3	5	7	7	5	3	2
4	0	0	0	0	0	0	0	0
3	0	0	0	0	0	0	0	0
2	0	0	0	0	0	0	0	0
1	0	0	0	0	0	0	0	0
	a	b	c	d	e	f	g	h

pawn mobility psqt(mg)

	a	b	c	d	e	f	g	h
8	25	30	32	37	37	32	30	25
7	16	19	21	24	24	21	19	16
6	7	10	12	14	14	12	10	7
5	4	5	7	9	9	7	5	4
4	0	0	0	0	0	0	0	0
3	0	0	0	0	0	0	0	0
2	0	0	0	0	0	0	0	0
1	0	0	0	0	0	0	0	0

pawn mobility psqt(eg)

Additional information: the bonus is given for the fact, that the free pawn has more available options at its disposal, namely to move forward. By moving forward, no matter what particular pawn it represents, it improves its board location, so more advanced ranks should be incentivised.

moving forward improves the location of the free pawn. On the diagrammed position, if the c6 white pawn advances, it will become a strong passed pawn on the 7th rank, just a single square away from promoting, if the a5 pawn is pushed, it will become a very strong blocked pawn on the 6th rank, and, if the e4 pawn is moved, it will start levering on the 5th rank.

Apart from vertical advancement, it is very important for free pawns to be more centrally placed in terms of files. The more central a free pawn is, the bigger its relative strength, as all kinds of pawns, from passers to any standard pawn, will have higher influence on the game, when pushed in the center. Central pushing will mean the possibility of creating an even stronger central passer, opening up vital lines in the center, when levering, placing own pieces on advanced central squares with possible lever captures, central more significant threats upon enemy pieces, etc. Edge or close-to-the-edge pushing, on the other hand, unless under special circumstances, will do quite the opposite. So, incentivising central pushes is another priority.

available free pawn pushes for the d5 and a5 passers are far from equal in significance, for the simple fact that a central d6 passer is immeasurably stronger than an edge a6 one. Similarly, free available pushes for the plain f4 and h4 pawns are quite different, as an f5 blocked pawn is much stronger than a h5 blocked pawn.

39

an e5 lever push will open the central e file, a b5 lever push, on the other hand, will activate simply developments along the much less significant b file

Frequency: very frequent

Available double pawn pushes

Definition: pawn on the 2nd rank on file c,d,e or f, with the squares in front of it on the 3rd and 4th ranks both free

the d2 pawn represents this condition, it has an available double pawn push

Value: small bonus, 8cps, just for the mg

Additional information: the extremely-well deserved bonus is due for the following reasons:
- such a pawn can quickly advance, taking central position and starting influencing the center
- in case it is on a file on the side where the enemy king is, it can quickly advance to the 4th rank and start exerting pressure upon the king as a storming pawn, also threatening with further advance

As both random central pawns and storming pawns are extremely important, the condition can hardly be overestimated.

Please note, that this is very much different from simply having a central pawn on the 2nd rank, as such a pawn might be more or less immobile.

the conditions of the c2 and f2 central pawns are quite different. While the c2 pawn can immediately advance with a double push to c4, in order for the f2 pawn to have this opportunity, first the white knight on f3 should go somewhere, even if modestly retreating on e1. That is why retreats are not always necessarily bad.

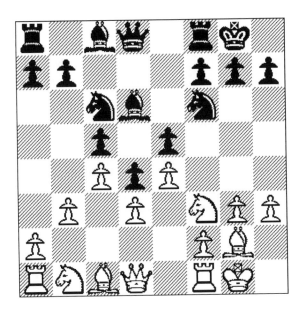

guess what the best move in this position is? Right, Ne1, threatening f2-f4.

Frequency: frequent

Low and zero mobility pieces

Low and zero mobility pieces are very important in chess, though seemingly, not all humans, and very few, even top programs, will be able to even partially make sense of them. Being low-mobile, of course, means being less active, at least currently, sometimes even long-term. Less activity, of even a single piece, is always to be avoided, as, in the struggle for supremacy, every single asset matters. The higher mobility of other pieces is not a guarantee that everything is fine, so that, apart from scoring general mobility as a sum for all pieces, taking into account singular piece mobility characteristics is a must. Occasions, when a single, badly-placed piece loses the game, are far from rare.

The situation is even worse, when a certain piece is a zero-mobility one, i.e. it has no available free mobile squares at its disposal at all. In such cases, the side having this negative, will mostly be playing with a piece less, albeit only for a limited period of time. Playing with a

piece less is not easy, is it? Not to mention possible long-term conditions.

Low mobility pieces on the edge

Definition: any non-pawn and non-king piece on the edge of the board, either the h or a files, or the 1st or 8th ranks, having just a single available mobile square

Value: penalty, -20cps, both for the mg and eg

Additional information: as said, low mobility pieces provide this side with fewer assets in a competitive environment. The outlook might not be utterly dismal, as the piece is still a bit mobile, and from the next mobile square it might find itself even more at ease, but the situation is to be avoided, whenever possible.

the white bishop on c1 is a low-mobility piece on the edge, as well as the black bishop on a2. Such pieces are easier to attack, and sometimes even trap.

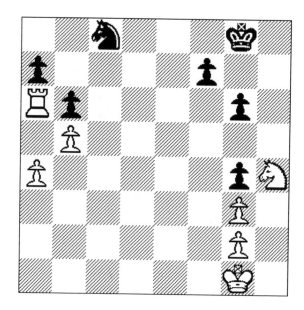

the rook on a1 is a low-mobility piece, b1 being its only accessible square, the knight on h7, although well-placed and attacking the enemy king shelter, is also a low-mobility piece on the edge, vulnerable to attacks and capturing, with f8 being its only accessible square

the knight on h4 and the rook on a6 are zero mobility pieces. They feel quite awkward, can not transfer to other parts of the board, if needed, are easily attackable and frequently trappable. Whether the condition will be more or less permanent will largely depend on particular board factors.

Zero mobility pieces on the edge

Definition: any non-pawn and non-king piece on the edge of the board, either the h or a files, or the 1st or 8th ranks, lacking even a single available mobile square

Value: penalty, -40cps, both for the mg and eg

Additional information: as noted, zero mobility is tantamount to playing without a piece, either short- or long-term. That is very negative, and sometimes even loses the entire game. With no additional specific conditions mentioned, the supposition will be that zero mobility will be just short-term, but that can in no way be guaranteed, hence the generalised custom-assessed value. Long-term zero mobility pieces are naturally due a significantly bigger penalty, and we will pay special attention to them later.

the white queen on h6 is trapped, and can be captured after Bb4-f8

the white bishop on h2 is trapped, though not permanently. After Ng1-e2, it can move via g1 to freedom.

Frequency: frequent

Zero mobility pieces not on the edge

Definition: any non-pawn and non-king piece not on the edge of the board, on files b through g and ranks 2 through 7, lacking even a single available mobile square

Value: penalty, -15cps, both for the mg and eg

Additional information: this happens much rarer, as in the center pieces are generally more mobile, due to the larger number of squares on an empty board they can go to from there. Still, the factor is important, as zero mobility, especially if permanent, at least means this piece can not be transferred to other sections of the board to perform different functions and pieces are mobile for precisely this very reason, to go around. Such pieces are also frequently trappable.

the white knight on e5, even though excellently placed and strongly-supported, as well as attacking the enemy king shelter, is trapped, enemy pawns cut its retreat and possible transfers to either the king or queen side. The black bishop on e8 ensures that the knight will not be able to advance, too. Thus, the knight is fully immobile, it can not be activated on other parts of the board, and that might prove decisive, as the focus of the game frequently shifts from one section to another. The opponent side will be able to mobilise all its pieces for different tasks, while the knight side will have to do without the services of the knight on a range of occasions.

Frequency: infrequent

Zero mobility king

Definition: king with no available mobile squares

Value: penalty, -10cps in the mg, -30cps in the eg

Additional information: this is a bad condition, though much more severe in the eg.
In the mg, having zero mobility will frequently mean the king is under strong

enemy attack, and attacks are already scored separately, but might also mean the king enjoys good sheltering. So, no generally valid conclusions might be drawn, but still having a bit of freedom of movement is to be encouraged. Zero king mobility might also indicate impending zugzwang.

In the eg, zero mobility is always bad, it can either mean the king is extremely inactive, under strong enemy attack, or even herald zugzwang. As resources in the eg are rather limited, the inactivity of each and every piece is doubly important.

zero mobility king in the mg under severe enemy attack

smothered mate also involves a zero mobility king

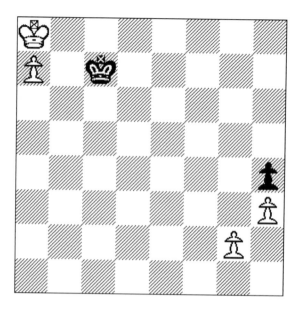

in the eg, zero king mobility will often happen in one of the corners of the board as an indication of a zugzwang

or, again in the corner, pointing at an inability to activate. White can not save that, simply because it plays without a king. The black king can enjoy a very long walk deep into the enemy camp, with the white bishop basically shuffling around. From afar, the win might not be immediately obvious, unless one has good evaluation.

Frequency: infrequent

Permanently trapped minors

In distinction to low and zero mobility pieces, that would always have very low mobility, but are not guaranteed to be trapped for a prolonged period of time, permanently trapped minors might even have better mobility, but will always necessarily be restricted to a small portion of the board in a longer time frame.

This space restriction, due to either limitations imposed by enemy pawns or own pawns, blocked by enemy ones, basically means that this particular piece will largely stay out of the game and will not be transferrable to other parts of the board, where it might be needed. Playing with a piece less for more than just a couple of moves points at a sure demise for the side yielding it. Thus, permanently trapped minors are a very major liability, to be avoided whenever possible, and due rather big penalties.

It is funny how even the top engines are so often fully clueless of some of their pieces being permanently trapped, obviously, they are lacking in knowledge for this specific feature.

There are different types of permanently trapped minors, below we will concentrate on the most useful and widespread instances.

White knight on b1, trapped by enemy pawns

Definition: white knight on b1, with white pawns on c2,b3, black pawns on c3,b4, or, alternatively, on the king side, white knight on g1, with white pawns on f2,g3, black pawns on f3,g4

white knight on b1, trapped by enemy pawns

Value: large penalty, -150cps, both for the mg and eg

Additional information: the penalty is obviously due for the permanent placement of the knight out of the game. As easily seen on the diagrammed position, all potentially available mobile squares for the knight, a3,c3 and d2, are controlled by enemy pawns, and in such a way, that one of those pawns is defended by the other, while the defending pawn will most certainly enjoy good protection, too, either by other pawns or even pieces. Additionally, the enemy pawns are blocked, which further restricts the knight, denoting that they will be attackable by fewer own pieces.

Above conditions signify prolonged limitations, and that is usually the case in practice. Situations like this can happen both in the mg and eg. The fact that the penalty is smaller than the material equivalent of a full piece is due to possible knight sacrifices for one or 2 enemy pawns.

Frequency: infrequent

White knight on a1, trapped by own pawns

Definition: white knight on a1, with own pawns on c2,b3, enemy pawns on c3,b4, or, alternatively, white knight on h1, with white pawns on f2,g3, black pawns on f3,g4

white knight on a1, trapped by own pawns

Value: large penalty, -220cps, both for the mg and eg

Additional information: the penalty is due for same reasons: prolonged mobility limitations. In distinction to the case of a white knight trapped by enemy pawns, here the corner knight is trapped by own pawns, which only increases the negativity of the phenomenon, as the enemy pawns, blocking the friendly ones and caging the knight, can only be destroyed by other own pieces, but not by a sacrifice of the knight itself.

The condition is permanent for same reasons: the knight-caging pawn construction is durable, due to the fact that the own pawns involved in it are fixed, while the enemy pawns well defended, with one of them by the remaining caging pawn, and the other either by another friendly pawn, or a friendly piece.

White bishop on b1 or a2, trapped by own pawns

Definition: white bishop on b1 or a2, with white pawns on c2,b3, black pawns on c3,b4, or, alternatively on the king side, white bishop on g1 or h2, with white pawns on f2,g3, enemy pawns on f3,g4

white bishop on b1 or a2, trapped by own pawns

Value: large penalty, -220cps, both for the mg and eg

Additional information: similar reasons as for the white knight on a1, trapped by own pawns, apply. In a way, this is even more funny situation, as the bishop is not a zero-mobility piece, it does have some freedom of movement within its cage, at least a single available mobile square at any particular time, but that is all. The bishop is limited to that very restricted section of the board. It will shuffle around from one cage square to the other to its heart's content, while battle rages on focal board points elsewhere, until finally, due to insufficient resources, the friendly side loses the game.

46

Strange as it might seem to you, it is hard to imagine how frequent such paradoxical situations might arise in engine play.

Frequency: infrequent

White knight on b1,a2,a3 or c1, trapped by own and enemy pawns

Definition: white knight on b1,a2,a3 or c1, with white pawns on d2,c3,b4, black pawns on d3,c4,b5, or, alternatively on the king side, white knight on g1,h2,h3 or f1, with white pawns on e2,f3,g4, black pawns on e3,f4,g5

white knight on a2, trapped by own pawns

on c1, the very same knight will already be trapped by the enemy d3 and c4 pawns

Value: large penalty, -150cps, both for the mg and eg

Additional information: again, the reason for the well-deserved penalty are mobility limitations in the long and very long term.
The knight can still go from a2 to c1, or, alternatively, from a3 to b1, but similar leaps will hardly prove useful to the game outcome. The knight will be badly needed somewhere else, and it will not be able to flash or even tortoise-walk there.
Sacrifices for one or 2 enemy pawns are still possible, hence the pawn and a half estimate.
This is also to be seen from time to time in engine games, especially when a human plays an engine, but who could vouch in purely human games such situations are inexisting?

Frequency: infrequent

White bishop on c1,b2 or a3, trapped by own pawns

Definition: white bishop on c1,b2 or a3, with white pawns on d2,c3,b4, black pawns on d3,c4,b5, or, alternatively, white bishop on f1,g2 or h3, with white pawns on e2,f3,g4, black pawns on e3,f4,g5

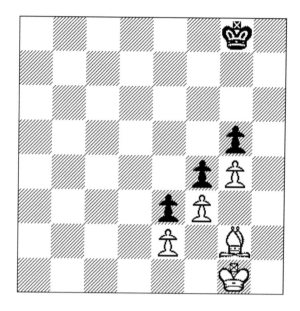

white bishop on g2, trapped by own pawns

Value: large penalty, -220cps, both for the mg and eg

Additional information: the penalty is due for long-term mobility limitations.

In distinction to other instances of trappings, here the caged bishop does really enjoy a rather spacious confinement, whole 3 available mobile squares, and can pseudo-slide from g2 to h3, f1 and even h1 for as long as it would not get bored, though that will hardly save the game.

Sacs by the bishop itself are also not possible, hence the evaluation estimate of close to 3 full pawns(of course, other friendly pieces can still sac for the bishop).

Frequency: infrequent

On occasions, a similarly-trapped minor piece can simultaneously trap another one, or even 2 other friendly pieces. This will, of course, tremendously deteriorate the situation, as the number of pieces out of the game receives over-dangerous proportions.

the b1 knight is trapped, but, what is even more disastrous, is that it simultaneously traps the own rook on a1. Thus, both pieces are out of the game. Sacs are urgently needed, many engines will spot this only too late.

and what about this one? It is not exactly clear which of the white pieces traps the remaining ones, but the picture is pitiful. You would guess that never happens in games? Of course it does, and even frequently, provided the defending player has no knowledge of similar tricks.

Bb7 is a self-trapped bishop

this is a real-life situation from one of my games. All too many, even very top, engines, will consider the position as fully equal, some even seeing black in the lead, but the truth is, that white enjoys a positional crush, of course. 3 black pieces on the queen wing, the rook on a8, the knight on b8 and the light-square bishop on c8, are factually trapped, out of the game and unable to support activities of the own army elsewhere. With time, white will attack on the king side, open the position and smash the remaining black forces. That takes time, possibly even many dozens of moves, and this might be the reason why top engines fail to recognise white's decisive edge, but is inevitable.

Self-trapped bishop

Definition: bishop on the 7th rank, defended by 2 own pawns, both blocked by enemy pawns

Value: penalty, -30cps in the mg, -20cps in the eg

Additional information: the large penalty is, of course, due for the very limited mobility of the bishop, combined with the permanence of the condition. As both pawns defending the bishop are immobile, it can not possibly go back, so its only alternative to move somewhere is to try doing that via the 8th rank. The 8th rank, though, deep into the enemy territory, will usually be very well controlled by enemy pieces, as is the case with the black rook on d8 above. So, in actual fact, the bishop is pretty much trapped, more precisely self-trapped, as it is own pawns that primarily limit its mobility.

Even top engines sometimes fail to understand such conditions. One of the most frequent instances of the phenomenon will happen with the bishop attacking the enemy king shelter, like on the position below:

the white bishop on g7 certainly looks very strong, but that is just an optical illusion. It is not only fully immobile, but, due to its peculiar location, as well as the location of the 2 own pawns defending it, the rest of the white pieces simply does not have access to the enemy king shelter, so attacking it is close to impossible. Of course, as engines are unable to see 30 moves ahead, they will generally think white has huge advantage.

Frequency: infrequent

Chapter III

Pawns

Strong pawns

Aligned pawns

Definition: a pawn that has another own pawn next to it on an adjacent file on the same rank

2 aligned pawns on b4 and c4 respectively

Value: bonus valid in terms of psqt

8	0	0	0	0	0	0	0	0
7	66	68	72	74	74	72	68	66
6	52	54	56	58	58	56	54	52
5	30	33	36	39	39	36	33	30
4	16	18	22	24	24	22	18	16
3	7	9	11	13	13	11	9	7
2	2	4	6	8	8	6	4	2
1	0	0	0	0	0	0	0	0
	a	**b**	**c**	**d**	**e**	**f**	**g**	**h**

aligned pawn psqt(mg)

	a	b	c	d	e	f	g	h
8	0	0	0	0	0	0	0	0
7	44	45	47	49	49	47	45	44
6	35	36	37	38	38	37	36	35
5	20	21	23	25	25	23	21	20
4	11	13	15	17	17	15	13	11
3	5	6	8	9	9	8	6	5
2	2	3	4	5	5	4	3	2
1	0	0	0	0	0	0	0	0

aligned pawn psqt(eg)

Additional information: aligned pawns are due bonus due to the following reasons:
- very flexible structure; if one of the pawns moves forward, it immediately becomes a well-connected defended pawn, and both pawns are able to move forward
- very nice square control in front of them; cumulatively, both pawns control 4 consecutive squares on the upper rank
- if passers, in the mg and eg alike, such pawns are a mighty asset, whose rush towards the square of promotion is extremely difficult to stop

Frequency: very frequent

Defended pawn

Definition: a pawn defended by an own pawn

defended pawn on d5

Value: bonus valid in terms of psqt

	a	b	c	d	e	f	g	h
8	0	0	0	0	0	0	0	0
7	52	54	56	58	58	56	54	52
6	30	33	36	39	39	36	33	30
5	16	18	22	24	24	22	18	16
4	7	9	11	13	13	11	9	7
3	2	4	6	8	8	6	4	2
2	0	0	0	0	0	0	0	0
1	0	0	0	0	0	0	0	0

defended pawn psqt(mg)

	a	b	c	d	e	f	g	h
8	0	0	0	0	0	0	0	0
7	35	36	37	38	38	37	36	35
6	20	21	23	25	25	23	21	20
5	11	13	15	17	17	15	13	11
4	5	6	8	9	9	8	6	5
3	2	3	4	5	5	4	3	2
2	0	0	0	0	0	0	0	0
1	0	0	0	0	0	0	0	0

defended pawn psqt(eg)

Additional information: defended pawns are due a nice bonus due to the following factors:

- they are strong, it is difficult for the opponent to capture such a pawn with a piece
- defended pawns still represent a connected feature, in case the pawn defending the defended pawn moves ahead, both pawns transform into a nice aligned unit, powerful in all stages of the game, especially when such pawns are both passers

Frequency: very frequent

Distant neighbours

Definition: a pawn that has another own pawn on the same rank across a file

a5 and c5 are distant neighbours (above, those 2 pawns make the black b7 pawn fully backward: upon trying to move forward, it simply can not, without being lost)

g4 and e4 pawns above are distant neighbours(similarly, f6 black pawn can not realistically advance to f5 square even with the help of the black g7 pawn)

Value: bonus valid in terms of psqt

8	0	0	0	0	0	0	0	0
7	20	30	40	50	50	40	30	20
6	12	17	25	32	32	25	17	12
5	8	12	17	22	22	17	12	8
4	4	6	8	11	11	8	6	4
3	2	3	5	8	8	5	3	2
2	1	2	3	4	4	3	2	1
1	0	0	0	0	0	0	0	0
	a	b	c	d	e	f	g	h

distant neighbour psqt(mg)

8	0	0	0	0	0	0	0	0
7	10	15	20	25	25	20	15	10
6	6	8	12	16	16	12	8	6
5	4	6	8	11	11	8	6	4
4	2	3	4	5	5	4	3	2
3	2	2	3	4	4	3	2	2
2	1	2	3	4	4	3	2	1
1	0	0	0	0	0	0	0	0
	a	b	c	d	e	f	g	h

distant neighbour psqt(eg)

Additional information: distant neighbours get their very well deserved bonus in view of the following reasons:
- on upper ranks, they would make enemy pawns backward, which is very important, especially in the mg
- on lower ranks, they would frequently stop enemy pawns' advance, which is particularly relevant in the center and when enemy pawns are storming pawns
- in their role as passers, or, at least when a single one of them is passer, especially on advanced and very advanced ranks, such pawns represent a tremendous asset, as they support each other across the file on their way to promotion

a5 and d5 are very distant neighbours

Value: bonus valid in terms of psqt, only mg

8	0	0	0	0	0	0	0	0
7	0	0	0	0	0	0	0	0
6	15	18	21	24	24	21	18	15
5	10	12	14	16	16	14	12	10
4	0	0	0	0	0	0	0	0
3	0	0	0	0	0	0	0	0
2	0	0	0	0	0	0	0	0
1	0	0	0	0	0	0	0	0
	a	b	c	d	e	f	g	h

very distant neighbour psqt(mg)

well, imagine, c3 and e3 distant neighbours stop the important d5-d4 black break

Frequency: frequent

Very distant neighbours

Definition: any pawn exclusively on the 5th and 6th ranks having another own pawn on the same rank 2 files across

Additional information: very distant neighbours deserve bonus due to the following considerations:
- as seen on the diagram, they frequently render enemy pawns on less advanced ranks partially backward, as usually the squares in front of the enemy pawns will also be controlled by own minor or other pieces
- they are a nice tandem themselves, even without the help of other own pieces, but with the support of own pawns; this could potentially lead to decisive passer creation
- very dangerous as passers, too, or even when only a single one of them is a passer, especially when their placement is in the

53

quadrant of the enemy king, as a free passer could additionally advance with a check to the enemy king, gaining tempo

Frequency: infrequent

Blocked pawns

Definition: a pawn with an enemy pawn on the same file one rank in front

f4 represents a blocked pawn

Note: blocked pawns are useful in many different ways, but here we are only interested in the conditions when such pawns would get a specific general bonus, and that would be when they are placed on advanced ranks, 5th or 6th(for the 4th rank, we have evaluation symmetry, for lower ranks, the bonus would become a penalty, basically the same as the opponent getting bonus for its advanced blocked pawns, and there are no blocked pawns on the 7th rank)

Value: bonus valid in terms of psqt

	a	b	c	d	e	f	g	h
8	0	0	0	0	0	0	0	0
7	0	0	0	0	0	0	0	0
6	15	18	22	50	50	22	18	15
5	7	9	11	13	13	11	9	7
4	0	0	0	0	0	0	0	0
3	0	0	0	0	0	0	0	0
2	0	0	0	0	0	0	0	0
1	0	0	0	0	0	0	0	0

blocked pawn psqt(mg)
(eg psqt is the same, with the only distinction being that central d6 and e6 squares get only 30cps instead of 50cps)

Additional information: blocked pawns perform a very wide range of roles. We can talk about simple advanced blocked pawns, blocked pawns when forming part of a larger chain, blocked pawns when being storming pawns at the same time, blocked pawns that could transform into an advanced passer, blocked central wedges in the mg, blocked pawns defining a larger blocked pawn structure/fortress, that should increase drawing chances, etc., etc., etc.
(very much tempted now to say "Blocked pawns are the soul of chess", but that would sound familiar, would not it?)

Simple advanced blocked pawns we are discussing now(other roles will be reviewed in different sections) get their bonus for the following reasons:
- being blocked means being more durable, and in this way the already existing asset of an advanced pawn is further amplified under this specific condition
- extremely favourable to the solidity and durability of longer pawn chains, consisting of 3,4,5 and more members. When longer pawn chains are blocked, both the restriction quality of longer chains upon enemy pieces and their boosting quality upon friendly pieces are considerably amplified, frequently to an extent entirely changing the logic of the game.

- a central blocked pawn on d6 or e6 in the mg represents an extremely powerful central wedge, which, even if not supported, has a tremendous influence upon the outcome of the game, as it basically splits the opponent half of the board in 2 parts, which are difficult to coordinate among and cramps the enemy position to a very large extent, no matter that this is just a single pawn

- if the enemy pawn blocking such a pawn on the 6th rank is captured, or if the blocked pawn on the 6th rank is supported by another own pawn which is free, and whose advance will challenge the enemy blocked pawn, the blocked 6th-ranker will immediately transform into a powerful passer

well, advanced b6 and c5 blocked pawns are simply more durable than if they were not blocked; in the general case, it is more difficult for the enemy to get access to and get rid of them

with larger blocked pawn chains, especially when they are central, the quality of the game completely changes, giving a substantial advantage to the side with the better-placed pawn chain(in this case the white pointed pawn chain, whose most advanced member, the f6 pawn, is closer to the enemy king than its counterpart on c4(and also taking a more advanced rank); please see Pointed chains section)

the central d6 blocked wedge splits to great effect the entire black position in 2

a6 blocked pawn above, supported by b5 free pawn, will easily mutate to an advanced 6th-rank passer, if b5-b6 break is played

Frequency: very frequent

Levers

Definition: a pawn attacking an enemy pawn is called a lever

white advanced lever on the 5th rank on b5 (the pawn tension between the b5 and c6 pawns will most likely open either the b, c, or even a file)

black advanced lever on the 6th rank on f3, additionally a storming pawn
(the pawn tension between the f3 and g2 pawns has the potential of opening the enemy king position, compromising the white pawn shelter, or at least driving a mighty pawn wedge at its most vulnerable place)

Note: general-purpose bonus is dispensed in terms of psqt only for 5th and 6th ranks. While this general bonus is the most obvious one, different specific conditions are also worth their points.

Levers easily capture human imagination, as you would have a clash of opponent pawns with the associated tension waiting to be resolved to influence the game, but assigning precise values is not that easy, unless you want to be too specific, as frequently levers take up a range of different roles on the same squares, acting as central breaks, wing breaks and storming pawns breaks depending on the circumstances.

Here we will briefly discuss the general purpose of advanced levers on the 5th and 6th ranks, and pay a bit of attention to some other types of lever pawns.

Value: general-purpose bonus for advanced levers on the 5th and 6th ranks in terms of psqt

8	0	0	0	0	0	0	0	0
7	0	0	0	0	0	0	0	0
6	24	28	32	36	36	32	28	24
5	12	14	16	18	18	16	14	12
4	0	0	0	0	0	0	0	0
3	0	0	0	0	0	0	0	0
2	0	0	0	0	0	0	0	0
1	0	0	0	0	0	0	0	0
	a	**b**	**c**	**d**	**e**	**f**	**g**	**h**

advanced lever psqt(mg)

	a	b	c	d	e	f	g	h
8	0	0	0	0	0	0	0	0
7	0	0	0	0	0	0	0	0
6	16	18	22	24	24	22	18	16
5	8	9	11	13	13	11	9	8
4	0	0	0	0	0	0	0	0
3	0	0	0	0	0	0	0	0
2	0	0	0	0	0	0	0	0
1	0	0	0	0	0	0	0	0

advanced lever psqt(eg)

Additional information: advanced levers get their not very big, but well-deserved bonus due to a combination of factors:
- they are very much conducive to opening lines, be it in the center, one of the wings, or in their capacity as storming pawns to attack the enemy king
- in case the pawn exchange is avoided by the opponent side by pushing the attacked opponent pawn further up to release the tension, or in case the lever side itself avoids trading by doing a further pawn push, if possible, the former lever immediately transforms into a mighty advanced non-lever pawn, or even passer
- those pawns are extremely helpful at breaking blocked positions/fortresses, involving the interlocking of many blocked own and enemy pawns, thus avoiding potential draws for the weaker side

Levers certainly do change their quality depending on whether they are supported by another own pawn or not, whether they are outer/inner levers(an outer lever would be a lever located on a less central file than the opponent attacked pawn, an inner lever would be the exact opposite, and, of course, in terms of centralisation, d/e files are more central than c/f files, which in turn are more central than b/g files, with a/h files being least central), the rank they are placed upon, etc.

Below, we will look at a couple of more salient evaluation features.

Outer central levers

An outer central lever is c4 pawn attacking d5 pawn, or, alternatively, f4 pawn attacking e5 pawn.

c4 outer central lever
(a very welcome situation; both pawns are situated on their 4th ranks, but the c4 pawn is less central. This means that after a possible exchange, white will remain with a more valuable central d pawn vs black's less central c pawn. This is also one of the reasons why 1.c4 is such a good first move: black simply can not play d7-d5)

Value: 20cps bonus, exclusively mg

Defended outer central lever

A defended outer central lever is an outer central lever, supported by another own pawn on less central file than the file the lever is placed upon.
Specifically, that would encompass the following board arrangements: white pawns on g3,f4, black pawn on e5; white pawns on f3,e4, black pawn on d5; white pawns on c3,d4, black pawn on e5; white pawns on b3,c4, black pawn on d5.

57

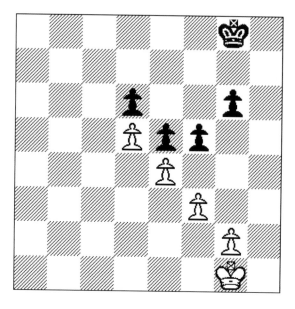

defended outer black central lever on f5 (Do you recognise the KID-like structure? It is not advantageous for white to capture e4-f5, as in this case black's pawn structure significantly improves, trading a central e4 pawn, 4th-ranker at that, for a much less central g6 one, 3rd-ranker at that, and black threatens f5-f4 push with enormous increase of the pressure.)

Value: 15cps bonus, only mg, presumably over the bonus for an undefended outer central lever, if that applies

Unopposed lever on the 4th rank

Unopposed lever on the 4th rank is a lever on the 4th rank that is not opposed by an enemy pawn on the same rank.
Small bonus will be due in view of the following reasons:
- as the pawn is not opposed, in case of a pawn trade, the file upon which the lever is will be opened, which usually will favour the lever side
- in case the trade is avoided, in most cases the unopposed lever will also have the chance to move forward and become a dangerous potential passed pawn, in case there are pawns to support it, as the squares to promotion are unoccupied by enemy pawns

b4 is an unopposed lever on the 4th rank (and yes, the b4-b5 push is a real threat)

Value: rather small, maybe some 7cps bonus, only for the mg

Lever on the 3rd rank

A lever on the 3rd rank, attacking an enemy defended pawn is worth some bonus points too, mainly for the fact that this threatens pawn exchange, in which case either the defended enemy pawn, advanced and valuable, will become undefended, or disappear altogether.

white lever on the 3rd rank on b3 attacking a defended black lever on a4(this situation definitely favours white, in spite of the fact that the b3 pawn is more central than the attacked enemy a4 pawn; a4-b3 capture will trade advanced a4 black pawn for modestly placed c2 white pawn, while b3-a4 capture is also a threat, this time trading 3rd-rank b3 pawn for 4th-rank b5 pawn)

Value: modest bonus, 10cps, both for the mg and eg

8	0	0	0	0	0	0	0	0
7	70	85	95	110	110	95	85	70
6	50	60	68	76	76	68	60	50
5	30	40	48	56	56	48	40	30
4	20	30	38	46	46	38	30	20
3	13	18	24	32	32	24	18	13
2	6	8	12	14	14	12	8	6
1	0	0	0	0	0	0	0	0
	a	b	c	d	e	f	g	h

passed pawn psqt(mg)

8	0	0	0	0	0	0	0	0
7	98	115	130	150	150	130	115	98
6	72	90	98	105	105	98	90	72
5	42	60	72	84	84	72	60	42
4	30	45	52	67	67	52	45	30
3	20	27	35	47	47	35	27	20
2	9	12	18	21	21	18	12	9
1	0	0	0	0	0	0	0	0
	a	b	c	d	e	f	g	h

passed pawn psqt(eg)

Passed pawns

Definition: a pawn that has no enemy pawns on more advanced ranks than the pawn itself up to the square of promotion on the file it is placed upon, as well as the 2 adjacent files

well, c5 is an advanced passed pawn for white, while a7 is a non-advanced passed pawn for black

Value: bonus, valid in terms of psqt

Additional information: passed pawns are one of the most valuable pawns in chess, of course, as promoting them would increase significantly the material of the promoting side.

There are different types of passed pawns, protected ones, connected ones, very large groups of connected passed pawns, other very specific, but important cases, etc.

Here we will look briefly at the most salient ones.

In general, passers would get their well-deserved bonus for the following weighty reasons:
- primarily, they are unopposed pawns, whose promotion leads to material increase
- advanced passers, especially if central too, would also tend to restrict enemy pieces' activity
- in different configurations, to be investigated separately, their value is even further boosted, sometimes to an enormous extent

Frequency: very frequent

Protected passed pawns

Definition: a protected(defended) passed pawn would be one supported by another own pawn

c6 is a protected passed pawn, very dangerous, for the obvious reason that it is strong and durable

Value: well, a bonus is due of course, over the plain passed pawn bonus, within our evaluation framework that would be seen by the existing bonus for a defended pawn

Frequency: very frequent

Connected passed pawns

Definition: any passed pawn that has another own passed pawn on adjacent file

c3 and d4 are connected passed pawns for white, g5 and f5 are connected passed pawns for black

Value: additional bonus is due, of course, that would be seen by the psqtised bonus for defended and aligned pawns.
Another ad-hoc bonus should be given only in the case, when a connected passer is neither defended, nor aligned.

c2 and d4 white pawns are neither defended, nor aligned, but still connected and valuable as tandem too.
f5 black pawn is also neither defended, nor aligned, but still connected and valuable.

60

The size of the bonus should be approximately 40cps, both for the mg and the eg.

Additional information: connected passed pawns get their bonus because:
- they are able to advance, support each other and frequently control a range of consecutive squares in tandem, which makes their position on the board much more stable, as well as their march towards the squares of promotion much more efficient
- in case a connected passer is supported, it will be more durable, difficult to attack by enemy pieces, while if it is an aligned pawn, in tandem with the other own aligned pawn next to it they will control a range of consecutive squares on the rank in front of them, also threatening a safe(defended) passer push with one of the passers reaching a more advanced rank by force
- even if such passers are neither defended, nor aligned, they still do threaten to become defended or aligned by relevant pawn pushes

Frequency: frequent

Minor pieces blockading passers

Note: a blockade would be the placing of a non-pawn piece on the rank immediately in front of the enemy passed pawn, so that its further advance is, at least temporarily, blocked.
No matter that one could doubt it, blockading of passers is an extremely useful and efficient feature, frequently underestimated by both top humans and top engines alike.

Definition: a minor piece, knight or bishop, taking up the square in front of the enemy passer

the white bishop on h2 blockades the well-advanced black h3 passer, while the black knight on b6 blockades the white b5 passer (as you see, the further advance of the passers is, at least temporarily, stopped)

Value: small bonus, valid in terms of rank.
- 20cps, both mg and eg, when the blockading minor piece is on its 4th rank
- 10cps, both mg and eg, when the minor blockader is on its 3rd rank
- and 5cps, for both stages, when the blockader takes the 2nd rank

Additional information: as said, this is a very useful feature, indeed. As a passer promotion is a tremendous asset for the promoting side, any effort at preventing that would be very welcome. Stopping the further advance of the passer, as soon as possible, before it reaches more advanced ranks, basically achieves 2 things:
- the establishment of a stronger passer on a more advanced rank after a pawn push
- and making the enemy passer a more vulnerable target for attacking pieces, as in general any fixed/immobile object is easier to reach and destroy

Frequency: frequent

On occasions, the minor piece blockade might be even more efficient, if the blockading side restrains 2 or even more enemy passers, as under such conditions the cumulative effect of the blockade would be bigger.

excellent black knights on a7 and b6 stop the advance of the, otherwise mighty, white a6 and b5 passers(as you can easily see, even though a6 and b5 are connected, and a6 defended, and both pawns being advanced too, they somehow look pitiful and the blockade very efficient)

Another important blockading feature of minor pieces primarily, but different pieces too, is the attempt to fully close the game and thus achieve a draw.

well, although white might be a pawn up, the excellently placed Nh6 fully closes the game and a draw by fortress is extremely likely, no matter the disposition of the remaining white and black pieces(thus, for blocked position purposes, not only the number of pairs of blocked and symmetrical twice backward pawns is important, but also the existence of files where a passer would be blockaded by an enemy piece)

well, as you see, on occasions, other non-minor pieces are also quite efficient in achieving a fully blocked/fortress position(as Kh6 is above)

Centralised blocking minors

Definition: Knight or bishop on the central c3,d3,e3,f3,c4,d4,e4 or f4 squares, blockading an enemy passer

Bc3 and Nd4 blockading enemy c4 and d5 passers in the center

Value: sufficiently large bonus, valid in terms of psqt, only for the mg

8	0	0	0	0	0	0	0	0
7	0	0	0	0	0	0	0	0
6	0	0	0	0	0	0	0	0
5	0	0	0	0	0	0	0	0
4	0	0	40	50	50	40	0	0
3	0	0	30	40	40	30	0	0
2	0	0	0	0	0	0	0	0
1	0	0	0	0	0	0	0	0
	a	b	c	d	e	f	g	h

centralised blockading knight psqt

8	0	0	0	0	0	0	0	0
7	0	0	0	0	0	0	0	0
6	0	0	0	0	0	0	0	0
5	0	0	0	0	0	0	0	0
4	0	0	30	35	35	30	0	0
3	0	0	20	30	30	20	0	0
2	0	0	0	0	0	0	0	0
1	0	0	0	0	0	0	0	0
	a	b	c	d	e	f	g	h

centralised blockading bishop psqt

Additional information: this is an extremely useful feature in the mg, almost always not taken into account by both humans and engines. Reason might be the very positional nature of the term, as well as the high depths associated with it. Often, why this term is useful, will become evident some 20-30 moves from now.

Bonus is given in view of the following considerations:

- of course, the advance of the enemy passer is stopped and, as it is a central one, this function is even more important

- while blocking the center, the initiative of the stronger side(usually the side with the blockaded passer) on that section of the board is also largely thwarted, and, as we all know, the center is where most things happen

- the blockading minor pieces themselves are placed on perfect centralised squares, meaning that such pieces would efficiently cumulate functions to great effect, apart from blockading, attacking important squares in the enemy half of the board/the enemy king shelter, defending the own king shelter, sometimes supporting the advance of other own passers, etc.

- on very special occasions, with deep positional considerations, such minors will efficiently block the whole center together with other own pawns, preventing counterplay there and, while using their added surplus value, giving the own side excellent attacking chances

an excellent blockading knight on e4 largely prevents counterplay in the center(the e file is blocked, after all), attacks the f6 square of the enemy king shelter, defends the f2 and g3 squares of the own king shelter and simultaneously supports the white passer on c5: tremendous functionality, no one can deny it!

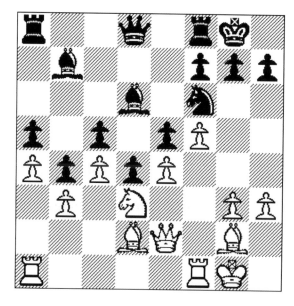

with fully blocked positions, the surplus value of such centralised minor blockaders will often incentivise kingside attacks(as you can easily see on the diagrammed position, the mighty Nd3 fully blocks the position, making impossible a d4-d3 push opening up the game and, although, seemingly, black plays with a whole pawn up, an impressive central passer at that, it is white that is winning, or at least having a substantial advantage)

Frequency: infrequent

Pieces attacking the square in front of an own or an enemy passer

Pieces attacking the square in front of an own or an enemy passer get a small, but well-deserved bonus, in the following way:
- 15cps, both mg and eg, if the piece is a minor

- 10cps, both mg and eg, if the piece is a rook(the condition would also apply with an own rook placed behind the passer on the same file, attacking the square in front of the passer on an x-ray)
- 5cps, both mg and eg, when the piece is a queen

Obviously, the bonus will be due for the ability to thwart the enemy passer's advance or support the advance of the own passer.

Ba5 supporting the advance of the own c6 passer by controlling the c7 square in front of the passer, Rc1 doing pretty much the same, but on an x-ray, and Nf1 thwarting the further advance of the enemy g4 passer by controlling the g3 square in front of it

King supporting passed pawn

Definition: king, defending own passed pawn

the white king on b5 supports the white c5 passed pawn

Value: bonus, 10cps, just for the eg

Additional information: the bonus is given for the following reasons:
- the pawn is defended by the king, and this is an important pawn
- the king can support the advance of the passer towards the square of promotion, if it controls the square in front of it
- at the same time, the passed pawn can shelter the king from enemy attacks

Frequency: very frequent

Restricting passer

Definition: passer, on ranks 5, 6 or 7, protected by an own pawn, blocked by an enemy pawn

restricting white passer on c5

Value: bonus, applied in terms of ranks

- 12cps, both for the mg and eg, for the 5th rank
- 18cps, both for the mg and eg, for the 6th rank
- 30cps, both for the mg and eg, for the 7th rank

Additional information: this is a very true term indeed, though skeptics might say it is just a figment of someone's over-exaggerated imagination. Bonus is due for 2 main reasons:
- the passer is well-protected and stable there, going to last for a long time(of course, well-protectedness will be valid for any other protected passer, too, but the distinction here is with durability, as the condition of the protecting pawn being blocked by an enemy pawn significantly adds to it, as the blocking enemy pawn kind of perpetuates the construction, making enemy attacks upon the defending pawn much more difficult, as the enemy blocking pawn will shelter it from direct attacks of heavy pieces along the closed file, where both pawns are, but also significantly restrict the access of other enemy pieces to it)
- precisely because of the same blocked construction, enemy pieces will have very

hard time dealing with the passed pawn, trying to get access to it and blockade it, while, own pieces will be reversely helped by the above-mentioned condition, as well as the supporting function of the passer concerning penetration into the enemy camp, especially with more advanced passers

Of course, above conditions also suppose, that the side with the passer will naturally have more time to organise efficient attacking regrouping, while the opposite side will mainly shuffle around.

Such passers are especially dangerous when on more advanced ranks, as the restricting effect is severely amplified.

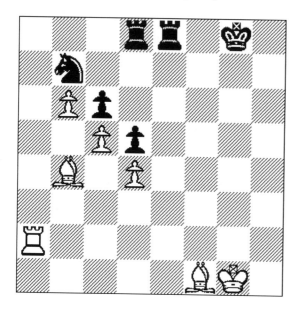

on the 6th rank, such passers often have cramping effect

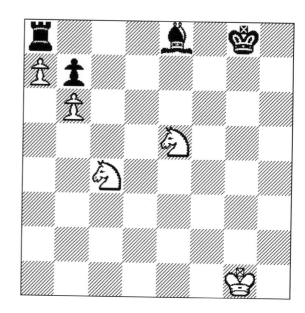

and, on the 7th rank, they are simply thrashing

Frequency: frequent

Spearhead connected passer

Definition: a spearhead pawn, with the pawn defending it blocked by an enemy pawn, and the pawn defending that pawn, all 2 part of the longer chain, also blocked by an enemy pawn, and another own passed pawn present on the other adjacent file

b5 is a spearhead passer. It is a spearhead pawn, the head of the d3-c4-b5 long pawn chain, the pawn defending it, c4, is blocked by an enemy pawn, c5, and the pawn defending c4, d3, is also blocked by an enemy pawn, d4, with both being part of the longer chain, and the b5 pawn has another own passer on adjacent file, a4.

another spearhead passer, f6, this time on the 6th rank. Maybe you can check the relevant conditions yourselves.

Value: large bonus, 70cps in the mg, 35cps in the eg

Note: only spearhead connected passers on the 5th through 7th ranks will be counted, as otherwise less advanced pawns are not so dangerous

Additional information: this is an extremely interesting feature, of which both top humans and top engines seem to be completely unaware of. The primary reason for that might be the lack of sufficient knowledge, the unresearched phenomenon, as well as the astounding depths involved in the variations.

The very-well deserved bonus is due for the following reasons:
- the longer pawn chain, of which the spearhead is the leading pawn, with most of its members blocked by enemy pawns, creates a situation, where the access of

enemy pieces to blockading, trying to stop the further advance of the 2 connected passers, is made much more difficult, because of lack of sufficient space
- the very same blocked condition, and that on a larger scale, will, on the other hand, significantly benefit the regrouping and coordination of own pieces, supporting the advance of the passed pawns, as well as their general activity
- at least the first blocking enemy pawn next to the spearhead passer on the same rank and adjacent file, e6 on the second diagram, will remain undefended and a much easier target for attack, because it will be squeezed between 2 opponent defended pawns

Couple of examples with similar arising structures:

well, on the second-posted diagram, accompanying the definition, any minor piece sacrifice on g6 will bring us to the appearance of the term; if engines or humans are unaware of its relevance, they might very well also not take their chance and sacrifice

taking the first-posted diagram, accompanying the definition, any minor piece sacrifice on a5 will bring us to the condition, or, alternatively, a knight sacrifice on c5, followed by a bishop capture on a5

So, usually, the feature will be reached after a sacrifice, but other paths are possible as well.

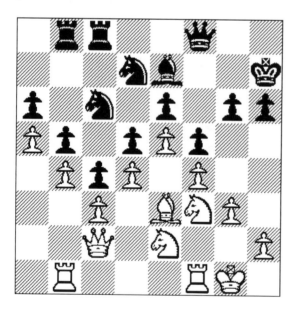

well, if either side does not find a way to open the position, the game will probably end in a draw, because of the blocked character of the position. Many might indeed think the game is more or less drawn, be it humans or engines, but, in actual fact, black has a very-well thought

sacrifice on b4, after which, no matter what minor piece is sacrificed first, it should get a big, winning advantage.

For the minor piece, black gets 2 strong, connected passers, c4 and b5, both currently defended, one of them advanced on the 5th rank, both free in their movements, and both supported in their movement forward by the pair of rooks on the c and b files, as well as other pieces, plus, after breaking white's chain pawn structure, both the d4 white pawn, and especially the a5 pawn, becoming isolated, transforming into vulnerable targets.

Certainly, the compensation is more than sufficient. Besides, the larger supporting black long chain pawn structure, in the form of the d5 and e6 pawns, both blocked by enemy pawns, kind of suffocate the bigger number of white pieces, making their coordination much more difficult. The friendly pieces, on the other hand, enjoy significantly greater freedom of movement and better coordination, because of the same fact, and that condition will only improve as the game progresses, as the passers start moving forward, squeezing even more white's position, and the black pieces manage to regroup better.

Overall, white has almost no chances to save the game.

How many very top engines would see a minor piece sacrifice on b4 and evaluate it as winning? How many humans will think a sac on b4 wins by force?

68

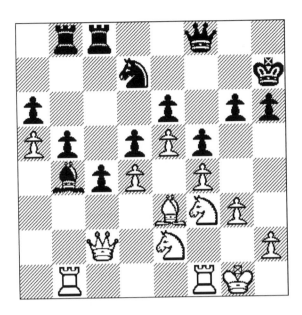

here the position after the possible knight sacrifice. Black has quite some advantage and will win, but that might take a lot of time, frequently beyond the search horizon of an engine.

the bishop sacrifice is winning, too, but associated lines are also very deep, certainly beyond the horizon of many engines and humans

The mg bonus is significantly higher, as in the mg the restricting effect of the long pawn chain and the blocked structure upon the larger number of enemy pieces will be much more severe.

As a whole, one evaluation term for people and entities that like deep, entertaining and beautiful play.

Frequency: infrequent

Rollercoasters

Definition: a large group of connected passers or passers and candidate passers on adjacent files, 4, 5 or 6 of them

c3-d4-e4-f5 is a rollercoaster of 4 connected passers

a rollercoaster of 5 connected passers, a2,b2,c2,d3 and e3

69

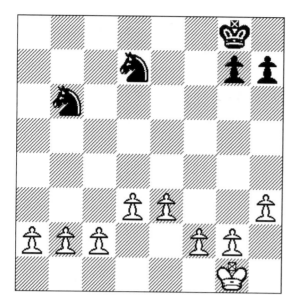

now, the rollercoaster pawns are already 6, with 5 passers, plus the f2 candidate passer

another mix of passers and candidate passers in a 4-pawn rollercoaster. d5 and e5 are passers, while c4 and f4 are candidate passers.

Value: sufficiently large over-bonus, dispensed in terms of the quantity of the pawns

4 connected pawns: 40cps, both for the mg and eg
5 connected pawns: 60cps, both for the mg and eg
6 connected pawns: 80cps, both for the mg and eg

Additional information: fact is, that with such extremely large connected pawn formations the existing bonuses for passed pawns, candidate passers and connected pawns, defended or aligned ones, are definitely insufficient.

The large formations, over 4 pawns, represent additional assets, for which the over-bonus is given:
- a compact mass of pawns, able to defend and advance in supporting each other
- massive control of the squares in front of the pawns, with no existing gaps, so enemy pieces will have very hard time coming closer, trying to attack them
- for the very same reason, the task of enemy pieces trying to blockade them is extremely arduous, if not impossible at all
- because of the inability of enemy pieces to come closer, in moving forward, such formations are able to very efficiently gain space

The bonus is the same, no matter if the pawns are only passers, or a mix of passers and candidate passers, for the simple reason that, with such large formations, with pawns supporting each other and restricting enemy pieces, candidate passers are able to quickly transform into fully-fledged passers in a short while almost automatically. So, in this sense, it is difficult to make a distinction between passers and candidate passers.

The mg and eg bonuses are equal, as, while in the mg such pawns will have a major restricting role upon the larger number of enemy pieces present, in the eg their advance will be generally easier.

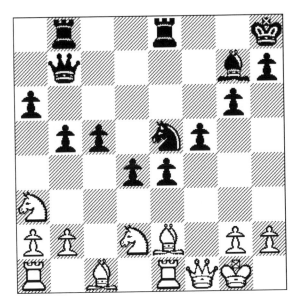

although white has 2 pieces more, with the material equivalent being 2 minor pieces for just 4 enemy pawns, it is definitely black who has the advantage.

I am not certain how much time top engines will need to fully realise that, but the fact is indisputable.

Quite frequently, as seen above, such constellations lead to beautiful positions with accompanying astounding, tactically relevant and quickly changing play.

Frequency: infrequent

Unstoppable passed pawn

Definition: with the existence of at least one own and one enemy passer, the most advanced passer on the board, provided that it is at least 2 ranks more advanced than the most advanced passer for the opponent side

Value: bonus, 20cps in the mg, 30cps in the eg

Additional information: the bonus is due, because such passed pawns are much stronger than the rest, closer to promotion, and play a vital role in deciding the game.

an engine, or even a human, might decide, that white is ok, because it has many more pawns. However, the most advanced passer of those pawns, the one on e3, is significantly less advanced than the black b3 passer, so in actual fact black is much better.

with queen endings, this condition might frequently lead to draws, in spite of one side having significant material advantage. Although black has 3 more passed pawns than white above, the game will end in a draw, as the single white passer is way ahead of the huge black pack.

Frequency: frequent

71

More pieces with passed pawns

Definition: at least one side having at least a single passed pawn, with unequal number of pieces for both sides

Value: sufficient bonus, 20cps in the mg, 40cps in the eg, for the side with more pieces

Additional information: the bonus is very-well due, because more pieces are useful in dealing with passers in 2 ways:
- by efficiently supporting the advance of friendly ones, and
- by efficiently stopping the advance of enemy ones

in spite of the evident material deficit, only black could have advantage above, as the strong centrally placed black passers are excellently supported by the friendly pieces.

The black predominance in numbers of pieces of lower power allows the lower-power pieces to efficiently protect the own passers, when under attack by enemy higher-power pieces and, even more decisively, be extremely beneficial to their advance, by controlling squares on the path to their promotion. When a heavy piece on the path of the passed pawn to promotion is attacked by a minor piece, it

will have to retreat, so the march of the passer is more or less forced.

it is not possible for black to win that one. In spite of the huge material deficit, white is holding the draw by just shuffling the rook to f3/h3 and back to b3. The b4 passed pawn can not advance any further, as it is very efficiently stopped by the larger number of white pieces of lower power, with the bishop on d5 and the rook both controlling the square in front of it.

Frequency: frequent

Passer-makers

Definition: unopposed pawn on the 4th or 5th ranks, defending an own pawn on one adjacent file, that is blocked by an enemy pawn, which pawn in turn is not a defended one, and with no enemy pawns on the other adjacent file in front of it

Value: bonus, dispensed in terms of rank

- 4th rank: 7cps, both for the mg and eg
- 5th rank: 15cps, both for the mg and eg

Additional information: the bonus is given, as such pawns, after a push, might help in creating an advanced passed pawn in the like of the friendly defended pawn.

b4 is an unopposed passer-maker on the 4th rank.

After the b4-b5 push, in the case of a6-b5 capture, the passer-maker is sacrificed, but a much stronger advanced passed pawn on a5 arises instead, ready to continue its march to promotion with a5-a6 at any time.

the condition the enemy pawn, blocking the friendly defended pawn on adjacent file, is not in turn defended by a pawn, is necessary, as otherwise, similar breaks in the center, might not lead to the creation of a passed pawn.

Above, after the d4-d5 break, and e6-d5 capture, the white e5 pawn is still not a

passer, as the black f7 pawn will be stopping its further advance.

the condition with an unopposed passer-maker on the 5th rank, as f5 is above, is even more beneficial.

After f5-f6 g7-f6 g6-g7, the white g pawn has almost promoted.

Frequency: frequent

Potential passers

Definition: a pawn that is not opposed, provided that the number of other own pawns on the same rank or less advanced ranks on adjacent files is not smaller than the number of enemy pawns on more advanced ranks on adjacent files

Note: of course, such a pawn should not be a passer, as passers already get their bonus

a3 is a potential passer for white(b3 vs b6 pawns on adjacent files), and g5 is a potential passer for black(again with equal pawn numbers on adjacent files, f3 and h3 vs f5 and h6 pawns)

Of course, there are always exceptions to the rule, as chess is simply too multi-faceted, but the general conception should hold.

and on the diagrammed position, although white g3 pawn does not formally satisfy the rule(a single white pawn on same or less advanced ranks supporting it, h3, vs 2 enemy pawns on more advanced ranks opposing it, f5 and h6), if white were to play, g3-g4 push would render g4 pawn very much potential passer/passer-like, with g4-g5 threatening

Value: bonus, valid in terms of psqt

8	0	0	0	0	0	0	0	0
7	0	0	0	0	0	0	0	0
6	25	30	34	38	38	34	30	25
5	15	20	24	28	28	24	20	15
4	10	15	19	23	23	19	15	10
3	6	9	12	16	16	12	9	6
2	3	4	6	7	7	6	4	3
1	0	0	0	0	0	0	0	0
	a	b	c	d	e	f	g	h

potential passer psqt(mg)

for example, although formally satisfying the conditions, c4 white pawn will have a very difficult time becoming a passer, as one of the pawns that could support its march forward, d3, is actually blocked by an enemy pawn and thus immobile

8	0	0	0	0	0	0	0	0
7	36	45	49	52	52	49	45	36
6	25	30	34	38	38	34	30	25
5	21	30	36	42	42	36	30	21
4	15	22	26	33	33	26	22	15
3	10	13	18	24	24	18	13	10
2	5	6	9	10	10	9	6	5
1	0	0	0	0	0	0	0	0
	a	**b**	**c**	**d**	**e**	**f**	**g**	**h**

potential passer psqt(eg)

Additional information: potential passers are bonised, of course, for the single reason that, at some future point in time, they could become passers

Frequency: frequent

Pair of potential passers

Definition: 2 potential passers for one side situated on adjacent files, with both of them having another own pawn on the other adjacent file looking away from the file the neighbouring potential passer is

well, d5 and e5 are just 2 potential passers on the diagrammed position, but in actual fact they hide much more in their interconnection as a cumulative influence; certainly, the possibility for the immediate building of a tandem of 2 connected

passers after f6-f5, e5-e4 and d5-d4 is quite realistic

Value: sufficiently large additional bonus, 30cps both for the mg and eg(well, when you give the bonus for one of the pawns, you actually assign it to the tandem)

Additional information: the bonus is dispensed for the fact that, quite often, this particular constellation will lead to the creation of 2 strong connected passers

Mainstays

Definition: a pawn on the central c4,d4,e4 or f4 squares, blocked by an enemy pawn, controlling the square in front of an enemy backward pawn and simultaneously defending an own passer

d4 is a mainstay pawn
(d4 is blocked by d5, supports own c5 passer and controls the e5 square in front of the enemy e6 backward pawn)

Additional information: an extremely valuable pawn, especially in the mg. A nice bonus is due in consideration of the following:
- such a constellation very favourably splits the opponent position in 2, while retaining all associated advantages, like

the passed pawn, enemy backward pawn; this split ensures much greater own pieces activity, while restricting opponent pieces activity, which might play a vital role, especially in the long run

- with bigger blocked pawn structures and closed-like game, the role of the mainstay further increases, as the central enemy backward pawn on the 3rd rank will be a major weakness with even bigger cramping effect upon the own pieces, and this could lead to a gradual, but very convincing king-side attack upon the enemy king

- the square in front of the enemy backward pawn is an ideal place for a minor outpost; a knight or bishop outpost will simultaneously attack the enemy king position and support the advance to promotion of the strong defended passer

Compact pawn structures

Definition: compact pawn structures are larger groups of at least 2 twice aligned, twice defended, defended aligned, defending aligned or long chain pawns

the b3,c4,d4 and e3 pawns are a larger group of 2 defended aligned pawns, c4 and d4

this time, the larger group of pawns includes one defended aligned pawn, d4, and one twice aligned pawn, e4

the larger group of pawns includes one twice defended pawn, b5, and one long chain pawn, c4

one twice defended pawn, f4, and one defending aligned pawn, g3

larger compact group of pawns, including one long chain pawn, c3, one defended aligned pawn, d4, and one defending aligned pawn, e4

very large compact pawn structure, consisting of 3 defended aligned pawns, b3, d4 and g4, 2 twice aligned pawns, e4 and f4, and one defending aligned pawn, c3

Value: such structures get their very nice bonus through the already existing bonus points for twice defended pawns, twice aligned pawns, defended aligned pawns, defending aligned pawns and long chain pawns. The larger the structure, the bigger the cumulative bonus.

Additional information: the bonus is given for the following reasons:
- the pawns co-exist as a compact mass, supporting each other, and thus being less vulnerable to enemy attacks
- the pawns are able to move forward in harmony and mutual support, posing bigger problems to the opponent in terms of stopping their advance
- the larger group very efficiently restricts enemy pieces' mobility, the larger the group, the more pronounced the effect, as the pawns almost leave no holes, undefended squares, which enemy pieces could use to penetrate

Such larger structures are very efficient both in attack and defence.

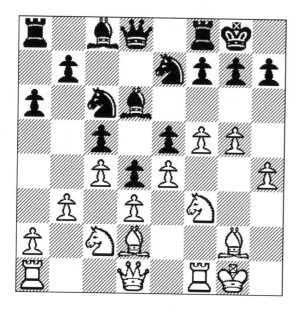

white has a compact very large pawn structure, including 5 connecting pawns: b3, long chain pawn, c4, twice defended pawn, e4, long chain pawn, f5 and g5, defended aligned pawns.

Much in contrast, although many humans and engines might not be quite able to realise it, black has only 2 connecting pawns: d4, which is twice defended, and g7, which is twice aligned.

In this way, white enjoys big advantage in terms of much more compact pawn structure. This is certainly decisive, and white has excellent winning chances.

Please note, how efficient the connecting white pawns on the king side are. f5 and g5 pawns are defended and strong, the g5 pawn supports a possible f5-f6 push, the f5 pawn, a possible g5-g6 push, those pawns plus the e4 long chain one considerably limit the mobility of a large pool of black pieces.

The compact mass of white pawns on the queen side, on the other hand, is very handy in preventing possible quick black counterplay there, as the b3 and c4 defended pawns are ready for any enemy pawn assault, just waiting and gaining time, as any enemy pawn attack, for example after b7-b5, or a6-a5-a4, is quite unsubstantial, as captures like b5-c4 or a4-b3 will only reproduce the attacked defended pawn after a recapture.

The structure as a whole also very much simulates closedness of the position, although there are just a few blocked pawns. The larger pawn structures are simply very much conducive to later fuller closure or at least will ward off for quite some time possible enemy tries at opening the game.

For this very same reason, the simulated closedness, the white king, although playing completely without pawn shelter, is feeling extremely well and healthy, with enemy threats just a distant reminder. So, larger compact groups of pawns are also extremely beneficial to king safety. This is a subtle king safety term, allowing for successful play with almost completely insecure king.

compact pawn structures are very useful in defence too.

Although black has substantial lead in development, and very robust pawn center, the game is about equal. The reason is that it is very difficult to break through the white defensive bastion of connecting pawns. Black has just a single connecting pawn, d5, which is twice aligned, while white enjoys the presence of 6! such pawns: b2, which is twice aligned, c2, which is defending aligned, d3, which is defended aligned, e3, similarly so, f2 and g2 defending aligned.

78

This compact mass of pawns wards off any possible enemy piece penetration, so black will have to work very hard to find a potential exploitable weakness.

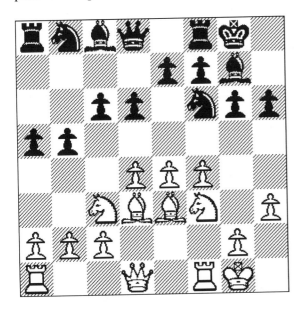

one last example for utter enjoyment.

In spite of the enormous lead in development and massive center, white is actually a bit worse. How many engines/humans would assess the position in this way?

Fact is, that white's pawns are quite broken-down in different very small groups, while black has a great number of interconnecting pawns. Look at the h6-g6-f7-e7-d6-c6-b5-a5 weaving snake! It is so inseparable and so powerful. I guess this time you will be able to make out yourselves what the 6 connecting black pawns are. This structure threatens attack on the queen side, counterplay in the center, significantly limits the mobility of the white pieces, and would not allow easy access to its king.

While white will have to spend quite some time searching for an exploitable weakness, black will be able to develop, and the white lead in development will disappear in and of itself. In this way, a single pawn feature turns the whole game around.

Frequency: very frequent

Twice aligned pawns

Definition: a pawn that has 2 other own pawns next to it on the same rank on adjacent files

twice aligned pawn on d3

Value: bonus valid in terms of psqt

8	0	0	0	0	0	0	0	0
7	0	30	35	40	40	35	30	0
6	0	19	22	25	25	22	19	0
5	0	10	15	20	20	15	10	0
4	0	6	8	10	10	8	6	0
3	0	3	4	5	5	4	3	0
2	0	1	2	3	3	2	1	0
1	0	0	0	0	0	0	0	0
	a	b	c	d	e	f	g	h

twice aligned pawn psqt(mg)

8	0	0	0	0	0	0	0	0
7	0	20	22	25	25	22	20	0
6	0	12	14	16	16	14	12	0
5	0	7	10	13	13	10	7	0
4	0	4	5	7	7	5	4	0
3	0	2	3	4	4	3	2	0
2	0	1	2	3	3	2	1	0
1	0	0	0	0	0	0	0	0
	a	b	c	d	e	f	g	h

twice aligned pawn psqt(eg)

Additional information: twice aligned pawns are an extremely powerful asset. They should get a beautiful bonus in view of a variety of reasons:

- very nice compact structure; no matter what pawn of the three moves ahead, the structure as a whole still remains very flexible and very valuable. Upon moving one square upwards, the twice aligned pawn becomes twice defended one, another asset, while if one of its neighbours goes forward one square, the twice aligned pawn is transformed into a defending aligned pawn, also an asset
- massive control of consecutive squares on the rank in front
- beautiful king shelter feature, if available
- if both the twice aligned pawn, as well as its neighbours are passers, they represent a tremendous force on their march to the square of promotion

Frequency: frequent

Twice defended pawn

Definition: a pawn defended by 2 own pawns

twice defended pawn on e5

Value: bonus valid in terms of psqt

	a	b	c	d	e	f	g	h
8	0	0	0	0	0	0	0	0
7	0	30	40	50	50	40	30	0
6	0	20	25	30	30	25	20	0
5	0	10	15	20	20	15	10	0
4	0	5	7	9	9	7	5	0
3	0	2	3	4	4	3	2	0
2	0	0	0	0	0	0	0	0
1	0	0	0	0	0	0	0	0

twice defended pawn psqt(mg)

	a	b	c	d	e	f	g	h
8	0	0	0	0	0	0	0	0
7	0	20	25	33	33	25	20	0
6	0	13	17	20	20	17	13	0
5	0	7	10	13	13	10	7	0
4	0	3	5	6	6	5	3	0
3	0	2	3	4	4	3	2	0
2	0	0	0	0	0	0	0	0
1	0	0	0	0	0	0	0	0

twice defended pawn psqt(eg)

Additional information: twice defended pawns get their well-deserved bonus due to a couple of weighty factors:
- they are extremely strong, meaning also durable
- they are flexible, in case one of the pawns defending the twice defended pawn moves ahead, the whole structure will still be valuable, with the twice defended pawn becoming defended aligned and still connected to 2 other own pawns
- of course, such pawns, if the defending pawns are also passers, represent a very powerful advancing unit

Frequency: frequent

Defended aligned pawn

Definition: a pawn that is defended by an own pawn placed on one of the adjacent files and has another own pawn next to it on the same rank on another adjacent file

defended aligned pawn on g5
(this one is additionally a storming pawn)

Value: bonus valid in terms of psqt

8	0	0	0	0	0	0	0	0
7	0	25	30	35	35	30	25	0
6	0	15	18	21	21	18	15	0
5	0	8	10	12	12	10	8	0
4	0	4	5	6	6	5	4	0
3	0	2	3	4	4	3	2	0
2	0	0	0	0	0	0	0	0
1	0	0	0	0	0	0	0	0
	a	b	c	d	e	f	g	h

defended aligned pawn psqt(mg)

8	0	0	0	0	0	0	0	0
7	0	17	20	22	22	20	17	0
6	0	10	12	14	14	12	10	0
5	0	5	7	9	9	7	5	0
4	0	3	4	5	5	4	3	0
3	0	2	3	4	4	3	2	0
2	0	0	0	0	0	0	0	0
1	0	0	0	0	0	0	0	0
	a	b	c	d	e	f	g	h

defended aligned pawn psqt(eg)

Additional information: salient pawn feature, part of a very nice compact and valuable structure. Should be bonised due to a mix of assets it creates:

- the pawn itself is strong, durable, and difficult to attack by opponent pieces
- binds together a beautiful compact structure, which is at the same time very flexible
- in case the pawn next to the defended aligned pawn moves forward, the defended aligned pawn is transformed into a long chain pawn, another valuable asset, while if the pawn defending it advances, the defended aligned pawn assumes the form of a twice aligned pawn, a cherished asset in all stages of the game(on the diagrammed position, if f5 pawn advances, we have the h4-g5-f6 white long pawn chain, with the g5 pawn at its center, while when h4 pawn advances, we have g5 at the center of the f5-g5-h5 aligned pawn structure)
- g5 itself moving ahead gets us to a more advanced defended pawn on g6

Frequency: frequent

Defending aligned pawn

Definition: a pawn that has one own pawn on the same rank next to it on one adjacent file and another own pawn that it defends on another adjacent file

b3 is a defending aligned pawn

Value: bonus valid in terms of psqt

8	0	0	0	0	0	0	0	0
7	0	0	0	0	0	0	0	0
6	0	15	18	21	21	18	15	0
5	0	8	11	14	14	11	8	0
4	0	4	5	6	6	5	4	0
3	0	2	3	4	4	3	2	0
2	0	1	2	3	3	2	1	0
1	0	0	0	0	0	0	0	0
	a	b	c	d	e	f	g	h

defending aligned pawn psqt
(same values mg and eg)

Additional information: bonised due to following considerations:
- binds together a compact structure, which simultaneously controls a number of consecutive squares
- apart from being compact, the structure is flexible; if the pawn next to the defending aligned pawn moves forward, it will be defended, while in case the defending aligned pawn itself goes forward, it transforms into a defended aligned pawn(see c3 and b3 pawns advancing above)

Frequency: frequent

Long chain pawn

Definition: pawn that is defended and defends another own pawn along the same diagonal

c4 is a long chain pawn
(see how beautiful, even outwardly, the structure is)

Value: bonus valid in terms of psqt

8	0	0	0	0	0	0	0	0
7	0	0	0	0	0	0	0	0
6	0	24	35	48	48	35	24	0
5	0	12	18	24	24	18	12	0
4	0	6	12	17	17	12	6	0
3	0	2	3	5	5	3	2	0
2	0	0	0	0	0	0	0	0
1	0	0	0	0	0	0	0	0
	a	b	c	d	e	f	g	h

long chain pawn psqt(mg)

8	0	0	0	0	0	0	0	0
7	0	0	0	0	0	0	0	0
6	0	16	25	33	33	25	16	0
5	0	8	12	16	16	12	8	0
4	0	5	8	13	13	8	5	0
3	0	2	3	4	4	3	2	0
2	0	0	0	0	0	0	0	0
1	0	0	0	0	0	0	0	0
	a	b	c	d	e	f	g	h

long chain pawn psqt(eg)

Additional information: Long chain pawns are extremely useful assets, whose real value is way underestimated by both top human players and top chess engines alike.

The lines such structures lead to are simply too deep and multi-branched.

Nice bonus over the bonus for a simple defended pawn is due because:

- the pawn itself is strong, and the pawn it defends is strong too
- being long and connected means the structure as a whole is compact, it is difficult for enemy pieces to break through such a bastion, and apart from that it supports a wide range of friendly pieces activities, which are sheltered in their movements and attacks upon the enemy side
- the structure is also reasonably flexible, in spite of the fact it might look otherwise; if the pawn defending the long chain pawn advances, the long chain pawn itself is transformed into a defending aligned pawn, while if the long chain pawn itself budges, it becomes a more advanced aligned pawn

Frequency: frequent

Very long chain pawn

Definition: a long chain pawn defending another own long chain pawn

this time, apart from being long chain pawn, c4 is also a very long chain pawn, and the bonus for a long chain pawn should be added to the bonus for a very long chain pawn(the chain structure is much larger now, you see, much stronger, occupies much bigger space, restricting enemy pieces and giving freedom to own ones, so it has a per se value, which the accumulation of simpler bonus points alone is not able to fully capture)

Value: bonus valid in terms of psqt

8	0	0	0	0	0	0	0	0
7	0	0	0	0	0	0	0	0
6	0	0	0	0	0	0	0	0
5	0	24	36	48	48	36	24	0
4	0	12	24	34	34	24	12	0
3	0	4	6	10	10	6	4	0
2	0	0	0	0	0	0	0	0
1	0	0	0	0	0	0	0	0
	a	b	c	d	e	f	g	h

very long chain pawn psqt(mg)

8	0	0	0	0	0	0	0	0
7	0	0	0	0	0	0	0	0
6	0	0	0	0	0	0	0	0
5	0	16	24	32	32	24	16	0
4	0	9	16	22	22	16	9	0
3	0	3	4	8	8	4	3	0
2	0	0	0	0	0	0	0	0
1	0	0	0	0	0	0	0	0
	a	b	c	d	e	f	g	h

very long chain pawn psqt(eg)

Additional information: very long chain pawns are valuable because:
- they are part of and represent an intrinsically solid structure
- the sheer size of the structure will largely restrict opponent pieces while supporting friendly ones at the same time
- the larger size of the whole structure determines to a great extent also its durability, and durability in chess is usually an asset

- yes, the structure is partially flexible too, in spite of its large size(see long chain pawns); of course, if one of the constituent pawns moves, the structure as a whole will crumble

Frequency: infrequent

Spearheads

Spearheads are the most advanced pawns of a long chain, consisting of at least 3 pawns.

b5 is the spearhead pawn of the d3-c4-b5 long chain

spearheads can also represent fully blocked chains

or partially blocked ones. This time, d4 black pawn is the spearhead of the b6-c5-d4 long chain.

or long chains, consisting of more than 3, or many more than 3 pawns. Above, c6 is the spearhead of the very long chain g2-f3-e4-d5-c6.

Spearheads are especially important in terms of conceptual definitions.

Value: within our evaluation framework, there is no need for any special bonus for spearheads, as they are already very well

84

seen by the already existing bonus points for advanced defended pawns, plus the bonus for long chain pawns, the connecting element, defining any longer chain

Weak pawns

Undefended pawns

Within our evaluation framework, pure undefended pawns are not considered, as it is much more correct to take into account different types of undefended pawns instead, as isolated ones, vertically isolated ones, backward ones, etc.

Undefended pawns that are part of a chain, their root or base, should not get penalty, as, in case they are backward, their penalty is already ensured, while, if this is not the case, the chain as a whole is a strong asset, so it is completely meaningless to give bonus to one of its parts, while penalising another.

Undefended pawns that are aligned are also too strong to assign them a negative.

Isolated pawns

Definition: a pawn that has no other own pawns on adjacent files

d4 is an isolated pawn

h5 is another isolated pawn, for black
(no white pawns on either c or e files, and no black pawns on adjacent g file)

Note: it very much makes sense to score isolated pawns in terms of opposed/unopposed flags, as unopposed isolated pawns are more easily attackable by virtue of the fact that the file the unopposed isolated pawn is placed upon is a semi-open file, where enemy heavy pieces could be placed to endanger the pawn(for example, d4 white pawn above is unopposed isolated one, attackable by an enemy rook or queen along the d file, while h5 black pawn is opposed isolated one, not attackable by white heavies along the closed h file)

Value: large penalty, valid in terms of psqt

8	0	0	0	0	0	0	0	0
7	-20	-25	-30	-35	-35	-30	-25	-20
6	-18	-23	-28	-33	-33	-28	-23	-18
5	-16	-21	-26	-31	-31	-26	-21	-16
4	-14	-19	-24	-29	-29	-24	-19	-14
3	-12	-17	-22	-27	-27	-22	-17	-12
2	-10	-15	-20	-25	-25	-20	-15	-10
1	0	0	0	0	0	0	0	0
	a	b	c	d	e	f	g	h

isolated opposed pawn penalty(mg)

8	0	0	0	0	0	0	0	0
7	-25	-32	-40	-45	-45	-40	-32	-25
6	-23	-30	-38	-43	-43	-38	-30	-23
5	-21	-28	-36	-41	-41	-36	-28	-21
4	-19	-26	-34	-39	-39	-34	-26	-19
3	-17	-24	-32	-37	-37	-32	-24	-17
2	-15	-22	-30	-35	-35	-30	-22	-15
1	0	0	0	0	0	0	0	0
	a	b	c	d	e	f	g	h

isolated opposed pawn penalty(eg)

8	0	0	0	0	0	0	0	0
7	-27	-33	-38	-45	-45	-38	-33	-27
6	-24	-30	-35	-42	-42	-35	-30	-24
5	-21	-27	-32	-39	-39	-32	-27	-21
4	-18	-24	-29	-36	-36	-29	-24	-18
3	-15	-21	-26	-33	-33	-26	-21	-15
2	-12	-18	-23	-30	-30	-23	-18	-12
1	0	0	0	0	0	0	0	0
	a	b	c	d	e	f	g	h

isolated unopposed pawn psqt(mg)

8	0	0	0	0	0	0	0	0
7	-33	-40	-50	-57	-57	-50	-40	-33
6	-30	-37	-47	-54	-54	-47	-37	-30
5	-27	-34	-44	-51	-51	-44	-34	-27
4	-24	-31	-41	-48	-48	-41	-31	-24
3	-21	-28	-35	-45	-45	-35	-28	-21
2	-18	-25	-35	-42	-42	-35	-25	-18
1	0	0	0	0	0	0	0	0
	a	b	c	d	e	f	g	h

isolated unopposed pawn psqt(eg)

Additional information: Isolated pawns are a very widespread and important positional feature. Along with doubled pawns, they are probably the easiest to recognise intuitively on the board.

Penalty is due in view of the following weighty reasons:

- they are weak(undefended), so easily attackable and capturable

- as there are no other own pawns on adjacent files, it is practically impossible to easily span the distance to other own pawns across files to build a valuable compact structure in the short term without resorting to major tactical arrangements,

while suitable tactics is far from always available; in this way, in order to render the isolated pawn non-isolated, one needs major other positional advantages in terms of specific factors

- in a range of cases, when the isolated pawn is blocked by an enemy pawn, or when the enemy has sufficient pawn and piece control of the square in front of it, in case it is not blocked, this pawn becomes an even bigger weakness, as both fixation by blocking and square control lead to impossibility of the pawn to move forward, which basically means greater difficulties of getting rid of it by a pawn push, challenging an enemy pawn, as well as much easier targeting by opponent pieces

f5 is a black isolated pawn, blocked by an enemy pawn, which makes its advance f5-f4 to try getting rid of the weakness impossible currently, as well as very difficult to arrange through different tactics; of course, such a pawn is additionally handicapped and should get over-penalty for this specific condition

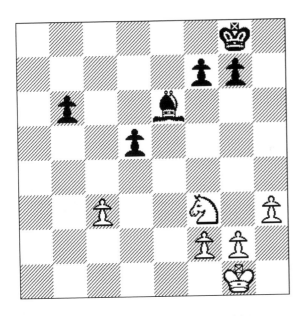

well, sufficient control over the d4 square by the white pieces makes d5-d4 pawn push extremely difficult or impossible to achieve either in the short or longer term; in this way, the weakness is amplified

Frequency: very frequent

Fixed isolated pawn

Definition: isolated pawn, on ranks 2, 3 or 4, that is blocked by an enemy pawn that is not isolated

b3 is a fixed isolated pawn on its 3rd rank. g4 is another such pawn on its 4th rank.

Value: small penalty, -2cps in the mg, -3cps in the eg

Additional information: well, such a pawn definitely constitutes an additional weakness, as the enemy pawn blocking it will restrict its movements, making it an easier, immobile target. Besides, it will be restricted on a less advanced rank, which will further highlight its fragility. The enemy pawn, on the other hand, blocking it, will not be vulnerable as much, as by definition it will be a non-isolated pawn, so other enemy pawns will support or potentially be able to support it.

Frequency: frequent

Knight and pawn immobilising enemy isolated pawn

Definition: knight and defended pawn simultaneously attacking the square in front of enemy isolated pawn

the knight on c2 and the defended pawn on c3 represent that condition

Value: small bonus, 5cps in the mg, 3cps in the eg

Additional information: the bonus is due for the fact, that in this way the enemy isolated pawn is highly probable to be immobile.

On the diagrammed position, for example, the black b5 pawn can not successfully advance one square, as it will be lost with no compensation. In case only the c3 pawn had been controlling the b4 square in front of it, the advance would still be possible, and that could open lines for attack.
The condition requiring the friendly pawn to be defended is necessary, as otherwise it too would be vulnerable, and the whole formula would not make much sense.

Frequency: frequent

2 pawns controlling the square in front of an enemy isolated pawn

the white b3 and d3 pawns control the square in front of the black isolated pawn on c5

Value: small bonus, 5cps, both for the mg and eg

Additional information: the bonus is due for the obvious reason, that the enemy isolated pawn is completely logically immobilised, as any its advance, unsupported by a friendly pawn that is unavailable on adjacent file, will lead to its

demise. Own pieces supporting the advance will help in no way either.

Frequency: frequent

Pawn controlling the square in front of enemy doubled isolated pawn

the c3 pawn controls the square in front of the black b5 doubled isolated pawn

Value: bonus, 8cps, both for the mg and eg

Additional information: the bonus is due for the ability of the pawn to stop 2 enemy pawns in their advance at the same time.
As easily seen on the diagrammed position, as both the b5 and b7 black pawns are isolated, with no friendly pawns on adjacent files capable of supporting their advance, the c3 pawn stops their forward movement single-handedly. The b5 pawn can not advance and, because of it, the b7 pawn going behind it, can not advance too.

Frequency: frequent

Pair of central isolated pawns

Definition: isolated pawns on e2 and e3, or d2 and d3

d2 and d3 are such a pair

Value: large penalty, -30cps, only for the mg

Additional information: the penalty is due not so much because of the structural weakness of such pawns, but rather because of their mg paralytical dysfunction. As such pawns are central, the pawn on its 2nd rank will block the friendly bishop on the same side of the board on its home square, while at the same time blocking the development of the friendly queen, positioned on the same file, too. With these 2 pieces blocked, the rest of the side's pieces will be blocked too, so this will have a very negative reflection on general piece development as a whole.

In the early middlegame, with lots of available piece attacks upon the king, that might prove decisive.

as easily recognised, the pair of central isolated pawns on d2 and d3 are a major liability.

Because of them, the white pieces are not only undeveloped, but very difficult to develop, too. The d3 pawn blocks the white bishop on e2, its counterpart on d2 does the same with the c1 bishop, but even more stringently, as, in order for the bishop to develop in the center, the d3 pawn should move first, and then the d2 one. This takes a lot of time. The white queen can not develop along the d file, too. As the bishop on c1 blocks the access of the white rook on a1 to the c file, it is certainly not an overstatement to say that more or less the entire white queen side is paralysed.

From that point of view, the one pawn material deficit of black is more than compensated by its superior development.

pair of isolated central pawns on the side where the own king is are sometimes even more negative, as this will have immediate bearing on king safety

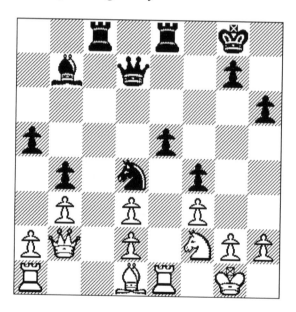

having the pawns blocked by an enemy pawn or minor piece is even nastier, as the pawns will be completely immobilised, thwarting friendly piece development for a longer time.

Black is winning with utmost ease.

Frequency: infrequent

Vertically isolated pawn

Definition: pawn that does not have other own pawns on the same rank, on the rank in front of it and on the rank behind it on both adjacent files, while still having at least one other own pawn on adjacent files on ranks different from the specified above

h5, g3, f5 are all vertically isolated pawns; a6 is another one

Value: penalty, valid in terms of psqt

8	0	0	0	0	0	0	0	0
7	-21	-22	-23	-24	-24	-23	-22	-21
6	-17	-18	-19	-20	-20	-19	-18	-17
5	-13	-14	-15	-16	-16	-15	-14	-13
4	-9	-10	-11	-12	-12	-11	-10	-9
3	-5	-6	-7	-8	-8	-7	-6	-5
2	-1	-2	-3	-4	-4	-3	-2	-1
1	0	0	0	0	0	0	0	0
	a	b	c	d	e	f	g	h

vertically isolated pawn penalty(mg)

	a	b	c	d	e	f	g	h
8	0	0	0	0	0	0	0	0
7	-22	-23	-24	-25	-25	-24	-23	-22
6	-18	-19	-20	-21	-21	-20	-19	-18
5	-14	-15	-16	-17	-17	-16	-15	-14
4	-10	-11	-12	-13	-13	-12	-11	-10
3	-6	-7	-8	-9	-9	-8	-7	-6
2	-2	-3	-4	-5	-5	-4	-3	-2
1	0	0	0	0	0	0	0	0
	a	b	c	d	e	f	g	h

vertically isolated pawn penalty(eg)

Additional information: vertically isolated pawns are one of the many types of undefended(weak) pawns. They are due penalty, though relatively small, because:
- they are weak(undefended), easily attackable and capturable by enemy pieces
- largely inflexible, although some possible pushes by such pawns or other own pawns would still lead to the building of a compact pawn structure, most will not, especially when the other own pawns on adjacent files are further apart in terms of ranks

On a range of occasions, bridging the gap to build a compact structure is even practically impossible, depending on enemy pawn control, see for example this one:

even though only 2 ranks apart, it is impossible for the g3 pawn to span the distance to the h5 friendly pawn and build

a compact structure by pushing g3-g4, as g4 will be met by a f5-g4 capture

Frequency: very frequent

Squeezed pawn

Definition: pawn, that is not defended, with enemy pawns on the same file, one rank in front of it, and one rank behind it

black e4 is such a pawn. It is squeezed between the pair of white e3 and e5 pawns on the same file on adjacent ranks.
white e5 pawn, on the other hand, is not a squeezed pawn, as, although conforming to the same conditions, it is defended by the f4 pawn.

Value: penalty, -10cps, both for the mg and eg

Additional information: the penalty is due, because such pawn is more vulnerable than usual, with enemy pieces having easier access to it, and own pieces a more difficult task in supporting it, because of the 2 enemy restricting pawns.
For example, on the diagrammed position, a black rook would not be able to defend it on the file the pawn is, as the e5 white pawn will prevent that.

even if not isolated, friendly pawns on adjacent files will have hard time defending it, too, as, in order to do that, they will first have to pass through the enemy sentinel behind it.

above, f7-f5, trying to support e4, might be met with ef6, and the pawn is still unsupported.

Frequency: infrequent

Doubled pawns

Definition: a pawn that has another own pawn on the same file on a less advanced rank

(of course, it is a matter of convention whether to define doubled pawns in terms of the more advanced or the less advanced pawn, here we will follow the first option, although the second one is perfectly reasonable too, it all depends on how you look at the board and how you estimate your other evaluation features)

doubled pawn on b4
(no matter what the other possible positional factors might be, it seems clumsy and unappealing both in the mg and eg)

Value: penalty valid in terms of psqt

8	0	0	0	0	0	0	0	0
7	-38	-18	-23	-28	-28	-23	-18	-38
6	-36	-16	-21	-26	-26	-21	-16	-36
5	-34	-14	-19	-24	-24	-19	-14	-34
4	-32	-12	-17	-22	-22	-17	-12	-32
3	-30	-10	-15	-20	-20	-15	-10	-30
2	0	0	0	0	0	0	0	0
1	0	0	0	0	0	0	0	0
	a	b	c	d	e	f	g	h

doubled pawn penalty psqt(mg)

8	0	0	0	0	0	0	0	0
7	-48	-23	-30	-38	-38	-30	-23	-48
6	-46	-21	-28	-36	-36	-28	-21	-46
5	-44	-19	-26	-34	-34	-26	-19	-44
4	-42	-17	-24	-32	-32	-24	-17	-42
3	-40	-15	-22	-30	-30	-22	-15	-40
2	0	0	0	0	0	0	0	0
1	0	0	0	0	0	0	0	0
	a	b	c	d	e	f	g	h

doubled pawn penalty psqt(eg)

Additional information: doubled pawns are the easiest to recognise on the board, even by complete newbies. You just have to see the one after the other on the same file pattern, but the ugly structure is even more salient.

Humans definitely estimate doubled pawns better than even top engines, but I guess both humans and engines alike largely underestimate what is hidden in this concept and its various implementations.

One can score doubled pawns in at least a dozen specific situations, but we will concentrate here on just the most important ones.

Doubled pawns get their well-deserved penalty due to a variety of reasons, among which the most salient ones are:
- the doubled pawn thwarts the advance of the less advanced pawn behind it
- in case the doubled pawn is also a pawn-blocked one, above feature is even more negative, thus rendering both own pawns awkward
- in the highly indicative case of a doubled pawn blocked by an enemy one with the other own pawn placed on the rank immediately behind the doubled pawn, the immobility weakness of the doubled pawn and its behind-walker are exaggerated to a point that makes them a tremendous liability
- in many cases, if not defended, doubled pawns are of course also easily attackable
- in the extremely negative case that the doubled pawn is simultaneously an isolated one, even adding the doubled and isolated penalties for the pawn will not be sufficient to completely capture the negativity of the phenomenon, so in this case an additional over-penalty is due
- a large additional over-penalty is also very much appropriate in the specific case, when the doubled pawn is opposed by an enemy pawn and there is symmetrical pawn placement of both own and enemy pawns on the 2 adjacent files(the single adjacent file in case the doubled pawn is an edge a or h file one), i.e. both files are open ones, one is open and the other one closed, or both files are closed; the penalty

is due to the fact that, practically, the side with the doubled pawn plays with a pawn less, as undoubling such a pawn is extremely difficult or practically impossible to achieve, even in the long term

blocked doubled pawn on d5
well, such a pawn simply can not advance to try undoubling with the help of own pieces, so it is a bigger negative(a few cps, maybe -5 or -6 in the mg, -8 in the eg)

blocked doubled pawn on f4 with its less advanced counterpart on the rank immediately behind it, and immobile
(this is a serious penalty, as both f4 and f3 pawns are immobile, more vulnerable

targets, more durable liabilities; -8cps additional penalty in the mg, -12cps in the eg, would be quite appropriate)

doubled isolated pawn on c4
well, this is a major weakness, due further over-penalty, maybe some -15cps or so in the mg, some -22cps in the eg; reasons:
- pawn is even more vulnerable to opponent pieces' attacks
- pawn is even more difficult to undouble

symmetrical doubled white pawn on h5;
symmetrical doubled black pawn on c4 (well, as you immediately spot for yourselves, this is a major weakness; the side with the doubled pawn effectively plays with a pawn less, this pawn is

extremely difficult to undouble, extremely difficult to advance, and more or less worthless, even in the very long run. I would assign some -20cps mg penalty, -40cps eg penalty for such a pawn)

Frequency: frequent

Distance between doubled pawns

Definition: available squares between the more advanced and the less advanced doubled pawn

3 available squares between the b2 and b6 doubled pawns, one available square between the d2 and d4 doubled pawns, and zero available squares between the g2 and g3 doubled pawns

Value: small bonus, assigned in terms of the square distance, equal for mg and eg

- 2cps, for one available square
- 4cps, for two available squares
- 6cps, when the squares are three
- 8cps, for 4 squares

Additional information: the bonus is given for 2 reasons:
- with bigger distance between the pawns, the less advanced doubled pawn, the pawn

going behind, will have more free available pushes
- more advanced pawns, already having crossed the center line, in spite of being weak, already gain space and are less of a liability

As easily seen on the diagrammed position, the most awkward constellation is that of the g2 and g3 doubled pawns, with the pawn going behind, g2, unable to move.

the c6 doubled pawn is a strong passer, so its weakness is not felt at all.
The h2 and h3 doubled pawns, however, are very weak, with both immobilised by the black blocking h4 pawn on adjacent squares.

Frequency: frequent

Restricting enemy doubled pawn on its 3rd rank

Definition: pawn on the 4th rank, controlling the square in front of enemy doubled pawn on its 3rd rank, provided that square is empty

the h4 pawn restricts the black g6 pawn

Value: small bonus, 6cps in the mg, 8cps in the eg, for the restricting pawn

Additional information: the bonus is given for the obvious very negative condition, making the doubled pawn unable to move forward without severely compromising the pawn structure, and thus less valuable.

On the diagrammed position, if g6 pawn advances, after hg5 fg5, a doubled isolated pawn will appear on g5, while, if f6 pawn advances, the doubled g6 pawn will lack the support of a friendly pawn to do a successful push, remaining logically immobile until a support from a friendly piece.
The condition is more severe, as the doubled pawn is not advanced.

Frequency: frequent

Blocking an enemy doubled pawn on its 3rd rank

Definition: pawn on the 5th rank, blocking an enemy doubled pawn on its 3rd rank

the g5 white pawn blocks the black g6 pawn

Value: bonus, 15cps, both for the mg and eg, for the advanced blocking pawn

Additional information: the good bonus is given for the almost permanent doubled and immobile condition of the doubled pawn until the opponent blocking pawn is possibly captured.

As easily recognised on the diagrammed position, if the f7 black pawn goes to f6, and then captures the blocking g5 pawn, a tripled very weak pawn will arise on g5 for black, while, after an f7-f5 push, the doubled pawn condition will remain unchanged.

The bonus is large, as the doubled pawn is immobilised close to its home rank.

Frequency: frequent

Pair of doubled pawns on adjacent files

Definition: a doubled pawn, with another own doubled pawn on adjacent file

f3 and g4 are such a pair

Value: sufficiently large penalty, -20cps, both for the mg and eg

Additional information: the penalty is due for the obvious structural deficiency of the pair, it is even more immobile than 2 separate doubled pawns on different portions of the board, as the adjacent pair and the friendly pawns going behind them are in each other's way. Besides, the awkward non-standard phalanx is easily stopped by a significantly smaller number of opposing pawns, 3, or even just 2.

Also, the pair will be very clumsily placed for any friendly piece wishing to play an active role in the region.

2 separate doubled pawns penalties will not be sufficient, the above-mentioned weaknesses necessitate an ad-hoc over-penalisation.

Frequency: infrequent

Tripled pawn

Definition: a pawn that has 2 other own pawns on the same file that are both less advanced

tripled pawn on e5
(usually, tripled pawns will be also
isolated, as such pawns come from
adjacent files)

Value: penalty, -30cps mg, -30cps eg

Additional information: of course, an over-penalty above that for the simple doubled pawn is due because:
- tripled pawns are even uglier, even more awkward and clumsier
- extremely difficult to untriple and also extremely vulnerable to enemy pieces' attacks, as such pawns will frequently be isolated too

Frequency: infrequent

Backward pawns

Backward pawns are so plentiful, that at least 30 to 50% of all available pawn features might have something to do with them. In fact, backwardness in itself means that the advance of a pawn, no matter its rank and location, might be stopped by an opponent pawn or any other piece, so that its further movement would lead to its loss. Under such a condition, almost any pawn that has enemy pawns on adjacent files that would stop its march to promotion, and even passers, whose squares to promotion would be sufficiently controlled by opponent pieces, could be defined as backward; the degrees of backwardness, however, would be extremely different in all the possible cases, ranging from couple of percent backward to almost a 100 percent backward.

Here, we will discuss only the most salient features involving backwardness, as, even for a master specialist in backward pawns, it is far from an easy task to make perfect sense how to specifically define all the backward conditions without going into an unimaginable extent of detail. One of the reasons for this is that square control is dependent on the strength of the different pieces attacking the particular square, and doing a full analysis of all piece attacks on all possible squares is currently impossible for top humans and top engines alike.

Standard backward pawn

Definition: a pawn defending another own pawn, blocked by an enemy pawn, with no other own pawns on adjacent files on the same rank as the backward pawn or on less advanced ranks

d3 is a standard backward pawn above

Value: Penalty, valid in terms of psqt (and it makes very much sense to split tables into opposed/unopposed flags, as unopposed standard backward pawns are easier targets to enemy heavy pieces along the semi-open files those pawns are on)

8	0	0	0	0	0	0	0	0
7	0	0	0	0	0	0	0	0
6	0	0	0	0	0	0	0	0
5	0	0	0	0	0	0	0	0
4	-10	-20	-20	-30	-30	-20	-20	-10
3	-15	-25	-25	-35	-35	-25	-25	-15
2	-20	-30	-30	-40	-40	-30	-30	-20
1	0	0	0	0	0	0	0	0
	a	b	c	d	e	f	g	h

backward opposed pawn psqt(mg)

8	0	0	0	0	0	0	0	0
7	0	0	0	0	0	0	0	0
6	0	0	0	0	0	0	0	0
5	0	0	0	0	0	0	0	0
4	-15	-25	-25	-35	-35	-25	-25	-15
3	-20	-30	-30	-40	-40	-30	-30	-20
2	-25	-35	-35	-45	-45	-35	-35	-25
1	0	0	0	0	0	0	0	0
	a	b	c	d	e	f	g	h

backward opposed pawn psqt(eg)

8	0	0	0	0	0	0	0	0
7	0	0	0	0	0	0	0	0
6	0	0	0	0	0	0	0	0
5	-3	-4	-5	-6	-6	-5	-4	-3
4	-12	-25	-25	-35	-35	-25	-25	-12
3	-18	-30	-30	-40	-40	-30	-30	-18
2	-25	-35	-35	-45	-45	-35	-35	-25
1	0	0	0	0	0	0	0	0
	a	b	c	d	e	f	g	h

backward unopposed pawn psqt(mg)

8	0	0	0	0	0	0	0	0
7	0	0	0	0	0	0	0	0
6	0	0	0	0	0	0	0	0
5	-5	-6	-7	-8	-8	-7	-6	-5
4	-17	-30	-30	-40	-40	-30	-30	-17
3	-25	-35	-35	-45	-45	-35	-35	-25
2	-30	-40	-40	-50	-50	-40	-40	-30
1	0	0	0	0	0	0	0	0
	a	b	c	d	e	f	g	h

backward unopposed pawn psqt(eg)

Additional information: standard backward pawns get their well-deserved penalty due to a variety of reasons:
- the pawn itself is undefended/easily attackable
- on many occasions, if this pawn is captured, and the other own pawn it defends is not supported by other friendly pawn, it will immediately get weak too
- as said, most of the penalty goes for the fact that such a pawn is not able to realistically advance without being lost; this means the side with such a pawn has less resources to influence the game
- standard backward pawns are extremely damaging on lower ranks, as having low-mobility pawns on the home rank or close to it is equivalent to a sort of receiving a cramped position on the section of the board where those pawns are, with the additional negative of not being able to use such pawns for attacking purposes by legitimately advancing them

Frequency: very frequent

Twice backward pawns

Definition: a backward pawn the square in front of which is simultaneously attacked by 2 enemy pawns, both of which are blocked by own pawns

Note: it is extremely curious that even top humans do not make very extensive use of this useful concept, and top engines have an extremely difficult time implementing and recognising the concept either.

Seemingly, this feature is so positional, involving such a long sequence of moves until its value is recognised, coming to fruition, that many would even entirely disregard it.

d3 now is already twice backward, involving a significantly bigger penalty
(as you see, moving forward is altogether impossible, even with the significant help of own pieces, making the twice backward pawn almost entirely useless)

Value: large penalty, valid in terms of psqt and opposed/not opposed flags

8	0	0	0	0	0	0	0	0
7	0	0	0	0	0	0	0	0
6	0	0	0	0	0	0	0	0
5	0	0	0	0	0	0	0	0
4	0	-30	-40	-50	-50	-40	-30	0
3	0	-35	-45	-55	-55	-45	-35	0
2	0	-40	-50	-60	-60	-50	-40	0
1	0	0	0	0	0	0	0	0
	a	b	c	d	e	f	g	h

twice backward opposed pawn psqt(mg)

8	0	0	0	0	0	0	0	0
7	0	0	0	0	0	0	0	0
6	0	0	0	0	0	0	0	0
5	0	0	0	0	0	0	0	0
4	0	-35	-45	-55	-55	-45	-35	0
3	0	-40	-50	-60	-60	-50	-40	0
2	0	-45	-55	-65	-65	-55	-45	0
1	0	0	0	0	0	0	0	0
	a	b	c	d	e	f	g	h

twice backward opposed pawn psqt(eg)

8	0	0	0	0	0	0	0	0
7	0	0	0	0	0	0	0	0
6	0	0	0	0	0	0	0	0
5	0	-20	-25	-30	-30	-25	-20	0
4	0	-35	-45	-55	-55	-45	-35	0
3	0	-40	-50	-60	-60	-50	-40	0
2	0	-45	-55	-65	-65	-55	-45	0
1	0	0	0	0	0	0	0	0
	a	b	c	d	e	f	g	h

twice backward unopposed pawn psqt(mg)

8	0	0	0	0	0	0	0	0
7	0	0	0	0	0	0	0	0
6	0	0	0	0	0	0	0	0
5	0	-25	-30	-35	-35	-30	-25	0
4	0	-40	-50	-60	-60	-50	-40	0
3	0	-45	-55	-65	-65	-55	-45	0
2	0	-50	-60	-70	-70	-60	-50	0
1	0	0	0	0	0	0	0	0
	a	b	c	d	e	f	g	h

twice backward unopposed pawn psqt(eg)

Additional information: twice backward pawns are due their penalty because:
- they are completely immobile, which would translate to the side having such a pawn practically playing without it; it is difficult to find a bigger waste of positional resources in chess, at least what concerns pawn evaluation
- undefended and easily attackable; in case such a pawn is destroyed, any other of the 2 own pawns defended by the twice backward pawn, if not supported by a second pawn, would immediately become undefended too, which is exceptionally

negative when both would be supported only by it

- very long term liability; in order for such a pawn to disappear from the board with advantageous consequences for the side having it, this side should have weighty tactical resources at its disposal, and tactical resources, as everyone knows, are not always readily available

- on a range of occasions, under specific conditions, for example when such a pawn is part of the own king shelter, or a central one, the burden on the side having it increases tremendously, up to a point to quickly lose the game

- not infrequently, a central d3 or e3 twice backward pawn would lead to a complete closing of the position with inevitable advantage for the opponent side, as the opponent side will have a pawn more on one of the wings, getting additional storming resources, while at the same time the twice backward side will be devoid of realistic counterplay, bearing in mind that the strongest counterplay ever is the one in the center

twice backward pawn on the 2nd rank is even worse

(by definition, under such a condition, the white position would be cramped, no matter the disposition of forces on other wings; this is even more negative in terms

of cramping than if a black pawn wedge was placed on d3)

well, imagine this situation: pawn numbers for both sides are equal, but, as d3 is twice backward in the center, white practically plays with a pawn less, d3-d4 break in the center to attain counterplay is impossible, and black has a pawn more on the king side to start a mighty king-side attack by pushing g7-g5, h7-h5, etc.

Frequency: infrequent

Twice backward feature

Definition: pawn, that is not twice backward, defending an own pawn, blocked by an enemy pawn, with the square in front of it controlled by 2 enemy pawns, and no own pawns on the same rank or less advanced ranks on adjacent files.

Otherwise, simply, a backward pawn, that is not twice backward, with the square in front of it controlled by 2 enemy pawns.

d3 is a twice backward feature. It is not a twice backward pawn(which will defend 2 own pawns at the same time), defends an own pawn, c4, and the square in front of it, d4, is controlled by 2 enemy pawns, c5 and e5.

f2 is another twice backward feature, this time part of the king shelter

Value: sufficiently large penalty, -25cps in the mg, -15cps in the eg, over the one for a standard backward pawn

Additional information: the penalty is obviously due for the peculiar almost complete immobilisation of the pawn. The condition is especially relevant, when such a pawn is a central one, or part of the own king shelter. In such cases, the full center gets immobilised, simulating closedness, which will have beneficial effect on the opponent side, if attacking, as it will have more time to regroup and bring new resources supporting the attack. Or, alternatively, the king shelter is less flexible and much more prone to enemy attacks, sometimes of a slow nature.

It is necessary to consider this pawn feature apart from standard backward pawns, as the condition is much more severe. It is also necessary to make a distinction with a full twice backward pawn, as this one already gets its separate, much higher penalty. The feature is frequent and important, so it will be a big mistake not accounting for it.

d3 is a twice backward feature in the center of the board that pretty much loses the game. Because of its nature, the center as a whole is completely immobilised, so black has all the time in the world to start a gradual kingside attack with g7-g5, Rf7-g7, etc., slowly building up pressure. That swings the balance of forces in a decisive way.
Some engines or humans might think white has the advantage because of its more prolific pawn shelter, as well as the good b5 outpost square for the white

knight on c3, but that is far from being the case.

So that, failing to consider similar subtle evaluation features might sometimes give a fully distorted picture of the position.

there is no other option but for white to lose the game, after a bishop sacrifice on h4, followed by bringing both rooks to the king side, Nf6-h7-g5-f3, etc., with a rout, but some engines or humans might think it is white who has the advantage, due to the missing black pawn shelter, the advanced white queenside pawns and somewhat better development.

Of course, this is not so, and the main reason for black's substantial positional advantage is the completely immobilised white pawn shelter, in the form of the f2 pawn, constituting a twice backward feature. Because of this shelter inflexibility, black has all the time in the world to slowly increase pressure, bringing up additional attacking resources to the king side of the board.

The mg bonus is substantially higher than the eg one, precisely because of the above-mentioned features, encountered exclusively in the mg.

Frequency: frequent

Semibackward pawn on the 2nd rank

Definition: a pawn exclusively on the 2nd rank, that is defending aligned, with the own pawn defended by it blocked by an enemy pawn

c2 is a semibackward pawn on the 2nd rank (c2 is defending aligned, and b3 is blocked by b4)

Value: penalty, -15cps in the mg, -10cps in the eg

Additional information: the penalty is due to following factors:
- usually, the square in front of such a pawn would be additionally controlled by enemy pieces, which would render this pawn effectively fully backward; the pawn is simply too unadvanced and chances are enemy pieces would already have reached this portion of the board earlier
- even if not so, a single push could be met by capture, while a double push by an en passant capture, which would mean the building of a particular pawn structure largely dependent on the discretion of the opponent; this is especially sensitive in cases involving the king shelter

Frequency: very frequent

Unbackwarded pawn

Definition: a pawn on the 4th rank, defended by an own pawn, which in turn is blocked by an enemy pawn

e4 is an unbackwarded pawn

(as you easily see, it simply can not possibly be made backward by the enemy d4 pawn, as it has already moved past the influence square of d4; this means, you guarantee yourself easier life)

Value: bonus, 10cps in the mg, 5cps in the eg

Additional information: unbackwarded pawns get their quite deserved small value for the fact that such a pawn has already moved past the control of the enemy sentinel pawn on the same rank next to it, so it practically can not become backward, at least not on low 2nd and 3rd ranks. This is an important asset, though many humans tend to disregard it, and what concerns engines, they have almost no clue about such pawns, unless there is something tactical to see alongside.

Such pawns are extremely useful in the mg with larger closed structures, both in trying to win the game using a wing attack and in attempting to draw, resorting to closing/blocking as many files as possible, while getting rid of any possible backward

weaknesses that would annul drawing chances.

well, why above position, the Chech Benoni, arising with a bit of transformations after for example 1.d4 c5 2.d5 e5 3.c4 d6 4.Nc3 g6 5.e4 Bg7 6.Bd3 Ne7 gives black complete equality, which both top engines and many humans fail to recognise: c5 and e5 black pawns are unbackwarded, they can not become weak backward pawns, it is impossible for white to break with c4-c5 on the queenside, as c4 is blocked, while at the same time black could easily draw by placing all black pawns on dark squares, f6,g5,h6, achieving symmetry and building an impregnable fortress; if white does not push f2-f4, after f7-f5-f4 black can even get better

same situation: this favours white, no matter how much surprised some humans, and especially some engines, might be. c4 and e4 are unbackwarded, central at that, the position is largely closed and, no matter that white significantly lags behind in development, f2-f4, creating a nice compact structure, involving chains/storming pawns at that, should easily decide the game.

Backwardmakers

A backwardmaker is any pawn that makes an enemy pawn backward, semi-backward or otherwise backward.

d5 is the backwardmaker, and e7 is the backward pawn

c5 is the backwardmaker, and b7 is the semi-backward pawn

Backwardmakers might be especially useful with conceptual definitions.

Unopposed backward-maker on the 5th rank

Definition: pawn that is not opposed, not a passer or a potential passer, takes the 5th rank, with an enemy pawn on the 7th rank(2nd rank from the opponent point of view) on adjacent file

well, b5 is an unopposed backwardmaker on the 5th rank

Value: bonus, 15cps in the mg, 10cps in the eg

Additional information: the bonus is given because:
- although not strictly backward, the enemy pawn on its home rank can not move advantageously, without being lost or creating further weaknesses
- even if the enemy pawn is not captured upon advancing, the backwardmaker might transform into an advanced passed pawn(see the diagrammed position)

Central unopposed chain backward pawn

Definition: exclusively, d3 or e3 pawns that are unopposed, with the condition that such a pawn is defended by a pawn and simultaneously defends another own pawn along the same diagonal, which in turn is blocked by an enemy pawn

e6 is an unopposed chain backward pawn

Value: penalty, -15cps, awarded only for the mg

Additional information: this is a strictly mg feature, with great effect on the game, as everything central. Penalty is given because, although such a pawn is defended, not vulnerable, it still can not advantageously advance along the central file to break open the game. As you can easily see from the diagrammed position, e6-e5 is impossible to play and, an attempt to break with f7-f6 and e6-e5 is frequently thwarted by a predominant control of white pieces upon the e5 square, for example Nf3 will often be present, and a white rook on e1 active on the semiopen e file.

Frequency: frequent

Central backwardmakers

Definition: white pawn on e5, black pawns on e6,f7,g7, black king on e,f,g or h file, or, on the queen side, white pawn on d5, black pawns on d6,c7,b7, black king on d,c,b or a file

central backwardmaker on the king side

central backwardmaker on the queen side

Value: sufficiently large bonus, 30cps in the mg, 10cps in the eg

Additional information: this is one of the most important terms at all. Its relevance is so big, and it is so frequently encountered, that excluding it from any evaluation framework, human or engine alike, would be simply a gross negligence.

Humans mostly should handle this purely theoretically sufficiently well, but, in actual fact, that is far from the case in a range of situations, as the associated variations are usually so deep, that calculating everything would be quite difficult even with the mighty help of pattern recognition. Even top engines, too, not to mention the rest, have generally a hell of a time with the feature, mostly completely ignoring it. The reason should be lacking refined evaluation, but also extreme depth of the lines, inaccessible to even the best searchers.

The very-well deserved bonus is dispensed for the following rather weighty reasons:
- the enemy pawn on adjacent file to the backwardmaker is a semi-backward one, and, as it constitutes part of the enemy king shelter, the weakness is further highlighted
- having a semi-backward pawn of the king shelter basically means the shelter will be inflexible, sometimes, in order to defend, a shelter pawn should move forward, and this will largely depend on the discretion of the backwardmaker, that has always the option of capturing; frequently, capturing will lead to severely weakening the pawn shelter, with isolated pawns left behind and also the number of shelter pawns decreasing, not moving the backward pawn at all, on the other hand, will hardly be tolerable in the long run
- as the backwardmaker is a central pawn, this presumes by definition a more closed character of the position, meaning the attacker will have more time to regroup its pieces

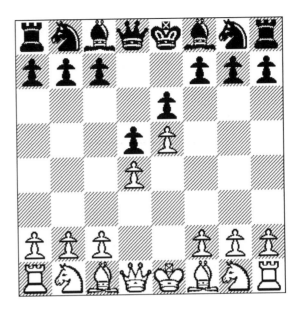

let's imagine now, what will happen, if black plays f7-f5, or f7-f6, trying to get rid of the clamp. White has the option of capturing ef6, and after gf6, the black shelter will shrink to only 2 pawns(f6 and h6), with h6 becoming isolated. In case black captures with a piece on f6, the shelter will again shrink to 2 pawns(g7 and h6), with the e6 pawn also possibly becoming isolated.

So, in each case, the shelter will suffer enormously.

This term has a tremendous theoretical importance. It is encountered, starting from the very first moves, in a great range of openings, and, if understood to the fullest, could become even more frequent phenomenon.

To start with, let us take the French as an example.

after 1.e4 e6 2.d4 d5, white can continue with 3.e5, reaching above position.

Do you recognise the pattern in the form of the e5,e6,f7,g7 pawns? It is already there, on the 3rd move, in a very popular opening. Of course, this might not be the wisest kind of play, as white will compromise on development, but is still strong.

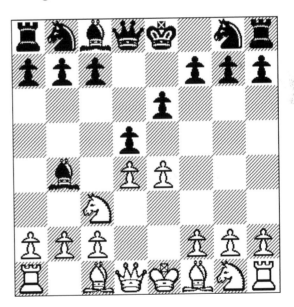

or, in the same French, emphasising development, with a better piece coordination, white might choose the McCutcheon, with 3.Nc3 Bb4. Again, white is faced with a choice, what to do in the center. Recognising our strong central pattern, the natural option would be 4.e5, which is indeed the best move, also

107

theoretically and statistically proven. Still, many humans will shun away from it, while, even the top of the top of engines will almost exclusively play ed5 ed5, exchanging in the center and losing all of white's advantage.

How can such engines be trusted?

Another very frequent opening occurrence of the term could happen in the English Opening, after 1.c4 e5 2.Nc3 Nf6, in case white continues with e3 instead of e4, giving black the opportunity to gain space advantage in the center and clamp white's king shelter by advancing e5-e4.

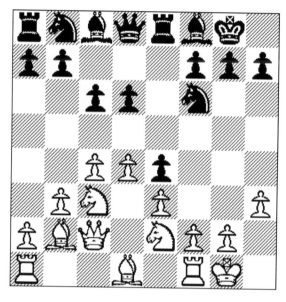

in spite of the big development advantage white enjoys, black has already a winning position. And the main reason for this is the familiar central pawn pattern in the form of the e4,e3,f2,g2 pawns. The central e4 black backwardmaker is having a cramping effect upon the entire white king side and renders the white shelter inflexible.

I am not very certain about humans, but, judging from the theoretical popularity of the English Opening lines, involving e3 instead of e4, humans mostly fail to understand the relevance of the feature, even after decades of analysis. Mainstream chess textbooks still do not recommend playing 3.e4 instead of 3.e3 in the mentioned line!

Top engines, of course, completely misunderstand and misplay the variation. Most of them will still assess above position as very favourable for white, but of course, black is winning. As the associated lines are very deep, engines basically see nothing and rely on their positional evaluation, which is far from perfect and, in many cases, like this one, rudimentary.

Winning is pretty much straightforward: black continues with slow attack on the king side, pushing pawns there, and gradually transferring pieces to this focal point, including the ones on the queen side. As the position largely carries a closed character, emphasised by the e4 central backwardmaker, black has all the time in the world for regrouping and coordination. White, on the other hand, can do almost nothing, as the white shelter is inflexible, and attempting to break free with f2-f3 or f2-f4 will easily backfire, creating multiple weaknesses.

Examples like that are rife, but there is no need to illustrate them all. What is more important is the pattern recognition. Precisely because of this term, the French is a bad opening for black, as widely recognised by modern top players, so one should choose one's openings very carefully.

The extreme importance of the central backwardmaker feature is also due to the fact that it starts appearing on the board with the very first moves, thus influencing the entire game.

Frequency: very frequent

Distant backward pawn

Definition: pawn on the 2nd rank, with no enemy pawns on the 3rd and 4th ranks on the same file, with another own pawn on the 4th rank on adjacent file, that is blocked by enemy pawn, and no other own pawns on the 2nd and 3rd ranks on the other adjacent file

c2 is a distant backward pawn. The squares in front of it on the same file are not occupied by enemy pawns, on the 4th rank on adjacent file there is another own pawn that is blocked by enemy pawn, b4, and on the 2nd and 3rd ranks on the other adjacent file there are no friendly pawns, that could support its advance.

Value: penalty, -10cps, both for the mg and eg

Additional information: the penalty is due for the obvious backwardness of the pawn. On c3, it would be a fully-fledged backward pawn, but, even on c2, one square less advanced, its backward condition is evident, though not that much severe. The pawn could advance once, becoming a full backward pawn, but not twice, on c4, where it will be lost by the b5-c4 capture, like any other backward pawn.
So, c2 is indeed a backward pawn, with less prominent character.

Frequency: very frequent

Backward long chain pawn blocked condition

Definition: long chain pawn, that is not blocked by an enemy pawn, with the pawn it defends and the pawn, defending it, part of the same chain, both blocked by enemy pawns

c3 is such a pawn. It is a long chain pawn, part of the b2-c3-d4 long chain, not blocked by an enemy pawn, and both the pawn it defends, d4, as well as the pawn defending it, b2, part of the same chain, are blocked by enemy pawns, d5 and b3 respectively.

g4 is another such pawn, this time

109

on the 4th rank

Value: small penalty, -8cps, both for the mg and eg

Additional information: this is not a full standard backward pawn in any conceivable way, but, although it is a defended, strong pawn, its partial backwardness is obvious. Indeed, as easily seen on above-posted diagrams, any advance of these pawns will be met by their loss.

So, the feature is real, the backward condition quite evident, but, as the pawn is a strong one, less vulnerable to enemy attacks, the penalty is naturally smaller.

Frequency: infrequent

Minor piece controlling the square in front of enemy backward pawn

Nd3 controls/attacks the square in front of black c6 backward pawn

Value: bonus, 8cps, mg and eg

Additional information: well, of course, minor piece control of such a square could very much decide how backward the pawn really is. If Nd3 was not present on the diagrammed position, c6-c5 push to get rid

of the backward pawn would be possible, with both Rc8 supporting that push on an x-ray and Qf8 directly supporting it. Now this push is simply banned, at least for the time being, and that gains white valuable time to achieve different goals.

Similar effect is achieved when such a square is attacked by a bishop.

Root pawn

Definition: the least advanced undefended pawn, part of a chain, short or longer one

c3 is the root pawn, or root, of the c3-d4-e5 longer chain.

h5 is the root of the h5-g4 short black chain.

Value: when not backward, root pawns only represent the bigger asset of the chain formation, and therefore should not be penalised

Frequency: very frequent

Attacking root pawns

Definition: any non-pawn and non-king piece attacking an enemy root pawn

Value: bonus, 10cps, both for the mg and eg

Additional information: the bonus is given for the obvious condition that, when such a root pawn is attacked and successfully destroyed, not only it perishes, but another enemy pawn, the one it used to defend, automatically becomes undefended too.

when the black bishop captures the c2 root pawn, the b3 pawn becomes automatically undefended and vulnerable

when the black knight captures the d4 root pawn, the c5 pawn becomes undefended.

When the black queen captures the g3 root pawn, the h4 pawn becomes undefended.

Frequency: frequent

Double root pawn

Definition: an undefended pawn defending 2 other own pawns at the same time

f2 is a double root pawn
(in this particular case being also part of the white king shelter)

Value: Penalty, valid in terms of psqt

8	0	0	0	0	0	0	0	0
7	0	0	0	0	0	0	0	0
6	0	-9	-10	-11	-11	-10	-9	0
5	0	-8	-9	-10	-10	-9	-8	0
4	0	-7	-8	-9	-9	-8	-7	0
3	0	-15	-18	-23	-23	-18	-15	0
2	0	-20	-25	-30	-30	-25	-20	0
1	0	0	0	0	0	0	0	0
	a	b	c	d	e	f	g	h

double root pawn psqt(mg)

	a	b	c	d	e	f	g	h
8	0	0	0	0	0	0	0	0
7	0	0	0	0	0	0	0	0
6	0	-9	-10	-11	-11	-10	-9	0
5	0	-8	-9	-10	-10	-9	-8	0
4	0	-7	-8	-9	-9	-8	-7	0
3	0	-8	-10	-13	-13	-10	-8	0
2	0	-10	-12	-15	-15	-12	-10	0
1	0	0	0	0	0	0	0	0

double root pawn psqt(eg)

Additional information: double root pawns should be penalised in view of the following factors:

- the pawn itself is weak, easily attackable and destroyable
- if captured, the 2 other pawns, defended by it, simultaneously become undefended and easy prey to enemy pieces
- this particular condition also means that the square in front of the double root pawn is pawn-undefended, a big disadvantage, especially with less advanced pawns

Frequency: frequent

Control of center

Control of center is one of the weightiest features available. Fischer said of central control: 'This is like hitting the ball with the bat'. When speaking about the center of the board, we primarily mean the 4 central-most squares, d4,e4,d5 and e5, the so-called focal center.

Control of center is more or less synonymous with friendly pawns exerting that control. So, when we speak of control of center, we primarily mean pawns.

Control of center basically has 2 forms: direct control and indirect square control.

Direct control will mean placing pawns on one of the 2 central squares on the 4th rank, d4 and e4, while indirect square control will be indirectly controlling with pawns the more advanced d5 and e5

central squares, either with the c4, or f4 pawns. Friendly pawns placed on d5 or e5 on the 5th rank within the enemy half of the board are pretty much irrelevant here, as this has already more to do with space advantage.

Direct pawn control within our evaluation framework is mainly seen by the relevant pawn, defended pawn, aligned pawn, etc. psqts, giving substantial bonus points for such pawns on d4 and e4, while indirect square control is provided for by terms like semi-central pawns attacking empty central squares, central bind and others.

Of course, minor or other pieces controlling the center simultaneously with own pawns also play a substantial role in center control, and are mirrored in a bunch of associated features.

Central piece attacks

Any non-pawn piece attacking an enemy piece or pawn positioned on one of the central squares gets the following bonus:

- 15cps for the mg, 8cps for the eg, if the enemy piece is on d4,e4,d5 or e5
- 8cps for the mg, 4cps for the eg, if the enemy piece is on c3,d3,e3,f3,c4,f4,c5,f5,c6,d6,e6 or f6(so-called extended center)

Reason is simple: a possible capture will place the attacker on a central square, and the center in chess is all-important. Values are not so big, as this is of largely tactical nature, and tactics in chess are usually very difficult to account for with general rules, in case you want to associate tactics with positional factors. Pawns are excluded from the set of attackers, as this would unnecessarily complicate the equation with a number of contradictory levers.

Nf3 getting an additional bonus for attacking e5 black pawn, Qf7 receiving the overbonus for assaulting white Nf3 and Rc4

Minor piece simultaneously attacking with an own pawn one of the 4 centralmost squares: e4,e5,d4,d5

Nf3 attacking the e5 square, simultaneously attacked by the own d4 pawn

Value: bonus, 7cps, only for the mg

Additional information: the bonus is due for efficient control of the center,

frequently preventing opponent breaks/counterplay there. As you can easily see on the diagrammed position, e6-e5 black central break is currently impossible precisely because of the double knight-pawn control over the e5 square; if Nf3 were not present, e6-e5 would be possible.

Despite its small value, this is an important feature, but only in the mg, where its influence spreads over a larger number of pieces involved in the struggle.

Frequency: very frequent

White pawns on e4,d4, black pawns on e5,d6; or white pawns on e4,d4, black pawns on d5,e6

first version of the term

113

second version of the term

a much much inferior central constellation for the defending side

Value: penalty, -7cps, only for the mg, for the side with the pair of aligned pawns

Additional information: no matter how paradoxical it might seem at first glance to penalise the side with more central pawns, this is a very efficient way indeed for the opposite side of challenging the enemy prevalence in the center. In fact, this may be the only wise way of doing so, as any other configuration, involving a central aligned pair for one side, and a central configuration different from the above 2, is very negative for the side lacking the pair.

For example, an aligned central pair on its 3rd rank, or just a single pawn on the central d and e files, barring big other relative advantages, would quite certainly compromise the position of the defending side. Something, of which most engines, and also many humans, are unaware of in a wide range of situations.

another possible very inferior central constellation for the defending side

I posted so many diagrams with just a couple of pawns present, as as many as 70% of all chess games might be decided based just on central issues, and this is one of them. Besides, as the pawn center is built-up very early in the game, this makes the feature even more important, as whatever side gets an early upperhand/manages to neutralise the opponent advantage, will be crucial to the whole game development.

no matter how passive the black position might look like, black does not have any difficulties holding, precisely because the central pressure is met the right way

Frequency: very frequent

The best move or semi-central pawns controlling the center

Definition: c4 pawn, attacking the d5 square, that is free, or, alternatively, f4 pawn, attacking the e5 square, that is free

Value: sufficient bonus, 20cps, just for the mg

Additional information: this is no doubt one of the most important terms at all. It arises right out of the opening, with the very first moves, and will determine the entire development of the game, so its significance can hardly be overestimated.

The extremely-well deserved bonus is dispensed for the following, rather weighty, reasons:
- the semi-central pawn will control a square where a central enemy pawn can land, the exchange will see less central pawn traded for an enemy central one, both on their 4th ranks, so this can, of course, only favour the side with the semi-central pawn
- when one semi-central pawn lands there, this is a preparation for possible establishment of a powerful central bind, in the form of the c4 and e4 pawns, or f4 and d4 pawns. Such binds almost always favour the binding side.
- as already declared, such moves happen right out of the opening, so their availability or lack will pretty much define the course of the game

yes, c4 is the best first move for white!
You might, of course, heartily laugh at this statement, but this is almost certainly the truth. In any case, 1.c4 is better than 1.e4 and even more so than 1.d4. Black almost lacks in satisfactory replies.

115

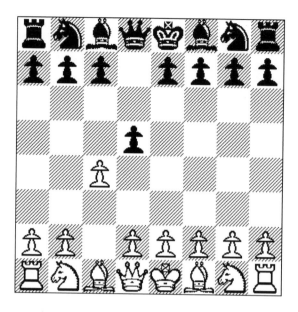

challenging the center with 1...d5.
This is certainly insufficient, as white has a very good reply in the form of the immediate c4-d5.

if black counters with 1...e5 instead, white can continue with 2.Nc3, and after 2...Nf6 3.e4!, we get to the above-posted position, almost never encountered in game play, which tremendously favours white.

Yes, substantially. Whether you believe me or not, is another matter, top engines also do not see that move, but in another 20 years, both humans and engines will understand 3.e4 is indeed the best possible move.

white has already won a pawn. Black will return it, of course, but will stay behind in development and, most importantly, as easily seen, white remains with a more valuable central d2 pawn, that will soon go to d4, vs a less valuable semi-central c7 pawn for black. That certainly makes a big distinction.

As easily seen on the diagrammed position, white has formed a central bind in the form of the c4 and e4 pawns, the d5 square is additionally controlled by the white knight on c3, and white has the choice after g2-g3 and Bg2 to fianchetto its light-square bishop on the king side, also controlling d5 on an x-ray, so black has almost no chance of pushing d7-d5 to break in the center and free its development. Thus, black will be totally pressed for space, the d4 outpost is quite an insufficient compensation in and of itself, and white can very successfully continue with f2-f4 kingside storm after a while, increasing the pressure.

you might doubt 1.c4 is the best first move for white, but the Sicilian, involving precisely this feature after 1.e4 c5, a semi-central pawn, c5, attacking the empty central d4 square, is more or less proven to be the best black reply on 1.e4, right?
This should certainly strike a bell.

1.f4 is not at all bad, too. Its only downside in comparison to 1.c4 is the fact that the f pawn is part of the white king shelter, and losing that pawn so early into the game without any clear-cut variations warranting it is certainly not the best of things.

countering with 1...e5 is insufficient. White gets quite an advantage after f4-e5, trading a less central pawn for an enemy more central one, but some still employ this gambit.

choosing 1...d5 instead provides white with full equality after, for example, 2.Nf3 Nf6 3.d4 Bf5 4.e3 c5 5.c3, though top engines will still assess this position as substantially favouring black

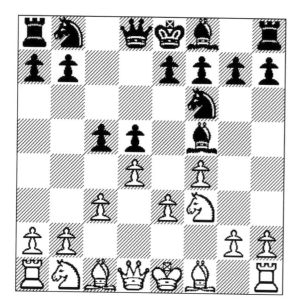

white has full equality. The game is closed, and the excellent black outpost square on e4 is largely compensated by the great white central bind upon the e5 square.

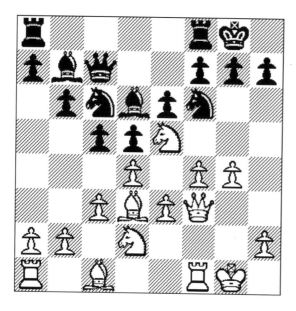

in the Stonewall Attack, white can even get much better. One pet Stockfish line for black runs as follows: 1.f4 d5 2.Nf3 Nf6 3.d4 e6 4.e3 c5 5.c3 Bd6 6.Bd3 Nc6 7.Ne5 Qc7 8.Nd2 b6 9.Qf3 Bb7 10.0-0 0-0 11.g4, and white gets a substantial edge. The obvious threat is g5, followed by Qh5, capturing on e5 is very dangerous and will create a mighty defended white pawn there, while the e4 outpost square is very well defended by white pieces, in the form of Bd3, Nd2 and Qf3.

Frequency: very frequent

Central bind

Definition: 2 own pawns, on c4 and e4, or, alternatively, on d4 and f4

central bind with f4 and d4 pawns

Value: large enough bonus, 40cps, only for the mg(this is above the also dispensed bonus for distant neighbours, as distant neighbours can not quite fully capture the specific condition, being dependent on other, non-central pawns too)

Additional information: this is an extremely valuable feature, wielding a significant influence on the whole game. The explanation lies in the fact that almost always such a pair of pawns in the mg will bind the center to great effect, making very difficult to impossible an opponent central break. Without a break, of course, it is difficult to find counterplay. In this way, binding the center in the aboveshown way is one of the most efficient paths to getting an upperhand, and should be strived at whenever possible, the earlier the better.

Almost any promising opening line includes such a constellation, although many, even top players, and engines as a whole, still fail to completely appreciate it. For example, the Maroczy Bind in the Sicilian is one of the best ways to counter the Sicilian, giving white large advantage, the Stonewall Attack is an extremely efficient white weapon, no matter it might look as bit passive at first glance, and, yes, black gets full equality in the Dutch by implementing the Stonewall System.

a typical Maroczy Bind structure; d6-d5 pawn break in the center is very difficult to achieve, and therefore white has substantial advantage

a typical Dutch Stonewall
(many humans would prefer white in the Dutch Stonewall, and all engines would

give substantial white edge, but the truth is, the position is fully equal. White can place an excellent central outpost on the e5 square, but that is more than compensated for by the black bind of the d5 and f5 pawns upon the e4 square. Even when white plays Ne5, followed by f2-f3, the e3-e4 break is extremely difficult to achieve(Nf6 controls e4 too), but apart from that, in view of the inflexible white pawn structure in the center, black has much better chances to start a promising kingside attack by pushing g and h pawns.)

Frequency: frequent

Closed position considerations

Closed center

Definition: a closed center would be defined by one of the following pawn arrangements:
- white pawns on d4,e5, black pawns on d5,e6
- white pawns on e4,d5, black pawns on e5,d6
- white pawns on c4,d3,e4, black pawns on c5,d6,e5
- white pawns on d4,e3,f4, black pawns on d5,e6,f5

119

a closed center feature

another closed center feature

white space advantage with closed center

Value: as in similar positions with a closed center the importance of long-term positional factors increases, while the importance of shorter-term dynamic ones definitely decreases, it makes very much sense to scale down/consider lower at least mg piece mobility

Frequency: frequent

Space advantage with closed center

Definition: space advantage with closed center should be considered in one of the following 2 scenarios:
- white pawns on d4,e5, black pawns on d5,e6,f7, black king on either the f,g or h file
- white pawns on e4,d5, black pawns on e5,d6,c7, black king on either the c,b or a file

Value: bonus, 15cps, only for the mg

Additional information: this is a very salient mg feature indeed. If one of the sides manages to get such a structure, receiving the bonus, that would mean a very durable positional advantage, which might be converted much later into the game. There are 2 main reasons for that:
- one of the quoted pawns of the disadvantaged side, the least advanced one, is virtually backward and, as it will constitute part of the own king shelter, that backwardness is felt much more seriously; for example, the defending side should be very careful when moving that pawn, as the king shelter might be severely compromised, and, if it does not move it too soon, the pressure on the kingside with the deficient backward pawn might get too strong in the medium and longer term
- as the center is closed, such weakness is felt even stronger, as there is no possibility for a counter-break in the center

The sooner one gets a similar advantageous position in the opening, the better. On many occasions entire games might be decided on this single feature.

Frequency: frequent

Closed positions are an extremely interesting feature of chess. It is namely those positions that are the least investigated of all. Humans do tend to understand such positions better or much better than engines, but, believe me or not, even top humans play them suboptimally, or very much suboptimally, at least what concerns a wide range of different patterns. I would say, if there is progress to be achieved in chess in the future, a surprisingly big portion of it lies in appropriately handling such structures.

Closed positions do mean positions where the solution is to be found only after getting to a much higher depth than otherwise. They are associated with a lot of manoeuvering, gradual increase of the pressure, until the advantage of one side becomes obvious, but, if you know well the patterns, the advantage will be obvious to you much much earlier. It is precisely the depth-feature that makes such positions so difficult for humans and engines alike.

Of course, we can talk about closed position features, leading to a win for the stronger side, and closed position features, involving increased drawing chances with larger blocked pawn structures/fortresses. Here we will focus on the first, and definitely much more intriguing feature.

Pointed chains

Definition: pointed chains are an extremely appealing positional feature, frequently disregarded even by top humans, not to mention top engines.

The following conditions would see the presence of alternative pointed chains:
- white pawns on c3,d4,e5, black pawns on c4,d5,e6,f7, black king on either the f,g or h file
- white pawns on d3,e4,f5, black pawns on d4,e5,f6,g7, black king on either the f,g or h file
- white pawns on e3,d4,c5, black pawns on e4,d5,c6,b7, black king on either the c,b or a file
- white pawns on f3,e4,d5, black pawns on f4,e5,d6,c7, black king on either the c,b or a file

one possible pointed chain

another possible pointed chain, even closer to the enemy black king

121

a third variation, this time looking towards the queenside

Value: bonus, 50cps, only for the mg

Additional information: the well-deserved bonus is dispensed for the following reasons:
- the enemy pawn on the 2nd rank, part of the enemy king shelter, is necessarily backward to different extents(depending on whether there are other enemy pawns on the 2nd rank next to it), and this makes the enemy king shelter much more vulnerable and inflexible than otherwise(as the advance of this pawn is restricted, dependent on tactical factors, this in turn means much lower flexibility of the shelter, and lower flexibility would mean much stronger attacking chances for the opponent)

Note: the presence of the enemy backward pawn on its 2nd rank is an obligatory feature of all pointed chains, otherwise the feature would simply not work; it is not only the pointed chain itself, but the combination of the pointed chain with the enemy backward pawn that makes the pointed chain so efficient

- the closed center, with the presence of large blocked pawn chains, imparts durability to the positional advantage of the stronger side, as the center is closed, central pawn breaks to open the game are very difficult or impossible to achieve, even in the long term, and getting counterplay on one of the wings is much less effective, so this all means the stronger side has much more time to slowly regroup its pieces and start a decisive attack
- the durability of the structure is additionally highlighted by the fact, that the large central chains are blocked, with blocked features being much more constant and difficult to change, especially what concerns chains
- pawn storms for the side with the pointed chain are encouraged to great effect, as the enemy king shelter is less flexible to counter them because of the backward pawn, and also because of the slower, manoeuvering-like nature of the game
- provided the side of the board opposite to where the pointed chain looks to is fully or even partially closed, this will only make the pointed chain considerably more valuable, as counterplay on the opposite wing will be very difficult or even altogether impossible to achieve

well, maybe you will recognise here a typical King's Indian Defence pawn structure(with the valuable black pointed chain; once white manages to play g2-g4, the black structural advantage is nullified)

and this one could arise with the more central pointed chain variation; structurally, white is winning that

Frequency: frequent

Inchoative pointed chains of 2 pawns

Definition: white pawns on c3,d4, black king on e,f,g or h file, or, white pawns on d3,e4, black king on e,f,g or h file, or, alternatively, looking towards the queen side, white pawns on f3,e4, black king on d,c,b or a file, or, white pawns on e3,d4, black king on d,c,b or a file

one type of inchoative pointed chain looking towards the king side

another type of inchoative pointed chain, looking towards the king side

a type of inchoative pointed chain, looking towards the queen side

Value: small bonus, 7cps, just for the mg

Additional information: the very-well deserved bonus is given for the obvious fact that such constellations start building a pointed chain towards the enemy king, and pointed chains are always a valuable asset.

The bonus is only mg, as pointed chains are valid only in this stage of the game.

123

Larger inchoative pointed chains

Definition: white pawns on c2,d3,e4, black king on e,f,g or h file, or, alternatively, looking towards the queen side, white pawns on f2,e3,d4, black king on d,c,b or a file

larger inchoative pointed chain, looking towards the king side

larger inchoative pointed chain, looking towards the queen side

Value: bonus, 11cps, just for the mg

Additional information: the bonus is obviously due for initiating the process of building a pointed chain towards the enemy king. In distinction to inchoative pointed chains of just 2 pawns, here things are indeed a bit more advanced, so the value is larger.

This concept can be very useful in the mg, both for engines and humans alike. It is not infrequent, that both entities will miss out on good opportunities to play an opening along the lines of creating a bigger pointed chain looking towards the enemy king. Pointed chains are always a significant plus, and one of the mightiest positional elements in chess in trying to gain substantial advantage.

many would think white has quite some advantage, because of its powerful center, as well as the better development. The truth is otherwise, though. If any side, only black could have advantage above, and the reason is simple: black has already started building a pointed chain towards the enemy king with the availability of the inchoative larger pointed chain in the form of the c7,d6 and e5 pawns, that could be continued with f7-f5, and further f5-f4, slowly increasing pressure. Of course, creating the longer chain closer to the enemy king would have been impossible, if the whole process had already not been prepared by the existing embryonic chain.

Alternatively, if black wants to stop in some way the potential dangerous c4-c5 white counter-break on the queen side, it can first play c7-c5, blocking c4, and only then continue with the above-mentioned plan on the king side. A smaller, and still effective, inchoative pointed chain in the form of the d6 and e5 pawns is still there, so f7-f5-f4 is not a problem at all.

Pointed chains are indeed a very powerful attacking tool, so implementing them should never be neglected.

Frequency: frequent

Central chain knight blockade

Definition: white pawns on c3,e5, white knight on d4, black pawns on c4,d5,e6, or, white pawns on d3,f5, white knight on e4, black pawns on d4,e5,f6, or, towards the queen side, white pawns on f3,d5, white knight on e4, black pawns on f4,e5,d6, or, white pawns on e3,c5, white knight on d4, black pawns on e4,d5,c6

one variation of the feature, looking towards the king side

alternative variation of the feature, looking towards the king side

one more variation, this time looking towards the queen side

Value: sufficient bonus, 25cps in the mg, 10cps in the eg, for the side with the knight

Additional information: the bonus for the knight side is very well deserved because:
- the knight is defended by a pawn
- the knight attacks an enemy pawn
- the knight blockades an enemy pawn in the center, immobilising a valuable opponent asset

- most importantly, with this condition, the game frequently will assume a more closed character, and in case the side with the knight is the attacking side, utilising the assets of the position, the well-placed attacking knight and especially the more advanced friendly pawn, part of the structure, this will give it more time under the cover of the blocked central structure to regroup and organise a successful pawn storm and piece attack on the side of the board, where the more advanced friendly pawn is

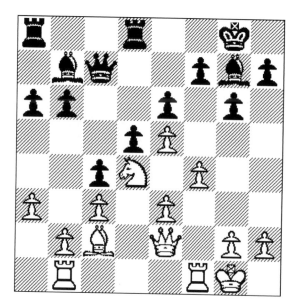

white has a winning position, although some engines and probably many humans might not be quite able to immediately apprehend that.

Making use of the fact, that the position bears a closed character, with c,d and e files in the center totally blocked, and the beneficial condition of the advanced friendly pawn on e5, part of the structure, white can start a forceful attack on the king side, pushing g2-g4, h2-h4, then g4-g5 or h4-h5, depending on circumstances, and then bringing both rooks to the king side, with a crushing attack.

In the meantime, black can do almost nothing, as the center is blocked, no possible pawn breaks or efficient piece counterplay there, and counterplay on the distant queen side is usually much less satisfactory.

Frequency: infrequent

Fully closed side with space advantage on the other side of the board

Definition: valid under the following conditions:

- a,b,c,d files all closed with pairs of blocked or symmetrical twice backward pawns(a symmetrical twice backward pawn would be one own and one enemy pawn that are both twice backward, and placed on the same file), white advanced pawn on e5
- a,b,c,d,e files all closed with pairs of blocked or symmetrical twice backward pawns, white advanced pawn on f5
- e,f,g,h files all closed with pairs of blocked or symmetrical twice backward pawns, white advanced pawn on d5
- d,e,f,g,h files all closed with pairs of blocked or symmetrical twice backward pawns, white advanced pawn on c5

one possible variation, with all pawns blocked(e5 is not necessarily a passer)

another possible variation, this time c3/c6 pawns are twice backward

and another one, with an f5 pawn

and one more, with the advanced pawn on the queen side and both kings castled opposite

Value: sufficiently large bonus, 50cps, only for the mg

Additional information: the bonus is dispensed for the simple, but extremely efficient reason, that while the advanced pawn on the 5th rank gives the side with the pawn attacking advantage on that side of the board, the fully closed feature of the opposite side would make attaining counterplay by the opponent there extremely difficult or impossible. This means the side with the advanced pawn has all the time in the world to gradually prepare and strengthen a mighty attack against the enemy king, with both storming pawns and pieces taking an active part. Under usual conditions, convenient regrouping would be difficult to achieve, but not under these particular conditions.

127

well, white has excellent winning chances with this pawn structure, considerably better than if the queenside was not locked with pairs of blocked and twice backward pawns

Frequency: infrequent

Weak spots

Weak spots(also known as holes) are an important square control feature.

Definition: a square on the 3rd rank, not attacked by an own pawn, with another own pawn placed on the same file on the 2nd rank

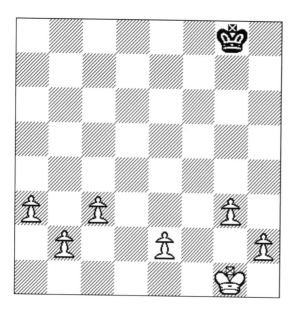

b3, e3 and h3 squares are weak spots

Value: penalty, -10cps, just for the mg

Additional information: the penalty is due for the fact, that such spots provide easy penetration for the enemy pieces. The pawn on the 2nd rank condition is necessary, as this has a twofold function, emphasising the weakness:
- further cramping the position for the side with the weak spot, as otherwise the square could be part of an open file, or at least an own pawn on this file would be too advanced to be backward
- ensuring that an own heavy piece along the file where the weak spot is, a rook or queen, would not be able to defend the weak spot, which might make it somewhat less prominent

Minor enemy pieces on a weak spot are naturally advanced outposts and only further emphasise the weakness, as in this way the pawn on the 2nd rank is immobile and due to stay there for quite some while.

the black knight on the e3 weak spot and the black bishop on the b3 weak spot immobilise the enemy pawns on their 2nd rank, highlighting the weakness

Weak spots, even if the square is not currently occupied by an enemy piece, are to be avoided, whenever possible.

Frequency: frequent

Own minor pieces controlling a weak spot

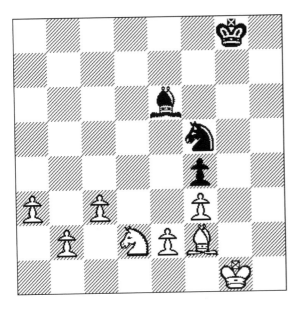

the white knight on d2 controls the weak spot on b3, so that the black bishop on e6 can not penetrate there; the white bishop on f2 controls the e3 weak spot, making penetration by the black knight on f5 there more difficult

Value: small bonus, different for the bishop and knight, just for the mg:
- 5cps for the bishop
- 3cps for the knight

Additional information: the bonus is of course due for the attempt at neutralising possible enemy piece penetration on the weak spot. A weak spot defended by an own minor is less of a weak spot.

Frequency: frequent

Symmetrical aligned pawns

Definition: 2 own pawns on the same rank on adjacent files, with another 2 enemy pawns 2 ranks in front and the same files, provided that the own pawns are on ranks 2 or 3

symmetrical aligned pawns on the 2nd rank

symmetrical aligned pawns on the 3rd rank

Value: small bonus, distinguishing between ranks

rank 2: 8cps in the mg, 2cps in the eg
rank 3: 12cps in the mg, 3cps in the eg

129

Additional information: the bonus is due for the uncanny ability of the pawns to close the game, whenever necessary. Thus, they are a very valuable defensive asset.

As easily seen on above diagrams, if the opponent side pushes one of its more advanced pawns, trying to attack and open the game, the defending side will have the good choice of not capturing, but blocking the other enemy pawn instead, with full closure of both files. For example, on the first diagram, if c4-c3 is played, white can answer with b2-b3, fully closing both b and c files, while, on the second diagram, g5-g4 could be answered by h3-h4, and h5-h4 by g3-g4, with similar closure.

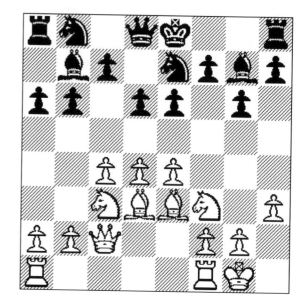

black has strong attack on the queen side and, in case it manages to open some files for attack there, it might get quite of an advantage. Unfortunately, because of the peculiar pawn configuration of the b3 and c3 symmetrical aligned pawns, opening the game there is simply impossible. c5-c4 is met by b3-b4, while b5-b4 by c3-c4, closing both files.

in the center, symmetrical aligned pawns are very helpful, too. d4-d5 break seems like a very strong move, and indeed, opening the game might have disastrous consequences for black, bearing in mind its considerable development lag. The valuable asset of the central symmetrical aligned d6 and e6 pawns, however, allows black to effectively close the game in the center, by answering d4-d5 with e6-e5. In this way, the considerable development advantage of white is annulled, at least temporarily.

Central symmetrical aligned pawns have, of course, large influence on the game as a whole.

Symmetrical aligned pawns are especially useful, when they are on the side where the opponent has storming pawns. This can prevent otherwise very unpleasant storming pawns breaks with opening the position, breaking up the king shelter and exposing the king.

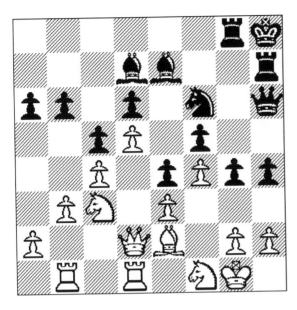

black has substantial positional advantage and is attacking on the king side. The h4 and g4 advanced storming pawns are particularly menacing. If black manages to open the position on the king side, even a single file, white is doomed, and that in rather quick fashion. Unfortunately for the attacker, the g2 and h2 symmetrical aligned pawns, part of the white king shelter, provide an extremely useful blocking possibility. Any attempt by black to open the game there will be futile, as h4-h3 is answered by g2-g3, while g4-g3 by h2-h3. In order to win, black will have to go the long way, preparing a break on the queen side, or resort to mighty tactical tricks.

Symmetrical aligned pawns have one more valuable application, that of guaranteeing full closure of the game and draw, in case they are placed on the last 2 remaining files that are still not closed by pairs of blocked pawns.

black has a large material and positional advantage in the eg, and would very easily win, were not it for the unfortunate circumstance of the presence of the pair of white symmetrical aligned a2 and b2 pawns, coupled with the fact that all remaining board files are closed with pairs of blocked pawns. In the current situation, this simply ends with a fortress position and a draw, as a4-a3 is answered by b2-b3, while b4-b3 by a2-a3, closing all files.

Frequency: infrequent

Pawn span

Definition: the distance in files between a side's leftmost and rightmost pawn

1 file distance between black's leftmost, d5, and rightmost, f5, pawn, 4 files distance between white's leftmost, b3, and rightmost, g3, pawn

Value: bonus, 5cps in the mg, 10cps in the eg, for any file in between the two pawns

Additional information: the bonus is due for the obvious reason that a bigger pawn span will usually denote the existence of a passed pawn, or at least a candidate passed pawn, for that side, and having such strong pawns with bigger distance between them will necessarily mean the opponent will have to allocate more resources for the defence against this strong pawn, which in turn will ensure the attacker will be able to concentrate more strength on the opposite section of the board, gaining positional advantages.

The extreme use of pawn span is easily seen in simple pawn endgames, where a bigger span almost certainly will lead to a win.

well, white is winning that, only because of the bigger span of its pawns. While the white king will be able to hold both of black's passers, his black counterpart will not be able to do that with the 2 white ones, far away from one another.

The white pawn span requires from black additional resources for defence, that black simply does not have.

adding a piece or two will still retain the advantage for the side with the larger span, but the edge will be much smaller and dependent on concrete tactical factors

132

candidate passed, instead of passed pawns, like a4 and h4 above, ensuring a bigger span, will also give the side with the larger span good winning chances, or at least a substantial advantage

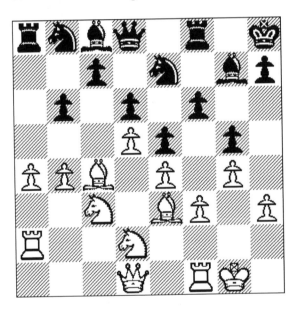

in the mg, pawn span is very much relevant, too. If white manages to install a passed pawn on a5, after a5 ba5 ba5, bringing the pawn span difference to 2 files, it will certainly have good winning chances, in spite of the equal material.

The eg value is twice higher than the mg one, as in the eg pawns defining the span will more frequently be dangerous passers.

Frequency: frequent

Space advantage on both sides of the board

Definition: having at least one pawn on the 5th, 6th or 7th rank on the queen side of the board, and, at least one other pawn on the 5th, 6th or 7th ranks on the opposite, king side of the board, provided the distance between them is at least 3 files

Value: bonus, 20cps in the mg, 10cps in the eg, for the side, gaining space this way

Additional information: the bonus is due, because:
- having advanced pawns, either in the mg or eg, is pressuring the opponent and, when such pawns are present on both board sections, the need to neutralise the pressure is even more urgent and will require more resources. Threats on a single focal point are usually easier to repel, in order to do that on different board sections, one needs more available strength.
- space gained by pawns on opposite sides is conducive to unlocking difficult to win positions, with a possible break at a propicious point in time, as breaking attempts will be available on more locations

having space advantage on both sides of the board, in the form of the advanced h5

133

and c5 pawns, with more than 3 files distance between them, severely pressures black, who has to defend more weaknesses, further apart. That certainly is a resource-drainer, and white has a number of good continuations.

At some point, if not something quicker, a break, either on b5, on the queen side, or f5 or g5(after g2-g4 is played) on the king side, will decide the outcome.

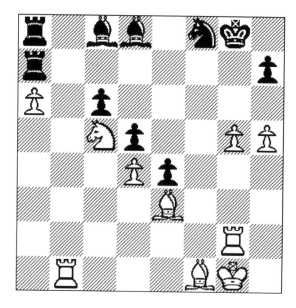

in the eg, having space advantage on both sides of the board will often take the form of advanced passers and potential passers.

The g5/h5 and a6 pawns on the king and queen sides respectively severely drain black's resources. Defence and communication between distant board sections will be difficult.

Note: the requirement the pawns should be separated by at least 3 files is necessary, as otherwise defending weaknesses close to each other is much easier

Frequency: frequent

Chapter IV

Outposts

Outposts are one of the most significant features in chess, placing second immediately after pawns. The reason is obvious: minor pieces, to which outposts primarily relate, are the second most numerous piece on the board after pawns, and their relatively small material value makes them especially good in gaining space advantage, with space advantage always playing a major role.

Definition: an outpost within the current framework is a minor piece(knight or bishop) on ranks 3 through 6 with no enemy pawns present on more advanced ranks than the minor piece itself on adjacent files

Note: however, this is just the general, and very restricted definition. Apart from minor piece outposts, there are rook outposts too, a wide range of semi-outposted features(involving the presence of an enemy pawn on more advanced ranks, that would however be in some respect immobilised or made unable to realistically threaten the outpost in another way), and also some outposts on the 7th rank.

white knight outpost on the central d5 square, black bishop outpost on the g3 square

Definition: a minor outpost that is not defended by an own pawn

Additional information: as said, outposts are very important. They receive a well-deserved bonus for a variety of reasons:
- stable, unattackable by enemy pawns, and in chess stability is frequently associated with surplus value, simply because a non-stable feature might easily disappear altogether
- in most cases, when on ranks equal or higher than 4th, also advanced, representing space advantage features, restricting enemy pieces' activity
- in a wide range of specific situations, outposts also perform very particular other valuable functions, like blocking the position for the purposes of attack and defence, representing durable king-attacking features, stopping enemy rooks from taking open files, supporting the advance of own passers, etc.

Frequency: very frequent

Further, we will examine the different outpost features.

Nc6 is such an outpost; Bf3 is another one

Value: bonus, valid in terms of psqt, making a distinction between knight and bishop outposts, as they all have their specifics

8	0	0	0	0	0	0	0	0
7	0	0	0	0	0	0	0	0
6	50	80	100	120	120	100	80	50
5	30	50	70	90	90	70	50	30
4	20	30	40	50	50	40	30	20
3	10	15	20	25	25	20	15	10
2	0	0	0	0	0	0	0	0
1	0	0	0	0	0	0	0	0
	a	b	c	d	e	f	g	h

no-pawn defended knight outpost psqt(mg)

8	0	0	0	0	0	0	0	0
7	0	0	0	0	0	0	0	0
6	22	33	42	55	55	42	33	22
5	10	20	27	38	38	27	20	10
4	7	10	13	17	17	13	10	7
3	4	6	7	9	9	7	6	4
2	0	0	0	0	0	0	0	0
1	0	0	0	0	0	0	0	0
	a	b	c	d	e	f	g	h

no-pawn-defended knight outpost psqt(eg)

135

	a	b	c	d	e	f	g	h
8	0	0	0	0	0	0	0	0
7	0	0	0	0	0	0	0	0
6	50	85	90	130	130	90	85	50
5	30	50	60	80	80	60	50	30
4	18	25	35	43	43	35	25	18
3	10	15	20	25	25	20	15	10
2	0	0	0	0	0	0	0	0
1	0	0	0	0	0	0	0	0

no-pawn-defended
bishop outpost psqt(mg)

	a	b	c	d	e	f	g	h
8	0	0	0	0	0	0	0	0
7	0	0	0	0	0	0	0	0
6	22	36	40	55	55	40	36	22
5	10	20	23	33	33	23	20	10
4	6	8	12	15	15	12	8	6
3	4	6	7	9	9	7	6	4
2	0	0	0	0	0	0	0	0
1	0	0	0	0	0	0	0	0

no-pawn-defended bishop outpost psqt(eg)

Additional information: no-pawn-defended outposts get all of the advantages of general outposts, with the additional downside that they represent less stable features than otherwise, as any enemy non-pawn piece could easily threaten them, forcing retreat, or even destroying them. Of course, if any friendly piece apart from pawn does defend them, that only enhances their value, as they become relatively more stable, though non-pawn defence tends to be a bit flimsy at times.

Frequency: frequent

Single-pawn-defended outposts

Definition: a minor outpost that is defended by a single own pawn

single-pawn-defended
knight outpost on e5

Value: bonus, valid in terms of psqt, while making distinction between knight and bishop outposts

	a	b	c	d	e	f	g	h
8	0	0	0	0	0	0	0	0
7	0	0	0	0	0	0	0	0
6	65	100	130	150	150	130	100	65
5	38	70	85	110	110	85	70	38
4	27	38	53	65	65	53	38	27
3	12	19	28	35	35	28	19	12
2	0	0	0	0	0	0	0	0
1	0	0	0	0	0	0	0	0

single-pawn-defended
knight outpost psqt(mg)

	a	b	c	d	e	f	g	h
8	0	0	0	0	0	0	0	0
7	0	0	0	0	0	0	0	0
6	28	45	60	70	70	60	45	28
5	15	28	35	55	55	35	28	15
4	9	14	18	25	25	18	14	9
3	5	7	9	12	12	9	7	5
2	0	0	0	0	0	0	0	0
1	0	0	0	0	0	0	0	0

single-pawn-defended
knight outpost psqt(eg)

	a	b	c	d	e	f	g	h
8	0	0	0	0	0	0	0	0
7	0	0	0	0	0	0	0	0
6	65	100	115	170	170	115	100	65
5	38	70	80	90	90	80	70	38
4	23	38	48	65	65	48	38	23
3	12	19	28	35	35	28	19	12
2	0	0	0	0	0	0	0	0
1	0	0	0	0	0	0	0	0

single-pawn-defended
bishop outpost psqt(mg)

	a	b	c	d	e	f	g	h
8	0	0	0	0	0	0	0	0
7	0	0	0	0	0	0	0	0
6	28	45	60	70	70	60	45	28
5	15	28	35	50	50	35	28	15
4	8	14	18	25	25	18	14	8
3	5	7	9	12	12	9	7	5
2	0	0	0	0	0	0	0	0
1	0	0	0	0	0	0	0	0

single-pawn-defended
bishop outpost psqt(eg)

Additional information: single-pawn-defended outposts inherit all advantages of general outposts, and get reasonably higher bonus than no-pawn-defended outposts for the simple reason that they are stronger and do represent substantially more durable feature

Frequency: frequent

Twice-defended outposts

Definition: a minor outpost that is defended by 2 own pawns

twice-defended bishop outpost on d6

Value: bonus, valid in terms of psqt, distinguishing between knight and bishop features

	a	b	c	d	e	f	g	h
8	0	0	0	0	0	0	0	0
7	0	0	0	0	0	0	0	0
6	65	100	150	180	180	150	100	65
5	38	70	100	120	120	100	70	38
4	27	38	53	65	65	53	38	27
3	12	19	28	35	35	28	19	12
2	0	0	0	0	0	0	0	0
1	0	0	0	0	0	0	0	0

twice-defended knight outpost psqt(mg)

	a	b	c	d	e	f	g	h
8	0	0	0	0	0	0	0	0
7	0	0	0	0	0	0	0	0
6	28	45	60	70	70	60	45	28
5	15	28	35	55	55	35	28	15
4	9	14	18	25	25	18	14	9
3	5	7	9	12	12	9	7	5
2	0	0	0	0	0	0	0	0
1	0	0	0	0	0	0	0	0

twice-defended knight outpost psqt(eg)

	a	b	c	d	e	f	g	h
8	0	0	0	0	0	0	0	0
7	0	0	0	0	0	0	0	0
6	65	100	130	220	220	130	100	65
5	38	70	85	110	110	85	70	38
4	27	38	53	65	65	53	38	27
3	12	19	28	35	35	28	19	12
2	0	0	0	0	0	0	0	0
1	0	0	0	0	0	0	0	0

twice-defended bishop outpost psqt(mg)

	a	b	c	d	e	f	g	h
8	0	0	0	0	0	0	0	0
7	0	0	0	0	0	0	0	0
6	28	45	60	70	70	60	45	28
5	15	28	35	55	55	35	28	15
4	9	14	18	25	25	18	14	9
3	5	7	9	12	12	9	7	5
2	0	0	0	0	0	0	0	0
1	0	0	0	0	0	0	0	0

twice-defended bishop outpost psqt(eg)

Additional information: twice-defended outposts inherit all the advantages of general outposts, but are due higher value than even single-pawn defended outposts, because:
- they are immeasurably stronger(completely impossible to destroy them without receiving severe positional penalties)
- because being stronger, they are also much more durable, so their influence on the game will be felt for a much more prolonged period of time
- any possible capture of such an outpost by an enemy piece will result in the building-up of an advanced own defended pawn on the square where the outpost previously stood, in some cases even passer(as the outpost is defended twice, the new friendly pawn on its place will also be defended, see the diagrammed position)

Note: twice-defended outposts will differ from single-pawn-defended outposts in their psqt values for just a number of central squares on the 5th and 6th ranks, where a capture by an enemy piece would install a major defended and centralised pawn, with other squares giving almost no added value. Still, for this particular number of squares, the distinction is pretty huge.

Frequency: frequent

Twice-defended knight outposts on the 5th rank with no enemy pawns on the same file as the outpost on more advanced ranks

c5 is such a knight outpost above

Small bonus, 10cps, only for the mg, is dispensed for the fact that any enemy piece capture of such a minor will lead to the creation of a strong, defended and advanced, friendly passer on the square previously occupied by the knight(see diagrammed position).

Possible squares for such a knight posting are b5 through g5; the reason that only knights get such a bonus is that, while all similar knights are central, a bishop placed on b5/g5, and even c5/f5 would definitely seem awkward and a bit misplaced(no possible to go back, both own pawns defending it will prevent that).

In the endgame, such a feature is largely irrelevant, as space advantage plays a significantly smaller role there and such knights could easily be tolerated.

Permanent minor piece outposts

Definition: minor piece outpost, with no enemy minor pieces able to attack them

Note: that will basically mean the lack of a knight, as knights are generally able to attack all board squares, independent of their colour, or, the lack of a bishop the colour of the square the minor piece is outposted on

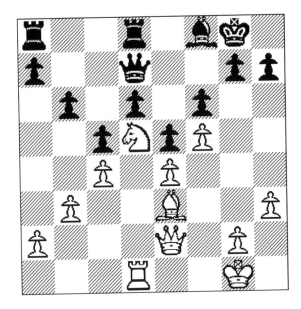

another permanent minor piece outpost, the knight on d5. As easily seen, no enemy minor pieces present, able to attack the d5 square, aiming at destroying the strong knight.

If any side, and despite being a pawn and the exchange down, only white could have advantage above.

the bishop on f5 is a permanent minor piece outpost, no enemy minor pieces on the board, that would be able to attack it

and one more, the bishop on e5

Value: sufficiently large bonus, over the already dispensed one for a general outpost, in terms of rank

5th or 6th rank: 50cps for the mg, 15cps for the eg

4th rank: 15cps for the mg, 5cps for the eg

139

Additional information: the very-well deserved bonus is obviously due for the following weighty reasons:

- as such an outpost will be unattackable by enemy minors, that will mean it will be undestroyable

- being undestroyable in turn means durability, and durability is always an asset, especially with strong features

- on occasion, due to the closed character of the position, such an outpost will be unattackable even by enemy rooks, so this will further boost its value

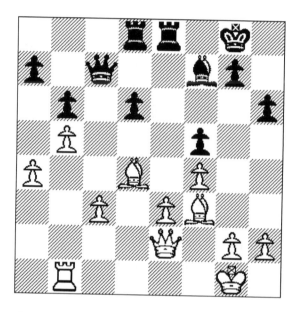

the strongly-defended permanent bishop outpost on d4, plus a bit more favourable imbalance, fully compensate the material deficit. White has clear advantage.

what a powerful outpost, the bishop on e6! Advanced, twice defended, and unattackable by enemy minors. White certainly has a winning advantage. About the best black could do is to sacrifice an exchange on e6, but that will hardly help too.

eternal knight on e5. The knight is sheltered by an enemy pawn, with the position being closed, so no enemy rook can ever attack it, trying to destroy it.

This only highlights white's advantage, and white will certainly win after the h3-h4-h5 break.

140

even in the eg, and even on the 4th rank, such outposts are undoubtedly very useful. If any side, only white can win the position above.

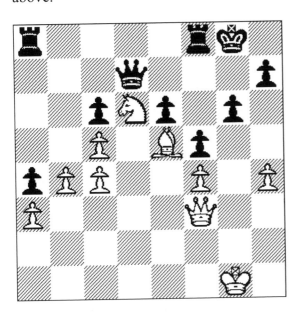

of course, it is even better to have 2 of those. The all-powerful knight on d6 and bishop on e5, unchallenged by enemy pieces, certainly more than compensate for the big material deficit.

The mg value is significantly larger, as outposts in general are much more relevant in the mg.

Overall, this is one feature, whose importance can hardly be overestimated.

Frequency: frequent

Outposts blocking enemy pawns

Definition: minor outposts on their 4th, 5th or 6th ranks, blocking enemy pawns

the knight on d5 is such an outpost on the 5th rank. It blocks the enemy d6 pawn.

one more similar outpost, this time on the 4th rank, the knight on c4 blocks the enemy c5 pawn

141

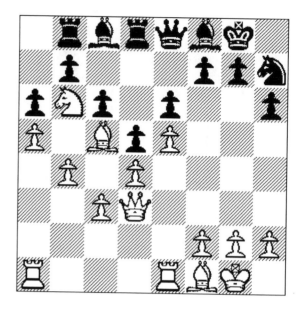

and one on the 6th rank. The knight on b6 blocks the enemy b7 pawn.

the knight on b6 immobilises the black b7 pawn, and this has a cramping effect upon the whole black position

Value: bonus, 10cps, both for the mg and eg

Additional information: the very-well deserved bonus is due for the following reasons:
- the enemy pawn is immobilised, which is especially of an asset, when it is closer to its home rank
- frequently, primarily in the mg, but also in the eg, this has a cramping effect upon the enemy pieces
- the outposted minor is unattackable by enemy heavy pieces along the file where it sits, as the enemy pawn shelters it
- when blocking an enemy pawn, part of the king shelter, the shelter as a whole becomes less flexible

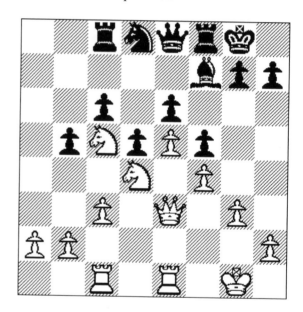

the knight on c5 is unattackable by the black rook on c8. Breathing space for the black pieces is also quite limited.

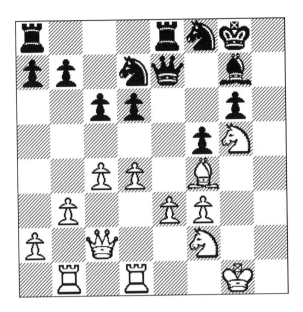

when blocking a shelter pawn, g6 above, such outpost additionally makes the shelter less flexible

even on the 4th rank, and even in the eg, such immobilisation definitely has its advantages

Frequency: very frequent

Useless outposts

Definition: minor piece outpost on the 5th or 6th ranks on files a or b, or h or g, on the side of the board, opposite to where the enemy king is, with all squares attacked by the outpost on more advanced ranks, not attacked by any other own pawn or piece, and attacked by at least one enemy piece

Value: sufficient penalty, -30cps in the mg, -10cps in the eg

Additional information: the penalty is because of the largely useless nature of such outposts. As the outpost will be placed far from the enemy king, it will not be able to attack it. What is even worse, because all squares on more advanced ranks the outpost can access are controlled by enemy pieces, the outpost will not be able to transfer from them to different sections of the board, including the center or king side. So, the most it can actually do, is stay where it is, doing nothing, or possibly go back on less advanced ranks in the own camp, but that is something no outpost would like to do. In this way, the outpost is completely disfunctional.

the knight on b4 is such an outpost.
All squares on more advanced ranks, a2,c2 and d3, are controlled by white pieces, even if only the bishop on b1, and not supported by any own piece. So, the most the outpost could do is stay where it is, and white has winning advantage.

Frequency: infrequent

143

Unretreatable knight outposts

Definition: knight outpost on its 5th or 6th rank, on files a,h,b or g, with all its mobility squares on less advanced ranks controlled by enemy pawns

the knight on a3 is an unretreatable knight outpost on the edge a file.

All the mobility squares of the knight on less advanced ranks than the knight itself, b5 and c4, are controlled by white pawns, c4 and b3 respectively.

Value: penalty, -15cps, both for the mg and eg

Additional information: the penalty is given because of the obvious mobility limitations of such outposts. Although otherwise excellently placed, they can not possibly retreat, as enemy pawns will prevent that, while more advanced mobility squares will usually be attacked by enemy pieces, as is the case with the white rook on b2 on the diagrammed position, attacking the b1 and c2 squares, so their functioning is pretty much limited to a very small section of the board, and sometimes, because of that, they are even trappable.

one more example, this time with a knight on its 5th rank.

All the knight's mobility squares on less advanced ranks, a6,c6 and d5, are under the control of enemy pawns, while its mobility squares on more advanced ranks, a2,c2 and d3, are restricted by the white bishop on b1.

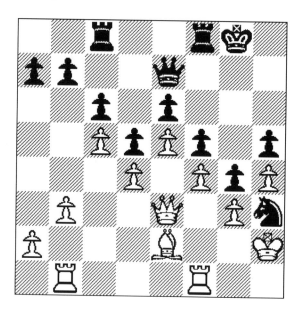

this condition is very negative, also when the outposted knight directly attacks squares of the enemy king shelter. Although one might think the black knight on h3 is very strong, in actual fact it is quite fragile, as it can not retreat, and after the white rook moves from f1 and its place is taken by the white bishop, the easily trappable knight comes under attack and

144

perishes together with the pawn defending it.

Frequency: infrequent

Semi-outposts

Definition: semi-outposts are outpost-related features, a knight or bishop on ranks 3 through 5, that are not pure outposts proper, in the sense that there are enemy pawns on more advanced ranks on one of the adjacent files, but those pawns do not represent immediate threat to the outpost, because they are either unable to move forward as being blocked by opponent pawns or pieces, or a possible pawn push is thwarted by an opponent pawn guarding the square in front of them

Such features are extremely different and wide-ranging. Below, we will briefly look at the most salient ones.

Minor piece behind an own pawn

Definition: a minor piece on the 3rd, 4th or 5th ranks with an own pawn placed immediately in front of it on the same file one rank above

Nd4 behind d5 pawn and
Bg3 behind g4 pawn

Value: small bonus, different for the knight and bishop
- 15cps in the mg, 5cps in the eg for the knight
- 12cps in the mg, 4cps in the eg for the bishop

Additional information: the bonus is given for the following reasons:
- the own pawn in front of the minor piece prevents any possible attack by an enemy pawn(on the diagrammed position, c7-c5 would be met by d5-c6, f7-f5 and h6-h5 thrusts also do not represent a danger to the bishop, as g4 pawn could capture both sides)
- the minor pieces are also protected from file attacks of enemy heavy pieces, with the pawn in front shielding them

Frequency: frequent

Minor piece with an own pawn diagonally in front of it

Definition: a minor piece on the 3rd, 4th or 5th ranks with an own pawn one rank upper on adjacent file

Nc4 and Bf5 represent such semi-outposts

Value: small bonus, different for the knight and bishop

- 10cps in the mg, 3cps in the eg for the knight
- 8cps in the mg, 2cps in the eg for the bishop

Additional information: bonus is dispensed as:
- an enemy pawn on the adjacent file where the friendly pawn is could not possibly attack the minor, as the friendly pawn blocks its further push(see the diagrammed position; d6-d5 push to threaten the knight is currently impossible because d5 pawn blocks d6, g7-g6 push threat to attack the white bishop on f5 is thwarted too, as g6 pawn blocks g7)
- even if enemy pawns are not present, the knight will support the own pawn push, while the bishop will defend the own pawn, which is particularly important, if the own pawns are passers

Frequency: frequent

Minor piece with an own pawn on the same rank across a file

Definition: a minor piece on the 3rd, 4th or 5th ranks with an own pawn on the same rank 2 files apart

Nb4 and Be5 are such semi-outposts above

Value: small bonus, different for the knight and bishop
- 10cps in the mg, 3cps in the eg for the knight
- 8cps in the mg, 2cps in the eg for the bishop

Additional information: the bonus is given due to the following considerations:
- the friendly pawn on the same rank across a file prevents an enemy pawn push to threaten the minor piece, as the enemy pawn could be captured(see diagrammed position; on c6-c5 push, there is a d4-c5 capture, while on f7-f6 push, a g5-f6 capture)
- if the minor is a knight, it will control on occasion the square in front of the friendly pawn, rendering a pawn push easier, while, in the case of a bishop, the bishop will additionally control the square for the enemy pawn push(on the diagrammed position, even though f7 black pawn is aligned/connected, and g7 supports the possible f7-f6 push, this push is thwarted, because of the double Be5-pawn g5 control of the f6 square)

Frequency: frequent

Minor piece on the 4th rank with an enemy pawn on its second rank on adjacent file that is backward

146

Ba4 and Ne4 are similar minors above (b7 and f7 are backward pawns)

Value: small bonus, different for the knight and bishop
- 8cps in the mg, 2cps in the eg for the knight
- 6cps in the mg, 2cps in the eg for the bishop

Additional information: bonus is due because:
- the enemy pawn on adjacent file could not possibly attack the minor, as it is backward, and any push could easily be captured by the opponent pawn making it such(see b7 and f7 pawns on the diagrammed position; they are both backward, b7-b5 thrust would be met by c5-b6 capture, while f7-f5 thrust by g5-f6 one)
- in the case of a knight, it would additionally control the square in front of the backward pawn, making a sally even more difficult

Frequency: infrequent

Minor piece with another own outposted minor one rank in front on adjacent file

Bb3 and Nf4 are similar semi-outposts

Value: small bonus, equal for the knight and bishop, 10cps for the mg, 3cps for the eg

Additional information: the bonus is given for the impossibility of an enemy pawn on adjacent file to attack the minor piece. As the square for a potential enemy push is currently occupied by the other opponent outposted minor, such a push is unrealistic(see how on the diagrammed position black c5-c4 push to threaten Bb3 and g7-g5 push to attack Nf4 are out of the question, as white Nc4 and Bg5 outposts take up the push squares).

Frequency: infrequent

Minor piece on the 4th rank with another own minor piece outposted on the 6th rank on adjacent file

Bb4 and Nf4 are such semi-outposts

Value: small bonus, equal for the knight and bishop, 8cps for the mg, 2cps for the eg

Additional information: the bonus is given for the impossibility of a potential pawn push, threatening the minor, of an existing enemy pawn on the adjacent file where the other own outposted minor piece is. As you can see on the diagrammed position, Na6 outpost thwarts the possible a7-a5 push with threat upon the Bb4, while Bg6 effectively blocks the black g7-g5 thrust, with a threat upon Nf4.

Frequency: infrequent

Knight on the 5th rank with enemy knight on the 6th rank on adjacent file

Nc5 is such a knight

Value: very small bonus, 5cps for the mg, 2cps for the eg

Additional information: the bonus is given for the fact that a possible enemy pawn push with threat upon the knight is made more difficult by the presence of an enemy knight in front of the enemy pawn, thus blocking its march(see Nb6 blocking own pawn on b7 and currently preventing the b7-b6 push). Usually, the situation is only short-term, though.

Minor outposts on the 7th rank defended by a pawn

Nc7 for white and Bb2 for black are such outposts

Value: sufficiently large bonus over the general psqt one, 30cps in the mg, 15cps in the eg, both for the knight and bishop

Additional information: the bonus is given for the following reasons:
- as in the case with other advanced outposts, though less markedly, such minor pieces do severely restrict the activity of the enemy non-pawn pieces, primarily queen and rooks
- in distinction to a non-pawn-defended minor outpost on the 7th rank, a pawn-defended one is much more durable and difficult to evict, hence the bonus; non-pawn-defended minor outposts on the 7th rank would have difficult task sticking to their place
- if such an outpost is captured by an enemy piece, its place is immediately taken by a very advanced passed pawn on the 7th rank, a single square away from promotion
- in case the defending pawn is a passer, the minor outpost will support its further advance to promotion(for example, on the diagrammed position, after Nc7-e6, the knight will control the d8 promotion

148

square, and Bb2 already controls black c1 promotion square)

Frequency: frequent

Twice defended knights

Definition: knight, on d5,e5,c5 or f5 squares, defended by 2 own pawns

Note: the knight should not be an outpost, as twice-defended minor outposts are already scored within our evaluation framework

Value: bonus, 15cps, just for the mg

Additional information: the very-well deserved bonus is given for the following reasons:
- unless attacked by an enemy pawn, the knight is very stable and durable there, and those are vital central and advanced squares, from where the knight enjoys sway over almost the entire board
- if the knight is exchanged for another enemy minor piece, an extremely well placed advanced defended pawn will appear on the square the knight previously held, again an indisputable advantage

twice defended knight on e5. The knight is very stable there, controlling almost all

important board squares, including an attack upon the black king shelter, and possible enemy minor captures will introduce a strong defended pawn on that very same e5 square.

Twice defended knights are extremely relevant for one more reason, namely that they can appear quite early into the game, having influence upon a wide range of openings, and thus the side that manages to attain such a positional advantage first will usually also gain an overall strategic advantage.

Missing this opportunity and going for an alternative line instead, that would be clearly inferior, is missing a lot, so this is certainly not a factor to be disregarded as a simple nicety.

a typical Dutch Stonewall construction. Many humans would avoid the Dutch Stonewall, for unknown reasons, and all engines, even the very finest, will consider above position as very favourable for white(close to or more than half a pawn advantage), but the truth is black is already slightly better.

The main reason, apart from the excellent central bind in the form of the d5 and f5 pawns, is the gorgeously placed twice defended knight on e4, immediately attacking the white king shelter. It is difficult to long tolerate such a knight, changing it will quickly send a strong defended black pawn on e4 instead of the knight, which will further very negatively influence the white king shelter, and trying to kick it with a pawn is also not easy and takes some time(the white knight on f3 should evacuate the f3 square first). Besides, some captures are even tactically impossible, for example, Nc3-e4 loses a minor piece by force.

Black threatens with a mighty assault after g7-g5, g5-g4, h7-h5, Rf8-f7-h7, etc., or, alternatively, placing the black rook on the g file, then bringing the rest of the pieces on the queen side to support the attack.

Frequency: frequent

Rook outposts

Definition: rook on the 4th or 5th ranks with no enemy pawns on more advanced ranks on adjacent files

white rook outpost on b5 on the 5th rank; black rook outpost on e5 on the 4th rank

Note: this is a bit pedantic, but might be of interest to truth-searchers

Value: very small,
- 3cps in the mg, 1cp in the eg for a rook outpost on the 4th rank

- 5cps in the mg, 2cps in the eg for a rook outpost on the 5th rank

Additional information: include this feature to spice up your engine evaluation, or to have a deeper understanding of ongoings on the board. Bonus is given for the impossibility of enemy pawns to attack the rooks, which makes the feature somewhat more durable and, as an advanced feature, attacking objects/squares in the enemy camp, it is valuable. Not very salient, though, as such outposts could still be attacked and neutralised by enemy minor pieces.

Frequency: frequent

Rook on the 6th rank, defended by pawn

Rc6 is such a rook

Value: bonus, 10cps in the mg, 5cps in the eg

Additional information: the bonus is given because:
- the rook is outposted there, stable and more difficult to attack
- in case such a rook is captured, by an enemy rook, or even by an enemy minor piece with possible sacrifices, on its place

will immediately land a powerful passed pawn(as easily seen on the diagrammed position, Rc8-c6 is not the best move)

Frequency: frequent

Rook on the 7th rank, defended by pawn

Rc7 is such a rook

Value: bonus, 15cps, both for the mg and eg

Additional information: the bonus is given for the following reasons:
- the rook is excellently placed there, durable and difficult to attack by enemy pieces
- in case it is captured, a very powerful friendly passed pawn, a single square away from promotion, will immediately take its place
- in the eg, the defending pawn will frequently be a passer, so the rook will support the advance of the pawn forward, while the pawn will help with the rook penetration

Frequency: frequent

Twice defended rook on the 6th rank

Definition: rook on the 6th rank, defended by 2 own pawns

Rd6 is such a rook

Value: bonus, 20cps in the mg, 10cps in the eg

Additional information: the bonus is due because:
- the rook is well-defended and stable there
- in case it is captured, either by another rook, or even by an enemy minor piece with possible sacrifices, its place will be immediately taken by a very strong defended passed pawn
- if such rook lands on a square of the enemy king shelter, different sacrifices are possible, too, going as long as to sacrifice the rook for a mere enemy pawn

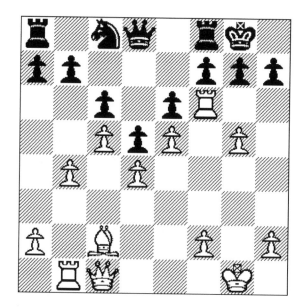

such rook frequently helps with the fight for an open file. Above, as capturing on d6 is close to impossible, as this will introduce there a powerful white protected passer, the black rook on d8 will have to retreat, after which white penetrates with an easy win.

and if such rook lands on a square of the enemy king shelter, flashy sacrifices, involving big temporary material losses, are often seen, too.

Capturing the rook above leads to a quick white mate after gf6 and Qh6.

Frequency: infrequent

Rook outposts blocking enemy pawns

Definition: outposted rook on the 5th or 6th ranks, blocking an enemy pawn

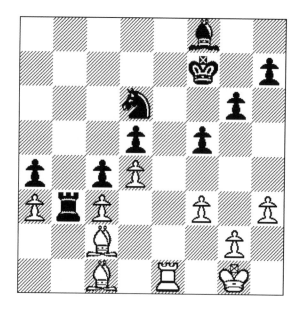

sacs are also possible. For example, on the diagrammed position, Bb3 quickly loses the game, after cb3, followed by Nc4.

the rook on g5 represents this condition. It is outposted and blocks the enemy g6 pawn.

152

Value: small bonus, 4cps in the mg, 2cps in the eg

Additional information: the bonus is due, because with this condition enemy pawns are immobilised, depriving the opponent of a valuable positional asset in the form of the ability to push pawns further.

the b7 pawn can not budge, is vulnerable, and thus, white enjoys big advantage

in the eg, such rooks are frequently a big plus, even with a material deficit

Frequency: frequent

Penetration points

Definition: square on the 5th or 6th ranks, that is empty, defended by an own pawn, and not attacked by an enemy pawn

Value: bonus, valid only for the mg, different for the 2 separate ranks:
- 6cps for the 5th rank
- 10cps for the 6th rank

Additional information: the bonus is due for the possible penetration of all kinds of own pieces upon this square, which is an advanced one and important therefore well into the enemy camp. The asset is just a potentiality, as a piece might also not quite get there sometimes, but very well calculated one.

Advanced squares are always a welcome haven, so it is just about natural that all pieces strive to reach them. Those might be future own outposted minors, but also minor pieces on the 5th rank that would not be outposts, as well as rook or queen.

An own pawn securing the place ensures the square will be mostly safe, when a piece lands there, and an enemy pawn not attacking it is a precondition for penetration. The condition the square should be empty is necessary because otherwise the feature could also encompass minor outposts and other pieces already having penetrated, which are separately scored.

The term is only mg, as in the mg there is an abundance of different pieces able to do the trip to such a square, and besides in the eg the relevance of such squares would almost fully vanish, as space advantage, an inherent element of penetration points, is much less significant in that stage of the game. A clear testimony to this is the diminishing value of minor outposts, as well as the much smaller importance of enemy king attack, where advanced well-placed heavy pieces close to the king will frequently have major role to play.

153

 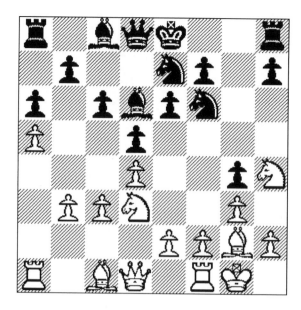

the b5 square is a penetration point for white on the 5th rank. It is attacked by the a4 white pawn, empty, and not attacked by a black pawn. Currently, the e2 bishop can go there, but, in just 2 more tempi, after Nb1-a3-b5, the white knight on b1 can also take it and, in the more distant future, with some simplifications, it is a possible target for the white queen and, under specific conditions, even a white rook.

In this way, even if it is not currently occupied, it is an extremely useful positional asset, allowing all pieces to change places, take it, and start pressuring the opponent.

e5 is another penetration point for white on the 5th rank, and e4 a penetration point for black on the same relative 5th rank. Both squares are attacked by own pawns and not under immediate attack of enemy pawns. They are a bit less safe than the b5 square, as enemy pawns potentially can still attack them, but still a very good spring-board for own pieces trying to penetrate the enemy half of the board.

b4 and c4 squares, on the other hand, are not penetration points for black, as, although defended by black pawns, they remain under attack of the c3 and b3 white pawns respectively.

b6 is a penetration point on the 6th rank for white. After some manoeuvering, the d3 white knight can go there, via b2 and a4, for example, the white bishop on c1 can join it, in a possible Bc1-a3-c5-b6 trip, and later in the game, other own pieces can follow too.

h3 is a penetration point on the relative 6th rank for black. Currently, it does not look very accessible, but, after some preparation, for example, h7-h5, Nf6-h7-g5, the black knight can start threatening penetrating there, and, later in the game, other black pieces would be able to join.

One peculiarity of this square is that it is also part of the white king shelter, so this makes it an even more valuable point of penetration.

e5 is a another penetration point for white on the 5th rank, and e4 for black.

Frequency: very frequent

154

Chapter V

Imbalances

Imbalances are one of the most interesting features in chess. Usually, they are so complicated and mostly not deeply researched, that only very few top engines will be able to play them only half-decently, because of lack of understanding, and almost no top human player will be able to reasonably implement their core values on the board, both because of an inherent lack of understanding, and due to the fact that humans are more error-prone in such constellations in view of the fast-changing nature of the game.

The scientific approach to imbalances will require building of a complete table of all possible piece imbalances with their relevant values, but, as such a table will hold up to some hundred thousands possible combinations, this is simply impractical. Therefore, the best that could currently be done is to rely on a small number of largely valid rules, that would not be perfect, but would still give a fairly good overview of board occurences.

If we had to briefly define what imbalances are all about, imbalances are the overvalue of pieces above their plain values that only the combination of 2 or more of them would be able to assign to them. In that sense, in order to have an imbalance situation, you would need at least 2 pieces for at least one of the sides, and, in order to meaningfully calculate them, you would need that one of the sides has at least one piece unmatched by a similar piece of the other side, otherwise calculation of imbalances for both sides would amount to pretty much the same thing.

Further, we will look at the most basic imbalances rules.

Pair of bishops

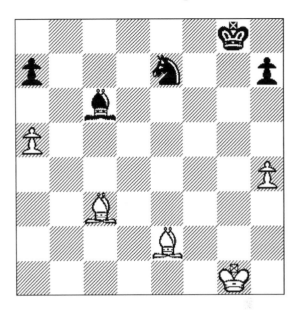

white has excellent winning chances, although one might think almost everything is equal: 2 pawns each side, 2 minor pieces each side; yet, the pair of bishops make big difference

Value: bonus, 30cps in the mg, 50cps in the eg

Additional information: the bonus is given due to the following considerations:
- the pair of bishops control in tandem all squares on the board easily, light and dark alternatingly, which a pair of knight and bishop simply can not do; the knight will access squares of colour different to the colour of the own bishop, but only randomly and much harder
- the pair of bishops is much faster in moving across the board than a pair of knight and bishop, for example
- it is possible to exchange one of the bishops for an opponent knight at almost any particular time in the game, gaining in the process an additional positional advantage, so big is the power of the pair; this always represents a further asset, as it increases the number of game options: the

155

bishop pair side can keep the pair, but it can also get rid of it to good avail

- in a range of particular situations, the pair of bishops is valuable in other respects, for example when simultaneously attacking the enemy king shelter, with opposite castlings on the board, when the pair is able to attack the enemy king and defend the own king at the same time as a king safety add-on, something a pair of bishop and knight can not do, for example, etc., etc.

The pair of bishops are especially valuable in the endgame(see above-diagrammed position), for the simple reason that in the endgame bishop mobility is much higher on average than knight mobility, and there are fewer opponent pawns to attempt restricting their activity.

It is a big misconception, though, that the pair of bishops lacks in significant value in earlier stages of the game, primarily the early opening. Even there, bishops are extremely strong, so it is always wise to try keeping them as frequently as possible, no matter the character of the position(more closed, more open) and the number of remaining own and enemy pawns.

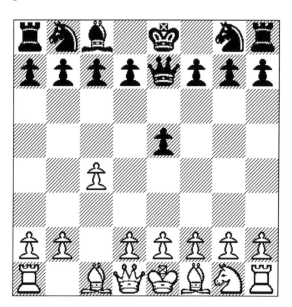

for example, take this position, arising in the English opening after 1.c4 e5 2.Nc3

Bb4 3.Nd5 Be7 4.Ne7 Qe7: white is largely winning, because of the bishop pair, although many top engines would assess it as almost equal, and quite probably so also many humans

Frequency: very frequent

Pair of bishops with enemy side having no bishops

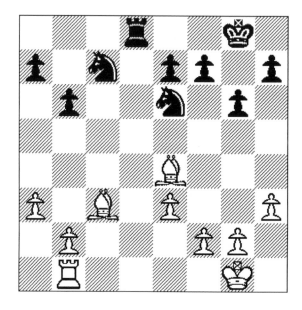

white has larger advantage than one would think; almost certainly a white win, although black possesses above some other relevant drawing advantages

156

a similar position with a bit different configuration

Value: bonus, 20cps, both for the mg and eg

Additional information: this is a very valid positional rule. In sharp distinction to the main 2 bishops rule however, to be found in almost any handbook on chess, it seems to be largely neglected and undiscussed.
Bonus is due for the following reasons:
- the opponent side does not have a bishop trying to match one of the bishops of the pair
- it is not possible for the enemy side to easily exchange one of the bishops of the bishop pair, as it lacks bishop, and equal exchanges(same piece for same piece, bishop for bishop) are most common in chess, with unequal ones(rook exchange or minor exchange, rook for bishop or knight for bishop) often requiring additional tactical assets; thus, the bishop pair seems to be much more durable

Frequency: infrequent

Pair of rooks vs queen

you might think position is almost equal, but in actual fact, white has large advantage

Value: bonus, 40cps in the mg, 30cps in the eg, for the rook pair

Additional information: the bonus is due because:
- the pair of rooks represent a nice tandem, they are able to attack together the enemy king shelter, specific enemy pawns, the enemy queen, etc., with the opponent queen quite lacking this capacity; in this sense, it is difficult to defend such objects
- the pair of rooks are able to defend each other well, so attacking and capturing them is much more difficult
- in the presence of other pieces too, this will only help the rooks side, as there will be more own pieces to coordinate among with all of the above-mentioned advantages; for example, on the diagrammed position, the pair of rooks will be able to coordinate with the white bishop on f3 too, so the bishop can defend the rooks, the rooks can defend the bishop, the bishop and rooks can concentrate their attack on a particular square of the shelter, particular enemy pawn, the enemy queen, etc.

believe it or not, white is almost certainly winning this

157

2 minor pieces vs rook

white has large advantage

Value: bonus, 20cps in the mg, 10cps in the eg, for the minors

Additional information: the bonus is given because:
- the minor pieces are able to coordinate among themselves, attacking in tandem enemy pieces, pawns and squares of the shelter
- the minors are able to defend each other, which the lone rook is quite unable to do

With the presence of more pieces on the board, the advantage of the minor pieces only increases, for the simple reason that opportunities for coordination, successful attacks upon enemy objects and successful self-defence further increase.

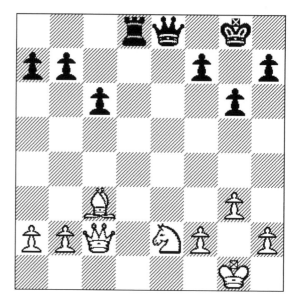

adding just one queen each side to the last-posted position, one might think the assessment of the position will remain more or less the same, but no, white's advantage has further increased

Frequency: very frequent

Queen and knight

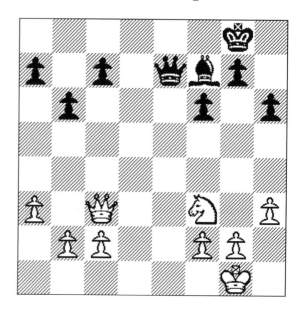

white's configuration, Qc3 and Nf3, is somewhat better than black's configuration, Qe7 and Bf7

Value: bonus, 15cps, both for the mg and eg

158

Additional information: the bonus is given because the queen and knight are able to successfully complement each other in a way impossible for any other 2 pieces. As the queen combines the powers of a rook and a bishop, controlling lines and diagonals, and we have a knight, the pair together combines the powers of all 3 basic pieces, rook, bishop and knight, simultaneously controlling a wider range of board squares. A similar feat would be impossible for a queen and a bishop, for example(see diagrammed position).

Downside: not always durable; the knight could be exchanged for a bishop, leaving only queens, or the queens, if present, could be exchanged, leaving knight vs bishop, for example, which will already generally favour the bishop side.

Of course, the rule holds true also with other possible configurations.

the bonus should be evaluated too, with the caveat that, in case queens are exchanged, that will already favour the rook side

Frequency: frequent

Queen and pair of knights

Qc3, Nd3 and Ne3 build an excellent triplet

Value: small bonus, 7cps, both for the mg and eg

Additional information: the bonus is given for the same reasons as for the queen and knight pair, good coordination, and involves pretty much the same downsides, associated with possible exchanges. In distinction to the plain queen and knight pair, here the queen already is able to communicate with 2 own knights.

Rook and bishop

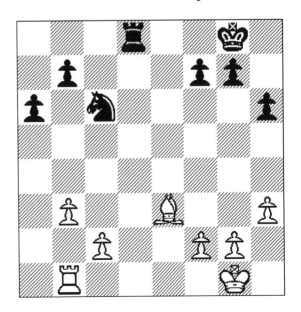

159

well, white already has quite a substantial advantage

Value: bonus, 10cps, both for the mg and eg

Additional information: the configuration is bonised because:
- both the rook and the bishop are sliding, long-range, fast-moving pieces
- as long-range, they are able to coordinate among each other even from afar, for example to defend each other, or to attack enemy objects/squares of the king shelter, which a tandem of opponent rook and knight can not quite always do

The rook and bishop pair will generally be even stronger in the endgame due to their long-rangedness and increased mobility, however, this feature is difficult to realistically account for, because of the very high probability to transit from the middlegame to the endgame with equal piece exchanges, very frequent, leaving the overall balance unchanged.

Frequency: frequent

Pair of rooks

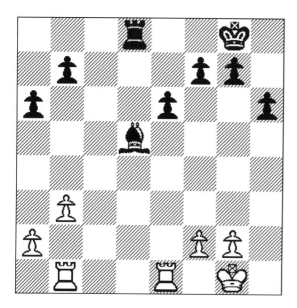

the white rook pair, although connected, looks pitiful next to the black piece tandem

Value: penalty, -10cps, both for the mg and eg

Additional information: you will find this feature in most wise chess handbooks. The obvious reason for the penalty is that the rooks are redundant, of same power, controlling squares only along files and ranks, and control of diagonals and knight powers are lacking.
Downside: possible exchanges of one of the rooks, getting rid of the redundancy, for example, on the diagrammed position, if rooks are exchanged, that will only benefit the pair of rooks side.

One must take into account that the pair of rooks could happen on the board in quite different configurations, with each configuration adding a different flavour to the mix. For example, on the diagrammed position, the redundancy penalty will be fully deserved, in an imbalance involving a pair of rooks vs 3 minors, for example, to the natural rook pair redundancy one should add the additional advantage a couple of lower-power minor pieces wield over the rooks, and in the case of a configuration including pair of rooks vs enemy queen, one should add the well-deserved bonus for 2 rooks vs queen to the ad-hoc dispensed redundancy penalty.

Frequency: frequent

Pair of knights

well, the knights are so pitiful, easily a win for the opponent side

Value: penalty, -10cps in the mg, -30cps in the eg

Additional information: the penalty is given for the same obvious reason: the knights are redundant, controlling only and exclusively squares, reachable by knight moves, and unable to access board squares along files, ranks and diagonals.

Apart from that, the knights are slow-movers, taking a lot of time to go from one edge of the board to the other, which is of particular significance in the endgame. Thus, having 2 knights, if not highly centralised and linked to some other relative advantages, simply means being twice as slow.

in the endgame, even though more in numbers, and with higher nominal material cumulative values, the white pair can easily concede a loss to the black side, precisely because of its extreme slow-movingness next to the fast-swinging rook

One must bear in mind though that, in spite of the fact that the redundant knight penalty is general, it receives particular flavours in a range of specific configurations. For example, in case of queen and 2 knights for one side, one should also add the bonus for the triplet to the general penalty, in case the 2 knights are part of a larger group of minor pieces or minor pieces and rooks pitted against an enemy queen, one should also add in the relevant bonus, and the same in case of couple of minors including the knight pair vs a pair of enemy rooks, etc.

Frequency: frequent

Rook, knight and bishop

Queen and bishop vs queen and rook

the white pieces beautifully coordinate among themselves

the white queen plus bishop are facing the black queen plus rook

Value: bonus, 10cps, both for the mg and eg

Value: small bonus for the queen and bishop, 8cps, both for the mg and eg

Additional information: the bonus is given, of course, for the excellent complementarity of the triplet: the rook, bishop and knight all have different powers, and control squares accessible along ranks, files, diagonals and through knight moves

Frequency: frequent

Additional information: the bonus is given because:
- the queen and bishop coordinate better
- in the queen and rook, you have a partial redundancy of a rook power, present in both the rook and the queen, while in the queen and bishop, quite the contrary, you have a partial presence of a pair of bishops, with the bishop power also available in the queen
- the bishop is a piece of lower power next to the rook, and pieces of lower power, when well coordinated, always have some relative advantages to pieces of higher power, mainly in the ability to attack them

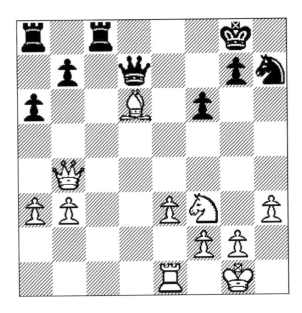

adding more pieces basically changes nothing: the white advantage has risen further

Please note, that the bonus is not given with the imbalance queen and bishop vs queen and knight, although the queen and bishop will still partially represent a pair of bishops, for the very simple reason that bishops have less influence upon enemy minors.

Frequency: frequent

Queen vs 3 minor pieces

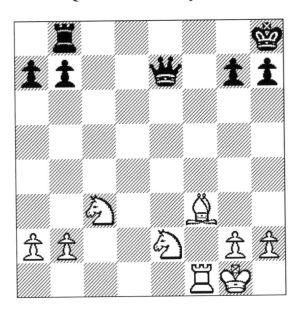

in spite of the seemingly materially balanced position, white is easily winning that

Value: bonus, 60cps in the mg, 20cps in the eg, for the 3 minor pieces

Additional information: this is one of the imbalances that capture the imagination. Even top humans have considerable problems playing it optimally, as transitions from one piece configuration to another are frequent and abrupt, and human perception usually has difficulties quickly adapting to changing unknown circumstances. Besides, gameplay is far from trivial. Machines, on the other hand, would play easier materially unbalanced positions with complicated exchanges and abrupt transitions, however, the problem there, with rare exceptions, is hugely insufficient material imbalance evaluation.

The 3 pieces are due a nice overbonus due to the following reasons:
- much better coordination in attack: the more numerous army is able to successfully aim at and conquer enemy objects, pawns and pieces, and squares of the king shelter, with defence of the opponent side being insufficient due to the presence of a single piece of higher power, the queen, which alone can not defend itself and particular board squares from multi-focused attacks
- pretty much along the same lines, much better coordination in defence: the more numerous army is able to very successfully defend its separate units, as well as vital points in its pawn structure and king shelter; with so many pieces, usually many of them will mutually defend each other, as well as a multitude of own pawns and otherwise vulnerable king shelter squares

The much lower endgame bonus is due to the fact that, the smaller the number of pieces for one side, the worse their coordination is.

this is pretty much a draw

and this is pretty much won for white, even if white did not possess the bishop pair

Frequency: infrequent

Queen vs rook and 2 minor pieces

white should easily win that one, although the material balance somewhat even favours black

Value: bonus, 120cps in the mg, 80cps in the eg, for the rook and 2 minor pieces

Additional information: another imbalance configuration that promptly captures the imagination. As with the 3 minor pieces vs queen imbalance, here most humans will have terribly hard time playing such positions optimally, while most, even top, chess engines, will fail to make the utmost of such imbalances, simply because of partially or entirely lacking chess knowledge, meaning the engines will rarely pick up lines involving similar imbalances, going for other, much inferior positions instead.

The very well-deserved bonus is dispensed for precisely the same reasons as with the 3 minor pieces vs queen imbalance:
- much better coordination in attacking enemy objects and particular board squares
- much better coordination in defence, including defence among pieces, and defence of specific board squares

The only bigger distinction with the above-mentioned imbalance is that here the drawing margin in terms of available board material comes significantly later for the queen side, as the opponent has a possession of more material even with no other pieces present, including a rook, and besides the presence of a rook will mean that this side has a piece attacking along ranks and files apart from pieces with minors' capabilities.

with more pieces on the board, that is an even easier win for the rook and 2 minors

Frequency: infrequent

Queen vs 2 rooks and a minor piece

in spite of the seeming material equality, white has excellent winning chances

Value: bonus, 150cps, both in the mg and eg, for the 2 rooks and minor

Additional information: the configuration is bonised because:
- the higher number of pieces provide much better coordination in attack
- the higher number of pieces provide much better coordination in defence

Bonus is equal for the mg and eg, as, even if no additional pieces present, the side with the 2 rooks and a minor already has a sufficient material availability to dangerously threaten the opponent.

more pieces would of course only increase winning chances for the side with 2 rooks and minor; in fact, white is easily winning that

Frequency: infrequent

165

Rook vs 3 minor pieces

in spite of materially balanced position, white should easily win that

Value: bonus, 70cps, both in the mg and eg, for the 3 minor pieces

Additional information: another intriguing imbalance. The bonus is given for the following reasons:
- much better coordination in attacking enemy pawns and pieces, as well as the enemy king shelter
- much better coordination in defence, including defence among pieces and defence of vital board squares, primarily the king shelter
- permanently fixing enemy pawns as backward, gaining valuable positional assets in the process

with more pieces present, the advantage for the side with the 3 minors further increases; white is easily winning that

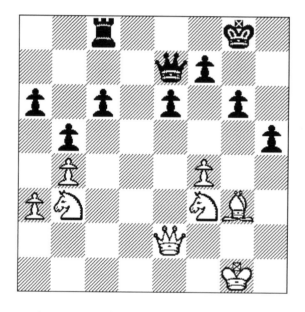

a clear example of how a big number of minor pieces for one side is able to make enemy pawns backward; if it were not for Nb3, controlling the c5 square, black would be able to push c6-c5, getting rid of the c6 weakness; if it were not for Nf3, controlling the g5 square, black would be able to push g6-g5, with some counterplay; even h5-h4 push is not possible, even though white does not have a pawn challenging black's h5 pawn advance, as both Nf3 and Bg3 control the h4 square; in this way, all of above black pawns are backward, and white can use these

166

positional assets to gain some more time in regrouping and delivering a decisive attack against enemy weak pawns, pieces and squares of the king shelter; what makes such opponent pawns backward is the lack of pieces of lower power as minors for the opponent side, able to support the advance of own pawns, therefore it is much preferable to have minor pieces than rooks in similar constellations

Frequency: infrequent

3 minor pieces vs 2 rooks

well, white will always have some additional small edge in similar positions

Value: bonus, 15cps, both in the mg and eg, for the 3 minor pieces

Additional information: the bonus is dispensed for the following reasons:
- better coordination in attacking enemy pawns and pieces, as well as squares of the king shelter
- better coordination in defence among pieces, as well as defence of vital board squares, basically the king shelter
- ability to make enemy pawns backward, pretty much along the same lines as in the case of an imbalance of 3 minor pieces vs rook

In distinction to the 3 minor pieces vs rook imbalance, however, here the bonus is significantly smaller, because the stronger side possesses just a single non-pawn piece more, which renders coordination among pieces somewhat better, but not to the extent as a plus of 2 non-pawn pieces would ensure.

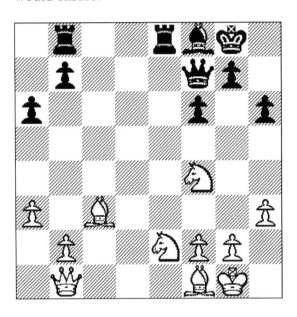

more pieces, of course, will only increase the edge for the side with the 3 minors

Frequency: infrequent

Rook and minor piece vs queen

white should easily hold that, in spite of the huge material deficiency

Value: bonus, 60cps, both in the mg and eg, for the rook and minor piece

Additional information: the bonus is given for the nice ability of the rook and minor piece to coordinate among themselves while attacking enemy objects, pawns, pieces and squares of the king shelter, and defending vital squares on the board, primarily the own king shelter, as well as for quite successfully defending each other. A lone queen, for example, can not capture a minor piece defended by a rook, or a rook, defended by a minor piece, nor it can take any enemy pawn supported by one of those pieces.

Similar configurations frequently lead to drawish fortresses in the endgame(see the diagrammed position).

With the presence of more pieces on the board, the relative advantage of the rook and minor piece only increases, as more pieces guarantee better general coordination.

some humans, and too many top engines too, might be surprised to know that above position is mostly drawn, at least very very close to being a perfect draw; I guess,

statistically, by perfect play, and a bit of randomness, black should not win more than 20% of the games, with the rest coming to a legitimate drawn conclusion

having a bishop instead of a knight changes nothing: still pretty much drawn

Frequency: frequent

2 minor pieces vs queen

in spite of the huge material deficit, white has excellent drawing chances; in any case, winning such endgames is extremely long-winding and difficult, frequently over the margin of the 50-moves chess rule, everything will depend on one or 2 small details, the eye-striking conclusion however will always be that the material lead by a couple of pawns for the stronger side is somewhat unreal

Value: bonus, 40cps, both in the mg and eg, for the 2 minor pieces

Additional information: the bonus is given for the better coordination of the 2 minor pieces. They are able to:
- much better defend each other, making enemy captures quite unlikely
- excellently defend different vital points on the board, as otherwise weak own pawns, squares of the king shelter, etc.
- frequently make enemy pawns permanently backward
- successfully support the march to promotion of possible own passed pawns, as they can control squares on the promotion path the side with lone queen simply can not defend

well, e5 pawn is permanently backward, e5-e4 obviously loses the pawn, c7 pawn is permanently backward, if it were not for the white bishop on d5, black could have pushed c7-c6, getting rid of the weakness, g5 pawn is permanently backward too, if it were not for the white knight on f2, black could have attacked on the kingside with g5-g4, now this is impossible

look at how pieces of lower power are indeed very good at supporting the march forward of own passed pawns; currently, white can play both c5-c6 and a6-a7, and the black queen can capture neither pawn, as the minors will support them

With more pieces on the board, the relative advantage of the side with the 2 minor pieces only increases, of course, due to improved coordination with the remaining own pieces.

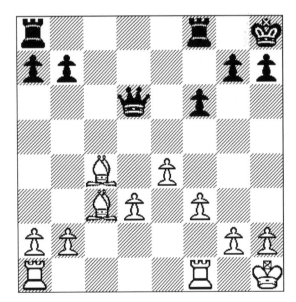

white has excellent winning chances, although some top engines and quite a few human players might be surprised

Frequency: infrequent

169

Queen pair

are the white pair of queens redundant, deserving a penalty, or, on the contrary, a welcome constellation, due some bonus?

Value: bonus, 40cps, only for the mg

Additional information: in my evaluation framework, a pair of queens is due a perceptible bonus, though most wise chess theory handbooks out there will tell you otherwise. Why should the queen pair be due a bonus?
Well, reason is simple: the pair has unmatched by opponent pieces properties of lightning-fast movement and coordination, which frequently leave the opponent king under very dangerous circumstances, especially when the position possesses a more open character. That is an undisputed fact.

Note: however, the queen pair bonus is meaningful, only if other relevant factors are considered too. So, for example, when one side has 2 queens, the other will usually have more rooks and minor pieces, where another additional bonus is dispensed, this time going to the imbalance of 3 minor pieces vs queen, rook and 2 minor pieces vs queen, etc. In this way, the presence of queens is first penalised, deservedly so, and then bonised. If the due

penalty for the imbalance queen vs 3 enemy pieces is not assigned, of course, this will only show up as a penalty for the queen pair, but that is another question, evaluation gaps and discontinuities are not a matter of the present work. It has to be figured out though, if both queens get penalised for the imbalance, and in what precise measure.

in the presence of more pieces and largely closed positions, the pair is usually weaker; above configuration is a most likely draw

with more open positions, especially when the enemy king is in the center, the queen pair is extremely dangerous, as the queens

170

move very fast across the entire board and different queen checks threaten all the time

Frequency: infrequent

One side having one piece more

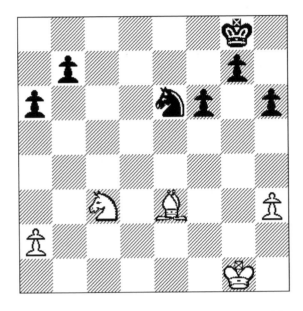

well, white is supposed to have big advantage, even in above simple endgame, where, according to theory, pawns get much more valuable

Value: bonus, 20cps, both in the mg and eg, for the side with the piece more

Additional information: this is a simple, but very sound, rule of thumb. The bonus is given of course for the fact, that the larger number of pieces will necessarily provide better coordination.
The more pieces on the board there are, the further the advantage of the side with a piece more increases.

this is most likely won for white, although the balance is just a single knight for 4 enemy pawns

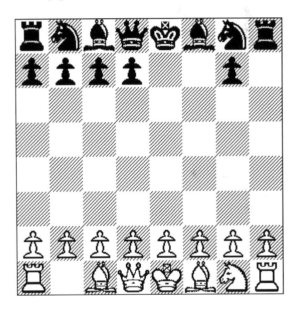

another good reason for assigning the side with the piece more, usually a minor, the bonus, is that the additionally available minor piece will provide quite a satisfactory cover to the own king, even in the absence of a pawn shelter, as on the diagrammed position, so that further boosts the friendly king safety

Frequency: frequent

171

One side having 2 pieces more

in spite of the generally accepted theory that pawns only get more valuable in the endgame, white has excellent winning chances

Value: bonus, 50cps, both in the mg and eg, for the side with 2 pieces more

Additional information: another very useful and true rule of thumb. Whenever you see one side has 2 pieces more, no matter what those pieces are, give this side a sufficiently big bonus.
The bonus is due, of course, for the significantly better coordination among the pieces prevalent in number, exponentially better compared to the case with just a single piece more, especially when the overall number of pieces is greater.
This is somewhat redundant to also assessing imbalance features as queen vs 3 enemy pieces, or, rook vs 3 enemy minors, but, it is necessary, as it also encompasses positional options as the one diagrammed above.

Frequency: infrequent

One side having 3 pieces more

white should be winning this, with utmost ease

Value: bonus, 100cps, both in the mg and eg, for the side with the 3 pieces more

Additional information: this is extremely rare, but still happens sometimes. The side with the much greater number of pieces is bonised, of course, due to the fact that those pieces provide exponentially better coordination than the other side. With such over-excellent coordination, the own king is completely safe, the pieces themselves quite safe too, even under attack, as defence by other own pieces is promptly available, the enemy pawns are over-easily stopped in their march forward and effortlessly attackable and capturable, much the same as the enemy non-pawn pieces.

Frequency: infrequent

172

Opposite colour bishops with one side having a piece more

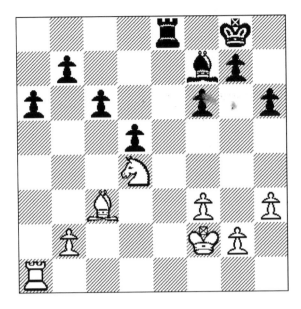

no matter how much surprised a bunch of top engines and many humans will be, in spite of the overall material balance and the presence of opposite colour bishops, that otherwise would only improve drawing chances, white is easily winning that

Value: bonus, 50cps, both in the mg and eg, for the side with the piece more

Additional information: the configuration will usually happen with one side having the piece more for a couple of enemy pawns. The bonus is dispensed for the fact that the side with the piece more will easily neutralise the advance of the enemy pawns, as the opponent bishop will not be able to support them on the squares of opposite colour, where the bishop of the side with more pieces will stop them unchallenged, on occasion also aided by another piece. In this way, while the pawns of the side with fewer pieces will remain largely blocked in their way forward and ineffective, the other side will gain valuable time to regroup, attain additional positional advantages and attack with its own pawns. The variations are always long-winding though, requiring a lot of manoeuvering, and probably this is one of

the reasons top engines do not promptly recognise the essence of similar positions granted the lack of correct evaluation.

The presence of more pieces will only improve the chances of the side with the piece more, of course.

Frequency: infrequent

Chapter VI

King safety

Well, here you are at the most interesting, as well as most complicated section of chess knowledge. Chess is basically all about king safety, mating the enemy king, so the importance of this section can hardly be overemphasised. When you learn how to attack the enemy king, you will get very good results, even if you misunderstand most of the other chess elements, for the simple reason that, when the enemy king is mated, it hardly matters how much material you and your opponent have, how many strong passed pawns, outposts, etc. you and your opponent possess. The game is simply finished. So, if you can learn one thing about chess, please do learn how to properly attack the enemy king.

Of course, enemy king attack is just one element of king safety, albeit the most salient one. King safety has many other elements, too, the presence of a pawn shelter for the friendly king, the availability of storming pawns, different other features too, which are also extremely important and can hardly be underestimated.

King safety is a challenge for both top engines and top humans. Although top engines play relatively well, or even extremely well many positions having to do with king safety, that will be only true of positions involving variations that are not very deep and including more or less forced series of moves like captures or checks. Whenever the associated lines are deeper, or do not necessarily involve a series of forced moves, top engines start to regularly miss out on the best moves. One reason being the depth, and the second one the lack of proper knowledge. Top humans, on the other hand, seemingly recognise a wide range of patterns conducive to enemy king attack and defence of the own king, but definitely not all. There are king safety patterns not a single top chess player has tried so far on the board, and other that only a few players have attempted. The major downside to human handling of king safety is however the very rapidly changing essence of what is going on on the board. Humans get accustomed to patterns and, with a lot of sacrifices usually happening in and around the enemy king shelter, the familiar patterns get transformed too quickly and unexpectedly, sometimes disappearing altogether, so that undistorted perception of transformations is very difficult to achieve. A very specific weak point in human attacking play is the inability, for whatever reason, to promptly recognise and employ sacrifices dealing with trading minor or other pieces for mere enemy pawns. Humans simply are unable to do that, probably because it is so unexpected to trade a knight or rook for one or 2 enemy pawns, so illogical at the first sight, that humans simply fail to consider it. Engines, on the other hand, do such tricks rather easy, one can certainly learn from engines in this respect. Humans also have significant problems with deep-running variations, especially when they involve unfamiliar patterns.

Further, we will examine to some length some of the most vital aspects of king safety.

Enemy king attack

Of course, enemy king attack may take the form of attack by friendly pieces and attack by friendly pawns, so called storming pawns. Here, we are only concerned with attack by friendly pieces.

King shelter

We have to introduce this notion before we go on with attacking explanations. The king shelter, strictly within our evaluation framework, but that will often overlap with many other frameworks, are the 8 squares immediately surrounding the king, the squares the king attacks, plus the 3 more squares 2 ranks in front of the king on the same file as the king, as well as the 2 adjacent files.

the white king shelter consists of the squares the king immediately attacks, h2,g2,f2,h1,f1(a bit less than 8 in this case, as the king is on its first rank and does not attack any squares behind), plus the 3 squares on the 3rd rank(2 ranks in front) on the same file and the 2 adjacent files, h3,g3,f3

The black pieces, that attack squares of the white king shelter, Ne5, Qf6 and Rh7, are said to be attacking the enemy king shelter. Ne5 attacks the f3 square of the shelter, Qf6 attacks the f2 and f3 squares, Rh7 attacks the h2 and h3 squares.

When the king is on an edge a or h file, the king shelter will consist of the squares the king immediately attacks, plus the squares 2 ranks in front on the same file as the king and the single adjacent file, plus the 3 additional squares on the same rank as the king, one rank in front and 2 ranks in front one file across the current king position. This rule will account for the fact that the king can quickly move from the edge to the adjacent file, with enemy piece attacks more or less remaining the same.

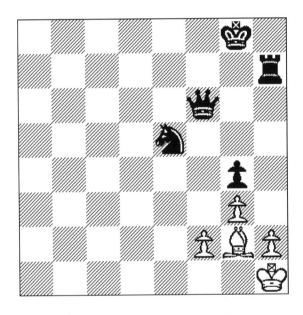

black piece attacks remain the same, although the white king is already on the edge h file

When the king is not on its first rank, then the enemy pieces will be attacking more squares, of course, including the squares behind the king.

now, the white king shelter consists of the h1,g1,f1,h2,f2,h3,g3,f3,h4,g4 and f4 squares; Rb1 attacks the h1,g1 and f1 squares behind the king, Nd2 attacks the f1 and f3 squares, while Qe6 attacks the h3 and g4 squares

Pieces attacking the enemy king shelter

Pieces attacking the enemy king shelter will get the following bonus in terms of specific piece:
queen: 50cps in the mg, 35cps in the eg
rook: 30cps in the mg, 20cps in the eg
knight: 20cps in the mg, 13cps in the eg
bishop: 15cps in the mg, 10cps in the eg

More or less, the pieces get bonus in accordance with their material significance. The slightly larger value for the knight next to the bishop is primarily due to the fact that it is more difficult to get the knight to an attacking position, the slow-moving knight should cross sometimes the entire board to achieve that, while the bishop can start attacking the shelter with a single movement, even from very far.

It is a major misconception that enemy king attack should not be considered, in case the attacking side does not have a queen. Of course, that does not matter at all. A combination of a couple of attacking pieces of lower power, say rook and 2 minors, will do just as fine and frequently even better.

Another major misconception is that enemy king attack should be considered only in the mg, or at least discontinued at some point later in the game. Not at all; on the contrary, as there is not anything more important than piece attacks upon the enemy king, such attacks, if present, should be counted in until the very last moment, well into the late endgame. Sometimes, a bare king plus rook is able to mate the opponent king, if on an edge file or under special circumstances.

X-ray attacks upon the enemy king shelter

Well, although x-ray attacks of any object or the king shelter are measurably less important than direct piece attacks, they are still valuable here, as squares of the king shelter are important targets.

Any sliding piece, x-ray-attacking the enemy king shelter, gets bonus in terms of specific piece in the following way:
queen: 25cps in the mg, 17cps in the eg
rook: 15cps in the mg, 10cps in the eg
bishop: 8cps in the mg, 5cps in the eg

As you quickly observe, the values are more or less half of the numbers for direct piece attack. Just a single x-ray-attacked square after the first own or enemy direct object in between the sliding attacker and this square is considered.

Bc7 directly attacks g3 square and x-ray-attacks h2 square of the white shelter, Rb2 directly attacks f2 square and x-ray-attacks g2 square, Qf6 attacks f3 square and x-ray-attacks f2 square

The knight attack that does not fit anywhere

Definition: knight on the 7th rank or b or g files, with enemy king on an edge file or rank next to the knight in the corner or on the same file or rank

above position represents this condition, with the g7 knight the protagonist

176

Value: bonus, 12cps in the mg, 3cps in the eg

Additional information: this should fill a gap in attack evaluation of the enemy king shelter. As easily seen on the diagrammed position, while the knight does not attack any square of the black king shelter, it is still within the shelter itself!
This seems like a bit of a contradiction and, as the knight is really very dangerous, it is legitimately due its over-bonus.

Frequency: infrequent

Unchallenged attacking bishop

Definition: bishop attacking 3 squares of the enemy king shelter, that are all empty

Value: bonus, 15cps, just for the mg

Additional information: the bonus is due, as the enemy pieces will have very hard time defending the own king. In the present situation, there will be no pawn on its 2nd rank in front of the enemy king, and also no pawn on the 3rd rank on the adjacent file towards the center, so that interposing pawns to lessen the strength of attack is close to impossible. Without defending pawns, of course, the sheltering task is even more difficult. Simultaneously, the bishop will attack one more square on the rank where the king is, ensuring further penetration.

the bishop on b2 attacks the f6,g7 and h8 squares of the black king shelter, that are all empty.
As easily seen, because of the impossibility of interposing pawns to defend, withstanding the attack is a futile task.

Frequency: infrequent

Bishop shelter attacks with opposite colour bishops

Definition: with opposite colour bishops on the board, bishop attacks on the enemy king shelter are scored higher

Value: double bonus for the bishop attacking any square of the enemy king shelter is given

Additional information: the bonus is due for a simple reason. As, with opposite colour bishops, bishops of different colour can only take part in the attack, but not in the defence of the own king, their attacking function only increases.
In that way, having a situation, where one bishop attacks the enemy shelter, while its counterpart does not do so, indeed very much favours the attacking side, as the defending bishop is completely useless in defence, unable to interpose, attempt

changing the attacking bishop to weaken the attack, or otherwise help the king.

Above considerations mean that, with opposite colour bishops, both in the mg and eg, sides should try at all costs to attack, even if sacrificing a pawn or 2 in the process.

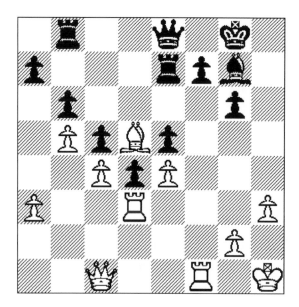

even though a pawn down, white is much better, as the white bishop attacks the vital f7 square of the black king shelter, while its counterpart on g7 currently attacks nothing, and will not be able to do so in the near future.

As the black bishop can in no way help in the defence, by supporting the f7 square, or by interposing somewhere, the attack is even more decisive. In this way, passivity of bishops in opposite colour middlegames is tantamount to self-destruction and should always be avoided.

in the eg, such condition is pretty much forceful, too.

In spite of being a pawn up, white is in a precarious situation.

Frequency: infrequent

Bishop pair with kings on opposite sides of the board

Definition: having the bishop pair, when kings are placed on opposite sides of the board, one of them on the queen side, and the other on the king side

Value: bonus, 15cps, only for the mg

Additional information: the bonus is due for the fact, that, with kings positioned on different sides of the board, and storms on different wings, communication between sides becomes even more important, and bishops, as long-range pieces, are capable of providing such efficient connection better.

Bishops will be able to simultaneously attack the enemy king shelter and defend the own shelter, support the advance of own storming pawns and stop the advance of enemy storming pawns, etc., while the slow-moving knight can only do one task at a time, either defend the own king on one side, or attack the enemy king on the

178

other. It will take the knight 2 or 3 moves to slow-jump between sides.

In tandem, also, the bishops constitute an excellent king cover.

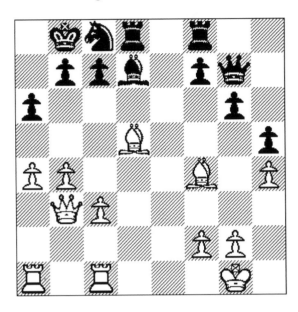

the pair of white bishops are performing much better with opposite-sided kings than an enemy constellation involving a knight. The pair of white bishops simultaneously attack the b7 and c7 squares of the black king shelter and defend the g3,f3,h2 and g2 squares of the own shelter, while the black knight on c8 only defends certain squares of the own shelter.
In order to take part into the attack, the knight will first have to go to e7-f5-h4, etc. This takes time, and time is vital, especially with opposite-sided kings in the mg. If not immediately advantageous, this condition is sure to bear fruit in the long run.

With kings on same sides of the board, a similar bonus is inapplicable, as knights need just a single move to jump from a defensive to an attacking square, with fronts being close by, while bishops, in order to attack, should be placed on the opposite side of the board, and thus unable to defend the own king.

Frequency: infrequent

Rook on open edge file with enemy king on adjacent file

Definition: rook on open edge h file with enemy king on adjacent g file, or rook on open edge a file with enemy king on adjacent b file

the white rook on h1 represents this particular condition; the h file is edge and open, and the black king is placed on the adjacent g file

Value: bonus, 40cps, only for the mg

Additional information: the very-well deserved bonus is given for the fact that an open edge file, in the mg, is a much more dangerous attacking alley than otherwise, because it is incomparably more difficult for defending pieces to organise sufficient defence there. It is not easy to quickly transfer pieces to the edge of the board and, once the attacker has placed a rook on such an open file, mate will be very difficult to avoid(see diagrammed position).
Many human opening positions involve such a strategy, but top engines are not so quick in discerning the value of similar

179

moves, as often the corresponding winning lines are rather deep, while the engines lack similar knowledge.

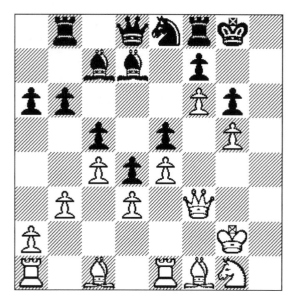

white is winning easily that, but quite often, even top engines have considerable problems in similar setting to recognise the impending danger, as some 10-12 preparatory/regrouping moves are needed until white transfers both one rook and the queen to the edge h file: white should first get the 2 minors, Ng1 and Bf1, out of the way of the white rook on e1, and then play Rh1, with transfer of the queen on h2 or h4, or, alternatively, play Kg3 or Kh1, then move the rook on e1 to h2 via the second rank, and only then put the queen on h4

Frequency: frequent

Rook on g or b open file with enemy king on adjacent edge file

Definition: rook on g open file, with enemy king on adjacent edge h file, or rook on b open file, with enemy king on adjacent edge a file

the white rook on g1 is on an open g file, with the black king placed on an edge h file; well, similarly, this one is quite dangerous, though the mating sequence is far too long

Value: bonus, 20cps, just for the mg

Additional information: the bonus is given for similar considerations: it is more difficult to organise successful defence close to the edge of the board, besides, the single enemy shelter pawn on the adjacent edge file covering the king is quite vulnerable and often an easy target

Frequency: frequent

Rook on the same closed file as the enemy king

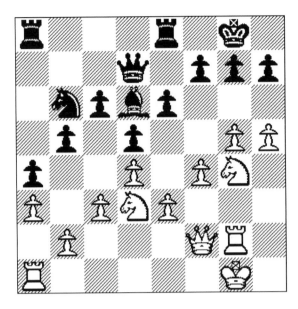

the white rook on g2 is placed on the same closed file as the enemy king

Value: bonus, 15cps, just for the mg

Additional information: the bonus is dispensed for the fact, that this represents a rather dangerous configuration, while it is not taken otherwise into account. For example, on the diagrammed position, Rg2 does not attack directly the enemy king shelter, as the files are closed, and even does not attack it on an x-ray, as the knight on g4 and the pawn on g5 stand in between, so attacking bonus for similar attacks is not due. At the same time, different things threaten, for example, Nf6 and Nh6 checks with opening the g file, etc.

Frequency: frequent

Rook on adjacent closed file as the enemy king

this time the white rook on h2 is placed on an adjacent closed file to the enemy king

Value: bonus, 12cps, just for the mg

Additional information: bonus is given for pretty much similar reasons as with the rook on the same closed file. This time, on the diagrammed position, h6 and g6 threaten, opening the h or g file.

Frequency: frequent

Queen on the same closed file as the enemy king

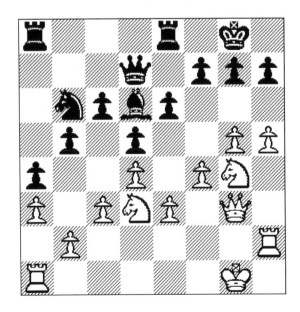

this time, the white queen on g3 is placed on the same closed file as the enemy king

Value: bonus, 8cps, only for the mg

Additional information: reasons similar to above-mentioned for the rook in the same situation apply. For example, on the diagrammed position, white already threatens Nf6 with queen capture or mate.

Rook on the same semi-closed file as the enemy king

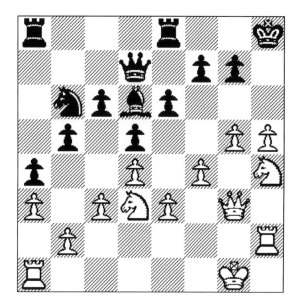

this time, the white rook on h2 is placed on a semi-closed file that is identical with the file of the enemy king

Value: bonus, 10cps, just for the mg

Additional information: the bonus is given for the fact that, while such a rook does not directly attack the enemy king shelter, as the file is semi-closed, it is still very dangerous. For example, on the diagrammed position, Ng6 or g6 threaten, with later opening the h file.

Rook on adjacent semi-closed file as the enemy king

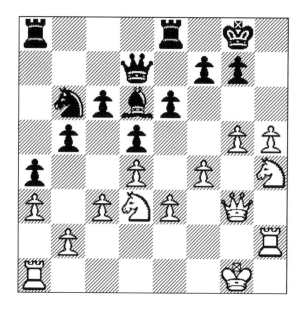

this particular time around, the white rook on h2 is on an adjacent semi-closed file as the enemy king

Value: bonus, 7cps, just for the mg

Additional information: similar considerations as for the rook on a semi-closed file identical with the file of the enemy king apply. On the diagrammed position, pretty much the same threats are available.

Frequency: frequent

Kingside presence of pieces

Definition: any non-pawn piece apart from the king itself present on the same side of the board as the enemy king. If the enemy king is on the king side of the board, that will make own pieces present on the h,g,f or e files, if the enemy king is on the queen side of the board, that will make own pieces present on the a,b,c or d files.

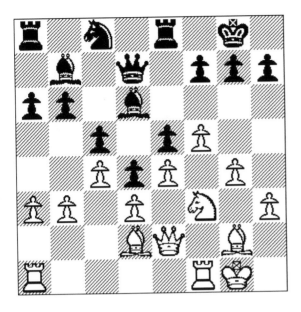

a whole lot of 4 white non-pawn pieces present on the side of the board, where the enemy king is: Rf1, Bg2, Nf3 and Qe2; the single black piece present on the side of the board where the enemy white king is situated is the rook on e8

Value: bonus, different for the specific pieces, is given in the following way, only for the mg:
queen: 20cps
rook: 15cps
knight: 10cps
bishop: 5cps

Additional information: this is equally important in closed and open positions alike. The bonus is dispensed for the simple fact that, even if not currently attacking the enemy king shelter, such pieces are much more likely to quickly start attacking it in the near future, as transfers from the same side of the board to attacking positions are easier and less time-consuming to do.

For example, on the diagrammed position, none of the white pieces, present on the king side, currently attacks the black king shelter. However, all of them can do so relatively quickly. The knight on f3 can jump to g5, starting to attack the shelter; in case the knight was placed somewhere on the queen side, such an attack would be impossible in just one move and would require many dislocations instead, even a knight on c2 would take 2 more moves to attack the black shelter, not to mention possible knights on b2 or a2. The queen on e2 can go through f2 or e1 to h4 square to directly attack the black shelter in just 2 moves; if it were somewhere on the queen side, b2 for example, such an attack would require one additional move. The bishop on g2, after h3-h4 and g4-g5 are played, can go to the h3 square, becoming very active, and later even start attacking the enemy king shelter, for example via f5, when game gets open; if that same bishop was somewhere on the opposite, queen side of the board, it could basically attack nothing related to the enemy shelter, even after a very long sequence of reasonable moves. The white rook on f1, after h4, g5 and Bh3 are played, can go to the g2 square via f2 to represent a valuable attacking feature, even though the game is closed; if that rook were on the queen side, such a manoeuver would necessarily require significantly longer to execute.

Frequency: very frequent

One open and one semi-open file or 2 semi-open files against the enemy king position

Definition: one side having 2 adjacent files, one of them open and the other one semi-open, or both ones semi-open, with the enemy king placed on one of them

183

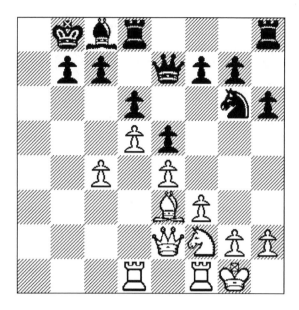 

above position represents such a constellation: a file is open, b file is semi-open for white

Value: bonus, 30cps, just for the mg

Additional information: the bonus is given for the fact that, although pieces for the side having this bonisable feature may not currently attack the enemy king shelter, they will certainly do so very soon, as the thoroughfares for attack already exist. For example, on the diagrammed position, although black has a pawn more and the white pieces do not predominantly attack the black king position at this point in time, they will certainly do so in the near future. The white rooks will be placed on the open a file, or on a and b files, with gradual thrashing attack. Black can not save that. For engines, that might mean seeing lines earlier due to improved evaluation, and for humans, one more useful attacking pattern to recognise.

this time, we have the feature in the form of 2 semi-open a and b files, with black having even 2 pawns more; still, white is winning this again, such is the power of the feature

Frequency: frequent

Storming pawns

Storming pawns are really one of the most significant elements of chess knowledge. Basically, immediately after attacks of pieces upon the enemy king it makes sense to consider storming pawns. Even before piece attacks upon enemy pieces, even before pawn attacks upon enemy pieces, and before pawn king shelter and every other feature. Reason is again very simple and quite evident: storming pawns constitute a major part of enemy king attack and, once you attack and mate the opponent king, it really does not matter at all what other things happen on the board. Storming pawns basically play 2 main functions in attack:
- opening up lines for attack of the pieces, primarily through levering, and
- by coming close to the enemy king, pressuring it, restricting the activity of opponent pieces in defence and providing valuable support for the own pieces in the

attack, often through controlling squares where those pieces could land

The first of the above-mentioned functions of storming pawns is largely due to free pawns, storming pawns not blocked by enemy pawns, while the second is a privilege of non-free pawns, storming pawns blocked by enemy pawns. Therefore, it very much makes sense to make a distinction between blocked and unblocked storming pawns in terms of evaluation.

Within the current evaluation framework, a storming pawn will be any own pawn on ranks 4 though 7 on the side of the board where the enemy king is placed. Thus, if the enemy king is on files h,g,f or e, the king side, storming pawns will be found on the same files on the above-mentioned ranks, while if the enemy king is on files a,b,c or d, the queen side, storming pawns will occupy pretty much the same files on above-mentioned ranks.

e4,g4,f5 and h6 are all storming pawns for white; the single storming pawn for black that could be considered is e5

Unblocked storming pawns

h5 is an unblocked storming pawn on the 5th rank, e6 is another unblocked storming pawn on the 6th rank. Both are levering and helping to open files for attack upon the enemy king; after hg6 hg6, the h file is opened, after hg6 fg6, the f file is opened, after ef7, the f file is opened, after fe6 instead, the same file is opened. Both pawns are also able to advance further, after h5-h6 or e6-e7. The free g4 storming pawn is also able to advance further, but, as it is not a lever, it is not capable of opening lines.

Unblocked storming pawns get bonus in terms of the following psqt:

8	0	0	0	0	0	0	0	0
7	0	0	0	0	130	120	120	100
6	0	0	0	0	30	90	60	50
5	0	0	0	0	40	80	70	60
4	0	0	0	0	25	60	50	40
3	0	0	0	0	0	0	0	0
2	0	0	0	0	0	0	0	0
1	0	0	0	0	0	0	0	0
	a	b	c	d	e	f	g	h

unblocked storming pawns with enemy king on the king side psqt(mg)

	a	b	c	d	e	f	g	h
8	0	0	0	0	0	0	0	0
7	0	0	0	0	65	65	60	50
6	0	0	0	0	15	45	30	25
5	0	0	0	0	20	40	35	30
4	0	0	0	0	12	30	25	20
3	0	0	0	0	0	0	0	0
2	0	0	0	0	0	0	0	0
1	0	0	0	0	0	0	0	0

unblocked storming pawns with enemy king on the king side psqt(eg)

	a	b	c	d	e	f	g	h
8	0	0	0	0	0	0	0	0
7	100	120	120	130	0	0	0	0
6	50	60	90	30	0	0	0	0
5	60	70	80	40	0	0	0	0
4	40	50	60	25	0	0	0	0
3	0	0	0	0	0	0	0	0
2	0	0	0	0	0	0	0	0
1	0	0	0	0	0	0	0	0

unblocked storming pawns with enemy king on the queen side psqt(mg)

	a	b	c	d	e	f	g	h
8	0	0	0	0	0	0	0	0
7	50	60	65	65	0	0	0	0
6	25	30	45	15	0	0	0	0
5	30	35	40	20	0	0	0	0
4	20	25	30	12	0	0	0	0
3	0	0	0	0	0	0	0	0
2	0	0	0	0	0	0	0	0
1	0	0	0	0	0	0	0	0

unblocked storming pawns with enemy king on the queen side psqt(eg)

Blocked storming pawns

h6 is a blocked storming pawn on the 6th rank, g5 is a blocked storming pawn on the 5th rank, and e4 is a blocked storming pawn on the 4th rank. Blocked storming pawns are especially valuable, when advanced. There, they are restricting the activity of the enemy pieces and greatly helping with the attack and building of mating nets. If a white queen is attacking simultaneously the g7 square, for example, it could promptly deliver mate to the black king precisely because of the support of the h6 pawn, if a white rook is targeting the very same square, it could at least deliver a dangerous check there, and any white minor, bishop or knight, can land with great effect on the f6 square, where it will be defended by the g5 storming pawn.

Blocked storming pawns get bonus in terms of the following psqt:

186

	a	b	c	d	e	f	g	h
8	0	0	0	0	0	0	0	0
7	0	0	0	0	0	0	0	0
6	0	0	0	0	40	110	90	70
5	0	0	0	0	30	80	60	50
4	0	0	0	0	15	50	40	30
3	0	0	0	0	0	0	0	0
2	0	0	0	0	0	0	0	0
1	0	0	0	0	0	0	0	0

blocked storming pawns with enemy king
on the king side psqt(mg)

	a	b	c	d	e	f	g	h
8	0	0	0	0	0	0	0	0
7	0	0	0	0	0	0	0	0
6	0	0	0	0	20	55	45	35
5	0	0	0	0	15	40	30	25
4	0	0	0	0	8	25	20	15
3	0	0	0	0	0	0	0	0
2	0	0	0	0	0	0	0	0
1	0	0	0	0	0	0	0	0

blocked storming pawns with enemy king
on the king side psqt(eg)

	a	b	c	d	e	f	g	h
8	0	0	0	0	0	0	0	0
7	0	0	0	0	0	0	0	0
6	70	90	110	40	0	0	0	0
5	50	60	80	30	0	0	0	0
4	30	40	50	15	0	0	0	0
3	0	0	0	0	0	0	0	0
2	0	0	0	0	0	0	0	0
1	0	0	0	0	0	0	0	0

blocked storming pawns with enemy king
on the queen side psqt(mg)

	a	b	c	d	e	f	g	h
8	0	0	0	0	0	0	0	0
7	0	0	0	0	0	0	0	0
6	35	45	55	20	0	0	0	0
5	25	30	40	15	0	0	0	0
4	15	20	25	8	0	0	0	0
3	0	0	0	0	0	0	0	0
2	0	0	0	0	0	0	0	0
1	0	0	0	0	0	0	0	0

blocked storming pawns with enemy king
on the queen side psqt(eg)

Unblocked storming pawns do occur on ranks 4 through 7, blocked storming pawns just on ranks 4 through 6, as a storming pawn on the 7th rank can not possibly be blocked by an enemy pawn.

Unblocked storming pawns are more dangerous on ranks 4 and 5, where they could additionally advance, while blocked storming pawns are more valuable on rank 6, due to the fact that, although they are stopped there, they have already reached a perfect square exerting maximum pressure upon the opponent king, with blocked usually meaning being more durable. Blocked storming pawns on ranks 4 and 5 are simply too unadvanced, while being stopped, and an unblocked storming pawn on the 6th rank is by definition a passer, often less durable, and besides passers already do get their quite nice separate bonus.

Both blocked and unblocked storming pawns are extremely frequent.

Storming pawns with kings on different sides of the board

One of the most intriguing aspects of chess play is the situation when both kings find each other on different sides of the board, one on the king side, files h,g,f or e, and the other one on the queen side, files a,b,c or d. This is the so-called opposite castling. Opposite castling is so extremely interesting, precisely because of the role of storming pawns. As the own king will be castled on the other side, the pawns that will storm the enemy king will not be part of the own pawn shelter, so this allows bravely thrusting them forward, sacrificing them more emphatically, which frequently leads to virulent, mind-boggling and eye-catching attacks.

As such storming pawns are easier to move and sac, it very much makes sense, of course, to assign them higher values. In the present framework, I would quantify storming pawns with opposite castling to be about one and a half times more valuable than normal storming pawns, for both blocked and unblocked storming pawns.

opposite-castled kings with a bunch of dangerous storming pawns for both sides; in such a situation, it is only quite natural to appreciate the storming value higher

Openers

Definition: a pawn that is an advanced lever and a storming pawn at the same time

h6 and e5 are openers for white; well, any capture, by either side, will lead to opening up the enemy king position, greatly facilitating piece attack

Value: bonus, valid in terms of psqt, only for the mg

8	0	0	0	0	0	0	0	0
7	0	0	0	0	0	0	0	0
6	0	0	0	0	25	30	35	40
5	0	0	0	0	15	20	25	30
4	0	0	0	0	0	0	0	0
3	0	0	0	0	0	0	0	0
2	0	0	0	0	0	0	0	0
1	0	0	0	0	0	0	0	0
	a	b	c	d	e	f	g	h

openers with enemy king
on the king side psqt(mg)

8	0	0	0	0	0	0	0	0
7	0	0	0	0	0	0	0	0
6	40	35	30	25	0	0	0	0
5	30	25	20	15	0	0	0	0
4	0	0	0	0	0	0	0	0
3	0	0	0	0	0	0	0	0
2	0	0	0	0	0	0	0	0
1	0	0	0	0	0	0	0	0
	a	b	c	d	e	f	g	h

openers with enemy king
on the queen side psqt(mg)

Additional information: openers are extremely useful in chess, both with same side and opposite side castles. Reason is obvious: opening up lines and diminishing the enemy king shelter is a major attack booster.

As this feature is redundant with the presence of advanced levers, one must be very careful when defining the size of the bonus for both features and deciding whether to dispense this ad-hoc bonus over the bonus for advanced levers or, alternatively, dispense one bonus only for the case when advanced levers are not storming pawns and a separate bonus for storming pawns that are levers. In the present evaluation framework, the bonus is given over the general advanced levers bonus.

Skipping the feature entirely with thoughts running along the lines of 'we have bonus for levers and another one for storming pawns, so why have a third one', is the wrong way to proceed, as storming pawn levers are quite apart from plain levers, their function is much enhanced, and very specific, and besides they are extremely frequent.

Frequency: very frequent

All storming pawns blocked

Definition: 3 own pawns on files a,b and c, or h,g and f blocked by enemy pawns, or some of those blocked by enemy pawns, with the rest being symmetrical twice backward pawns

h,g and f storming pawns all
blocked by enemy pawns

an alternative variation: h and f storming pawns blocked by enemy pawns, with the remaining g storming pawn being symmetrical twice backward pawn

Value: penalty, -50cps, just for the mg

Additional information: the very-well deserved penalty is dispensed for the obvious fact, that, in this very special case of storming pawns configuration, all possible lines of attack, both vertically and diagonally, are fully closed, this stalling the attack. In order for an attack upon the enemy king to be successful, one needs at least a single file against the enemy king remaining non-closed, semi-open or open. More files are even better, but at least a single file is essential.

As is very easy to discern on above diagrams, despite the presence of quite a few, in some cases advanced storming pawns, the opponent king really feels extremely safe.

Frequency: infrequent

Edge storming pawn blocked by enemy king

Definition: edge h storming pawn on h6, with enemy king on h7, or, edge h storming pawn on h7, with enemy king on

189

h8, or, alternatively, on the queen side, edge a storming pawn on a6, with enemy king on a7, or, edge a storming pawn on a7, with enemy king on a8

h6 storming pawn blocked by the enemy king on h7

alternatively, on the queen side and one square upwards, a7 storming pawn blocked by the enemy king on a8

Value: penalty, -80cps, for the storming pawn, only in the mg

Additional information: the very-well deserved penalty is due for the following weighty reasons:

- the file where the king-blocked storming pawn is is semi-closed, own heavy pieces can not attack along this file; additionally, even the square upon which the advanced storming pawn resides is unattackable by own pieces, so in a way it is better to have an opponent shelter pawn there instead of an own stormer
- the single remaining adjacent file to the attacked enemy king, even if open or semi-open, is far from sufficient to achieve a successful attack, as a single weakness is easily defended; any defending minor piece can easily stop enemy heavies trying to penetrate along that line
- it is true that the advanced king-blocked storming pawn exerts a considerable pressure upon the opponent king, but that is certainly more than compensated for by the vital file closure; as said, in this way the storming pawn is more of a burden than an asset

Edge king-blocked storming pawns are the only ones to be considered for this feature of king-blocked storming pawns, as, going towards the center, a g or b king-blocked storming pawn on g3/g2, b3/b2 would certainly be far more effective, as, although the file upon which that pawn resides would be closed, 2 adjacent files for attack still do remain, possibilities to repel attack along both are insignificant and thus the pawn only helps with the onslaught.

Frequency: frequent

Twice defended storming pawn on f5 or c5

twice defended storming pawn on f5

Value: bonus, 30cps, just for the mg

Additional information: the bonus is given for the following weighty reasons:
- this is a very strong, often durable stormer, close to the enemy king and exerting upon it considerable pressure
- the presence of such a stormer necessarily means that there are at least 2 other own storming pawns involved in the attack
- in case the storming pawn adjacent to the twice defended storming pawn on the file towards the edge of the board is free, this will significantly boost the pawn storm after this pawn itself advances(on the diagrammed position, see possible h2-h4, g4-g5 storm, with the g5 pawn becoming an aligned storming pawn, while the former twice defended storming pawn on f5 transforming into a defended aligned storming pawn); even if it is blocked by an enemy pawn, different pawn breaks, undermining the enemy blocking pawn are feasible, or, on occasion, rather efficient piece sacrifices

it is possible to open the h file after h2-h4 h7-h6 h4-g5 h6-g5, with the mighty f5 twice defended pawn still wielding a considerable pressure

it is also possible to sacrifice a piece, for example after Ng5 fg5 Bg5 or, the other way round, Bg5 fg5 Ng5, creating 2 tremendous unopposed storming pawns, one of which supported, both free and able to move forward, which usually gives more than sufficient compensation

This feature is especially useful in closed positions.

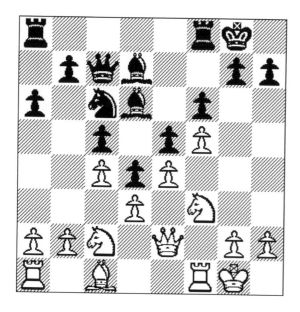

in above KID-like structure(basically a reversed KID), white already has the tremendous positional asset of the d3-e4-f5 pointed chain and, adding another positional asset with g2-g4, creating a twice defended storming pawn on f5, white will certainly win the game, even with best possible defence by black. Later, a gradual onslaught, involving h2-h4, Kh1, Rg1, Bd2, Rg2, Rag1, g5, etc., can follow, with a bust. Even top engines however, frequently have significant difficulties finding such moves, as a g4 thrust, apart from adding another storming pawn on g4, simultaneously leaves the white king with a pawn less within the shelter(former g2), carrying a penalty, and the associated variations are very deep. An useful evaluation feature can certainly attempt at resolving that. For humans alike, such patterns might be useful, as even top humans rarely do find such moves in a range of positions.

mainline KID structures frequently involve a twice defended storming pawn, see f4 above

The feature is equally useful on the queen side.

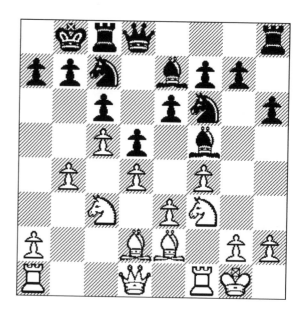

white has big advantage, partially because of the central bind, constituted by the d4 and f4 pawns, but also due to the tremendous twice defended c5 storming pawn

Overall, it is difficult to overestimate the great value of this particular feature.

Frequency: frequent

Minor piece controlling the square in front of an own or an enemy storming pawn

Definition: minor piece, knight or bishop, controlling the square in front of an own or an enemy storming pawn, provided that square is free

the white knight on f3 controls the g5 square in front of the g4 storming pawn, making the g4-g5 push possible; in case this knight was missing, g4-g5 would fail to h6-g5, losing a pawn

Value: bonus, 10cps, just for the mg

Additional information: the bonus is given for the fact that, quite often, such controls make further storming pawn pushes, sometimes with a break, possible. The condition the square in front of the pawn must be free is necessary, because otherwise this stormer would be immobile and its further advance irrelevant. Although the bonus is small, the situation is very frequent, and storming pawn advances are extremely important, so skipping that feature would be plain wrong.

within pretty much the same setting, now g4-g5 push is impossible, due to the defending side of this feature: opponent bishop on e7 controlling that very same g5 square

the value of minor pieces next to major ones in successfully providing this feature is easily seen above; in spite of the double black Qe7 and Rc5 control of the g5 square, g4-g5 is still possible, not losing material

Frequency: very frequent

Filling the gap

Definition: e2 or e3 pawn, with black king on the e,f,g or h files, or, alternatively, on the queen side, d2 or d3 pawn, with black king on the d,c,b or a files

Value: small bonus, 8cps, just for the mg

Additional information: the bonus is due, as, while such pawns are not considered by either pawn shelter with kings usually castled, or storming pawns, as being too unadvanced, they do play role in both functions.
So, this just fixes an ad-hoc evaluation problem.

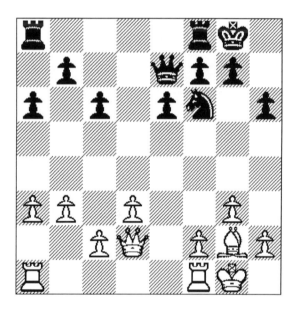

the black pawn on e6 is both useful as a defence for the black king close by, and as a potential storming pawn, when it reaches the e5 square. The white d3 pawn, on the other hand, enjoying the very same psqt, does and will do nothing of the above.
So the bonus is just about natural.

Frequency: frequent

Pawn shelter

Pawn shelter(also widely known as pawn cover) is an extremely important evaluation factor in chess. On the presence and number of own pawns close to the king, as well as their quality, will largely depend the safety of the king. Sometimes, having a lot of other good factors, but only lacking a sufficiently robust pawn shelter can have very negative consequences on the entire game, with one or 2 missing pawns around the king frequently outweighing a whole cohort of other terms. So securing the appropriate pawn shelter is always a priority, otherwise enemy pieces will make short work of the king.
Of course, the lack of sufficient number of own pawns around the king can be compensated for by a number of relevant substituting factors, like the presence of own minor pieces within the shelter instead of pawns, the availability of compact pawn structures on certain sections of the board, the more closed character of the position, etc. In this sense, the existence of a pawn shelter should not be absolutised, but only regarded as a nice asset within the much larger pool of evaluation parameters, many of which do pertain to the realm of king safety.

Definition: within our specific framework, the king pawn shelter will be any own pawn within the king shelter, i.e. the 8 squares immediately attacked by the king, plus the 3 squares on the file where the king is and the 2 adjacent files 2 ranks higher, provided that such a pawn is placed on ranks 2 or 3.
In case the king is on an edge h or a file, own pawns 2 files across towards the center, on f and c files respectively, on same 2nd and 3rd ranks, will be taken into account.
It definitely does not make sense to consider any own pawn on same rank and the 2 adjacent files on more advanced ranks than the 3rd, simply because such pawns constitute no cover at all, the king on more advanced ranks feels highly insecure, while such pawns are easily attackable and capturable.

the white pawn shelter consists of the
f2,g2 and h3 pawns; the black pawn
shelter consists of the f7,g6 and h7 pawns

this time, the g4 pawn is not part of the
white pawn shelter, neither the h4 pawn is
part of the black pawn shelter

Pawn shelter should always be considered
in the center, too. Frequently, a good
central pawn shelter might compensate for
the otherwise exposed location of the king.

with such a nice and sufficient pawn
shelter, the white king feels safe even on
the central e2 square, with same being also
true for his black counterpart on even more
advanced d6 square

It is a major misconception that the pawn
shelter should be considered only in the
mg. Of course, its relative value is higher
there but, as with piece attacks and
storming pawns, this king safety factor is
relevant right to the very end of the game,
even in very simple endgames. The king
always needs some cover.

Value: bonus, 30cps in the mg, 15cps in
the eg, for any own pawn within the king
shelter

Frequency: very frequent

Isolated pawn of the king shelter

f2 and h3 are isolated pawns of the white king shelter

Value: penalty, -20cps in the mg, -10cps in the eg

Additional information: the penalty is given for the obvious fact, of course, that such pawns render the shelter very vulnerable. There is no connection between the pawns, it is difficult to defend the pawns themselves, as well as for the pawns to successfully defend any own piece, and enemy pieces have very easy access to almost any of the king shelter squares.

Frequency: frequent

Doubled pawn of the king shelter

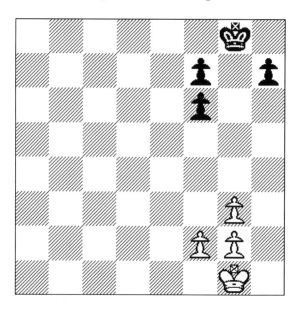

g3 is a doubled pawn of the white king shelter, f6 is simultaneously a doubled and an isolated pawn of the black king shelter

Value: penalty, -15cps in the mg, -8cps in the eg

Additional information: the penalty is due, of course, for the fact that the shelter with a doubled pawn is much less flexible. For example, on the diagrammed position, if f2 pawn moves, the doubled g3 pawn will remain undefended, while, in order for the g2 shelter pawn to take the g3 square, first the g3 pawn should move forward, and this takes time. Sometimes, in order to successfully repel an enemy attack, shelter pawns should have different moving options readily available, and this is not the case with doubled pawns. Besides, above, g4 square is difficult to defend without compromising the shelter, only option being f2-f3 push, which looks awkward; with a non-doubled white pawn on h2 instead, h2-h3 push would easily do the job.

In distinction to isolated shelter pawns, frequently both humans and top engines have difficulties with doubled shelter pawns, mainly because the associated lines are usually quite deep-running.

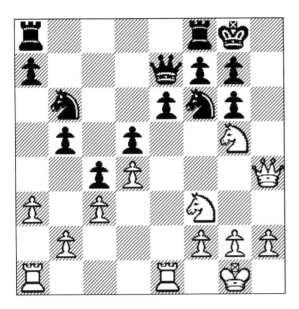

Value: penalty, -20cps in the mg, -10cps in the eg, over the penalty for the standard backward pawn

Note: only backward pawns on their 2nd rank are important, qualifying for the feature, backward pawns on squares of the shelter on more advanced ranks are significantly less of a weakness.

Edge h or a backward pawns on their second rank should probably receive considerably less penalty, maybe half of above values, as inflexibility along the edge files is much more difficult to exploit.

the doubled g6 black shelter pawn is so awkward, that, even though white plays with a pawn less, it should have little trouble winning the game, for example after g2-g4(cutting access for the black knight on f6 to the h5 square), followed by a Re3-h3 manoeuver. Many engines, however, will have hard time seeing this.

Frequency: frequent

Additional information: this is a very weighty feature, though frequently underestimated by both humans and engines. The penalty is due for the fact that such a pawn will make the shelter much more inflexible, depriving the side with it from possible valuable options. For example, on the diagrammed position, sometimes, in order to successfully defend, white will have to push the backward f2 pawn forward, but, under the specific circumstances, because of the backwardness, that will be very difficult or impossible to do. In this way, backward shelter pawns necessarily mean less flexibility. Which in turn means allowing the enemy more time to regroup its pieces and attack.

The feature is even more negative, when the backward-maker(the enemy pawn making the backward pawn such, controlling the square in front of the pawn) is a central e or d pawn.

Backward pawn of the king shelter

f2 is a backward pawn of the white king shelter

197

this time, the backwardness of the f2 pawn is felt even more, and the shelter as a whole is more inflexible, due to the fact that an enemy central backward-maker usually means the position bears a more closed character, and positions with more closedness do give more time for the attacker to regroup

Whole systems of play are frequently decided on the existence of a backward shelter pawn with a central enemy backward-maker. As the associated lines are deep or very deep, though, neither humans, nor even top engines will often have a clue one of the sides is already winning.

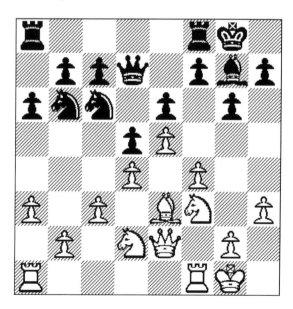

white has already basically positionally won the game, because of the black f7 backward pawn, part of the black king shelter, and the central e5 backward-maker, but I wonder how many humans will quickly give such an assessment, and how many engines will flash up a convincing winning score?

Thus, backward shelter pawns on their 2nd rank are tantamount to deep-running variations.

Frequency: very frequent

Twice backward pawn of the king shelter

Definition: exclusively, f2 or c2 twice backward pawns, when they are part of the king shelter

f2 is a twice backward pawn of the white king shelter

Note: due to specific considerations, possibility to open the edge h or a files, only twice backward pawns on the f and c files on their second ranks are considered. Other twice backward pawns of the shelter are completely irrelevant for the feature.

Value: significant penalty, -40cps in the mg, -20cps in the eg, over the penalty for a standard twice backward pawn

Additional information: this is one of my favourite evaluation features, and I have won a countless number of games with it against any of the top engines. The very-well deserved penalty is due for the following rather weighty reasons:
- the twice backward pawn makes the shelter extremely inflexible, much more so than with simple backward shelter pawns. As is easily seen on the diagrammed position, the f2 pawn can not possibly even budge from its place, as it will be immediately lost and a strong enemy passer created on the en passant square.
- usually, with such a constellation, the edge h or a file will be opened, or possibilities for realistically opening it up will be very high, which further increases attacking chances
- the feature includes by definition the presence of a central enemy backward-maker on either the e or d files, and central backward-makers are frequently associated with more closed positions, which in turn will give the attacker more time to regroup and launch a decisive assault
- a mighty minor piece outpost can be installed to great effect on the twice defended square on the 3rd rank in front of the twice backward pawn, smashing defences around. Usually, this will be a knight, but bishop outposting there is also sometimes possible. Capturing this minor outpost will help in no way, as this will automatically lead to its transformation into an extremely strong defended storming pawn.
- the square in front of the twice backward pawn is also a possible penetration point for enemy heavy pieces, be it a rook or even a queen. On occasion, such installation could be sacrificial, leading to a lot of fireworks display.
- finally, the twice backward pawn of the shelter assumes durability by definition, which only boosts attacking options

As is easily seen, this is a tremendous feature for the attacker to build, and a must-avoid element for the side with the pawn.

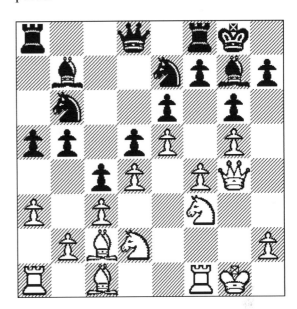

because of the black twice backward pawn on f7, part of the shelter, and the associated complete inflexibility of the shelter, white has already positionally won that, though I presume not many humans will see it, while practice shows that even the very top engines are fully clueless black is lost. White will transfer a knight via g4 to f6, proceed with opening the h file and win, though that might take quite some time, maybe 20-30 moves or so of regrouping. As the lines are deep, it is not easy to see, but the positional win is always there.

black has already won the game, because of the white twice backward shelter f2 pawn. I am not certain how many humans will think so, and most top engines will be very far from seeing a decisive black advantage, but the win is always there. It is true, though, that it will take quite a long time to achieve. Black should get its dark-square bishop to f6, sacrifice it on h4 for 2 enemy pawns, later transfer a knight via h7 to g5 and f3, with smashing attack. If necessary, both rooks could be enrolled in the approaching army to support the assault, by taking long-range aim along the h and g files.

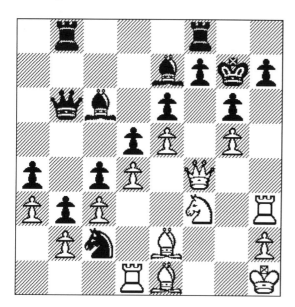

and this is from a game of mine against Stockfish, played on a computer chess

forum couple of years ago. Although many engines will doubt white's advantage, the gorgeous queen sacrifice, Qf6!, leads to a forced, albeit a bit longish, mate. Check all the variations yourselves, to get an idea of how strong an asset an enemy twice backward shelter pawn is.

In all, twice backward shelter pawns are interesting to play with and involve deep-running lines.

Frequency: infrequent

Semi-backward pawn of the king shelter

Definition: semi-backward pawn on the 2nd rank, when it is part of the king shelter

Value: penalty, -8cps, only for the mg, over the already dispensed one for any semi-backward pawn

Note: but this condition will exclude semi-backward pawns with the backwardmaker being a central e or d pawn, as this particular feature is already very-well penalised in evaluation by existing central backwardmakers

Additional information: the feature is penalised, as this makes the shelter less flexible, as with other backward shelter pawns.
In distinction to standard backward and twice backward shelter pawns, however, the liability is much less salient.

g2 is semi-backward pawn of the white king shelter, making it somewhat inflexible.

Any possible advance of this pawn, with existing captures of the f4 pawn, might severely compromise the shelter structure.

Frequency: frequent

Weak spots of the king shelter

Weak spots are an even bigger weakness, when they are part of the own king shelter.

f3 and h3 are weak spots, part of the white king shelter. The enemy bishop on g4

threatens to penetrate there, with decisive effect.

Value: double penalty as for a regular weak spot, -20cps, just for the mg

Additional information: the higher penalty is of course due to the fact, that enemy piece penetration on such squares within the shelter is even more dangerous and unwelcome.

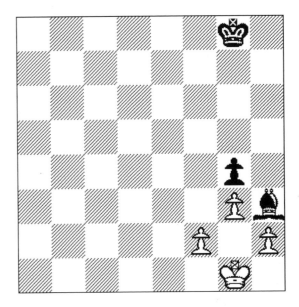

nothing more dangerous than an enemy piece on such a square. This makes the shelter much more inflexible, as the pawn on its 2nd rank, blocked by the enemy attacking piece, is immobile, precluding certain defence possibilities, associated with the pawn's advance.

a white knight on an f6 weak spot, part of the enemy king shelter, is often even more menacing

Frequency: frequent

Own minor pieces defending a weak spot of the king shelter

this time, the attack of the black knight on g5 upon the weak f3 and h3 spots of the white king shelter is not so dangerous, as the white bishop on g2 successfully defends both of them. This is one of the reasons why, although fianchettos are often associated with the creation of own

weak spots, they are still extremely useful and performing.

Value: small bonus, distinguishing between the bishop and knight:
- 10cps for the bishop
- 5cps for the knight

Additional information: well, the added value is obvious, defending a critical king safety point

Frequency: frequent

Colour deficiency with weak spots of the king shelter

Definition: one side having light-square bishop and enemy side having weak spot of the king shelter on a light square and no own bishop the colour of the weak spot, or, one side having dark-square bishop and enemy side having weak spot of the king shelter on a dark square and no own dark-square bishop

having no bishop the colour of the weak spot with the enemy side wielding such a bishop, able to attack it, usually means this spot will be very difficult to defend. Above, the f3 weak spot looks even weaker, indeed, penetration and x-raying through it by the enemy bishop seem unchallengeable, and the weakness is even bigger, as this is a square of the king shelter, closely related to king safety. Often, this will lead to mating attacks.

Value: sufficiently large penalty, -40cps, only for the mg

Additional information: this is a very tricky situation for the side with the weak spot. Repelling an attack by enemy pieces, with the enemy raking bishop the colour of the weak spot playing a leading role in it, is an enormous task, often unmanageable at all. This often allows for the side with the attacking bishop to even play with material down, and still organise a powerful mating assault.

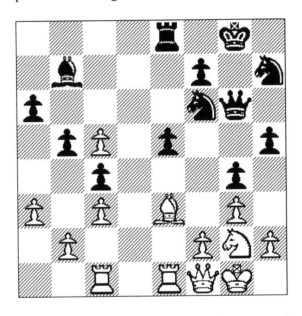

even though down the exchange and having no shallow immediate threats, black should win at some point, due mainly to the above-mentioned positional feature: black has the b7 bishop, the colour of the white weak spot on f3, while white does not possess bishop of the same colour

This is sometimes difficult to play for humans, but, quite often, even more so for top engines, that do not quite possess such knowledge. As the associated lines are usually deep-running, engines will frequently stumble, mainly in picking up the wrong variations.

If the weak spot is in the center, the advantage of the opposite side only increases.

black has quite some edge, although it trails down materially by a considerable margin. One of the main reasons for this edge is the unchallenged bishop on h6, firmly controlling the e3 weak spot of the white king shelter.

Note: the feature should not be considered with a weak spot on h3 or a3 on an edge file, as in this case the weakness is simply too small to be exploitable

Frequency: infrequent

King safety related queen pins

Definition: exclusively, white bishop on g5 or h4, black knight on f6, black queen on e7 or d8, with black king on e,f,g or h file on the king side, or, alternatively, white bishop on b5 or a4, black knight on c6, black queen on d7 or e8, with black king on d,c,b or a file on the queen side

the king side option

and the queen side alternative

Value: sufficiently large bonus, 80cps, only for the mg

Additional information: this is a very subtle feature, indeed. Many humans might still have problems with it, even at the very top level, and almost all top programs completely fail to recognise such configurations. The reason is simple: the associated lines are usually so deep and surprising, that precisely calculating some 20-30 moves is beyond the power of both humans and silicon monsters.

The very-well deserved bonus is dispensed for the fact, that the pin is closely related to the king safety of the side with the pinned knight. As seen on both posted diagrams, the black knights on f6 and c6 are part of the black king shelter(pertain to squares of the shelter), so if the queen has to move somewhere else from where it will not be able to defend the knight, or if the attacking side piles up more pieces to attack the knight, after the possible bishop capture of this knight, the pawn structure of the black king shelter will suffer enormously, with pawns being doubled, which will severely compromise the black king safety. Apart from that, usually another black shelter pawn will get isolated, highlighting the weakness. And additionally, this is still a pin, so moving the knight is also out of the question.

white threatens d3-d4, e4-e5, winning. If it is black's turn, that would not save the game either. For example, after h7-h6, Bg5-h4, g7-g5, white has already a winning sacrifice: Ng5! hg5 Bg5.

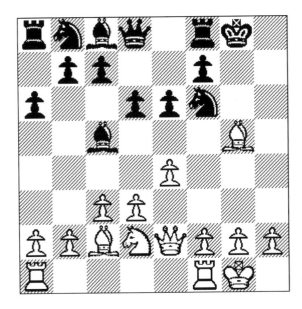

with a piece more, but totally broken king shelter, lacking in pawns, and the mighty nasty queen pin still there, black simply can not save that. It might take a while for a human or engine to see it, if at all, it might take some time, even a bit more, but, no doubt, white will win in the end. The pin is simply so obnoxious!

Such sacs frequently lead to beautiful play. Is not above position a beauty?

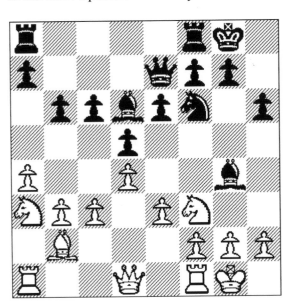

although this position might look more or less equal, in actual fact black has excellent winning chances, and one of the main reasons for that is the tremendous black pin of the g4 bishop.

Sometimes, the associated lines are so deep and wide-ranging, as well as difficult

to fully recognise, that it is an utter joy to immerse oneself in them.

Frequency: infrequent

No pawn shelter

Definition: the lack of even a single own pawn within the king shelter on ranks 2 and 3

the black king possesses a nice pawn shelter, consisting of the g7 and f7 pawns. The white king, on the other hand, does not have even a single pawn within its shelter: the e3 pawn is away 2 files across, while both the g5 and f5 pawns are too advanced on the 5th rank to be considered legitimate shelter pawns. This represents the so-called no pawn shelter.

Value: large penalty, -70cps, only for the mg

Additional information: this is a major feature indeed, though many humans tend to sometimes underestimate it, while even the strongest programs have regular problems with it. Of course, the penalty is very-well deserved for the obvious fact that the king remains fully without pawn cover, which, in the mg, usually leads to disastrous consequences. The king can still find sufficient cover with only a single own pawn present around in a range of situations, though extremely rarely when no pawns at all are present.

black will win this at some point, although this is not currently easily recognisable. The reason is precisely the complete lack of a pawn shelter for the white king(with the f4,g5 and h4 pawns all advanced), while its black counterpart still enjoys the immediate contact of 2 own shelter pawns, g6 and f7. It might take 30, 40 and even 50 moves, but at some point, the position will be opened, the black pieces will penetrate and mate the white king. The white king does not have any pawn shelter on its current place, the king side, as well as in the center, while walking to the queen side is simply impossible because of impending attacks.

Frequency: infrequent

No own pawn on the 2nd rank within the shelter

well, the white king does not have a single own pawn on its second rank within the shelter, both h3 and g3 shelter pawns being on their 3rd rank, while the black king still has one pawn on its second rank, g7

Value: penalty, -20cps, just for the mg

Additional information: the penalty is given, of course, for the fact, that pawns on the 2nd rank tend to shelter the king much better than other pawns and the lack of even a single pawn there quite often means the king will find only a partial cover. As is easily seen on the diagrammed position, the white king is quite exposed, it should go to the 2nd rank in order to find cover, and the 2nd rank is usually much worse for the king than the 1st rank. Also, a g2 pawn could stop an attacking enemy black bishop along the a8-h1 diagonal, while any of f2 or g2 pawns could challenge an enemy rook on its 7th rank, with both the long diagonal and the 7th rank now entirely open to attacks.

Frequency: frequent

206

Single own pawn on the third rank within the shelter

both the white and black kings enjoy the presence of single shelter pawns, g3 and g7 respectively. There is a big difference however. The single black pawn on its 2nd rank still sufficiently covers the king, while its white counterpart on its 3rd rank far from successfully will do that.

Value: penalty, -10cps, just for the mg

Additional information: the penalty is due for the obvious fact, that a shelter pawn is much less effective on its 3rd rank compared to the 2nd rank, and the truth that 2 own pawns on the 3rd rank, with no other shelter pawns, are still able to successfully hold in a range of cases, while this will almost never be the case with a single shelter 3rd-ranker

Frequency: infrequent

Minor piece shelter

Minor piece shelter is very important indeed, especially in the mg. A minor piece within the shelter will always strengthen it, while, in the absence of sufficient number of own pawns, minor pieces will still do fine as a cover for the king.

Definition: a minor piece, bishop or knight, on a square attacked by the king, i.e. one of the adjacent 8 squares

minor pieces will only strengthen the shelter, even it is already sufficiently robust, as above

a minor piece is a useful cover, even when the shelter is compromised

207

and in the center, too, even with the complete absence of own shelter pawns

Value: bonus, 15cps in the mg, 7cps in the eg

Frequency: very frequent

Minor piece on the 3rd rank within the shelter

Definition: minor piece, bishop or knight, on the 3rd rank within the shelter, provided that the square it takes is not attacked by the own king, i.e. the king is on its 1st rank

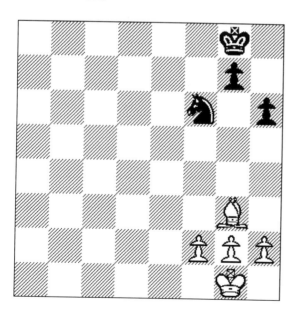

both the white bishop on g3 and the black knight on f6 provide additional cover for their respective kings

Value: bonus, 8cps, just for the mg

Additional information: this feature is less significant than the case with the minor piece immediately next to the king, but still useful

Frequency: very frequent

Minor piece shelter defence

Definition: minor piece, that is not part of the own king shelter, on square, adjacent to the king, or on square on the 3rd rank of the shelter, defending a square of the shelter, adjacent to the king

Value: small bonus, 5cps, just for the mg

Additional information: the bonus is given because this might sometimes be vital for defence.

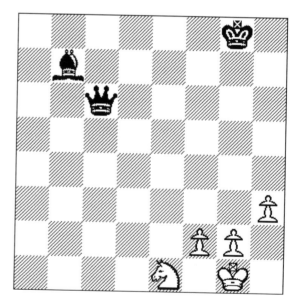

although the knight on e1 is not part of the white king shelter, it still plays a very useful role by defending the g2 shelter square, adjacent to the king.
In the present situation, the knight wards off the powerful queen and bishop battery

along the a8-h1 diagonal, but, even if not immediately under threat, minor piece shelter defence is always good, as enemy attack could come at about any moment.

the bishop on b7, even very far away from the white shelter, by defending the h1 shelter square, adjacent to the king, is able to ward off the rook battery along the h open file, that would otherwise simply deliver mate

Frequency: frequent

Minor outpost stopping enemy rook on an open file, with own king on the same or adjacent file as the rook

Definition: minor outpost on its 4th, 5th or 6th rank, supported by a pawn, with an enemy rook on the same open file attacking it, provided the rook is more advanced from the point of view of the minor, and positioned on the same or an adjacent file to the enemy king

Value: bonus, 15cps, just for the mg, for the outposted minor, over the already dispensed one for the regular condition

Additional information: the bonus is due because, apart from stopping enemy rook

penetration, such minors are also very much conducive to the own king safety.

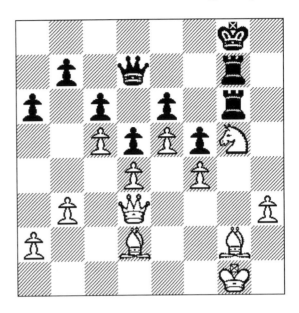

the pair of black rooks on the same open file as the white king are efficiently stopped from penetration and severely compromising the white king safety by the excellently placed white outpost knight on g5, heavily supported by the pawn on f4.

In case the knight was not there, the situation of the white king would have been very dangerous. In that way, even with a very much shattered pawn shelter, the king feels secure.

Frequency: infrequent

Immobile shelter pawns

Definition: pawns on the 2nd rank, part of the king shelter, blocked by an enemy piece

209

h7 is an immobile shelter pawn on its 2nd rank

f7 is another one

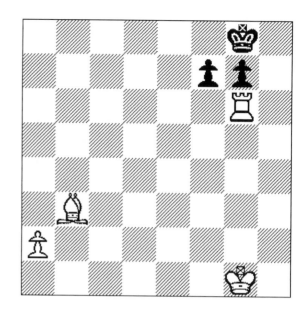

and g7 too

Value: penalty, -20cps, just for the mg

Additional information: the very-well deserved penalty is due because:
- immobile shelter pawns make the shelter less flexible, as shelter pawns need to move sometimes, in order to defend
- the shelter pawn immobility is very much tactically relevant, as they deprive the king of precious breathing space

Although nothing immediately menacing might be visible at the moment, this condition certainly bodes nothing well for the king.

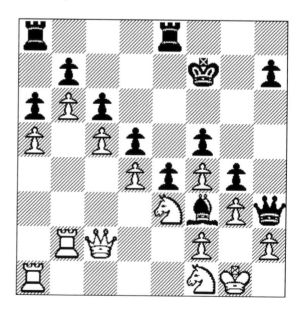

although white is a whole minor piece up, and nothing specific threatening the white king is seen at the moment, black is going to win after Re6-h6, Ra8-e8-e6, followed by a queen sacrifice on h2.

And white can do nothing to prevent this. The main reason for the loss will be precisely the extremely inflexible white king shelter, where none of the pawns can move at all. In order to defend, pawns should be able to move, and this is not the case in the present situation.

On the other hand, the pawn storm h7-h5-h4 gives nothing, as after hg3 fg3, the f shelter pawn is gone and already not inflexible, making the shelter much more acceptable as a whole and connecting both white heavy pieces on the 2nd rank on the queen side to the defence.

in case the shelter had not been that immobile, and the king had a safe haven square somewhere on the 2nd rank.

This feature is always tactically relevant.

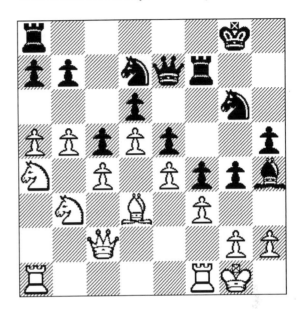

timely immobilisation of the shelter always helps. Black wins by force after Bg3!, immobilising the shelter g2 pawn and threatening Qh4. In case the g2 pawn is not immobilised, white could have found some counterplay after, for example, fg4 hg4 g3

Frequency: frequent

King on a fully closed side

Definition: own king on one of the a,b,c or d files, with a,b,c and d files all closed with pairs of blocked pawns; or, own king on e,f,g or h files, with e,f,g and h files all closed with pairs of blocked pawns

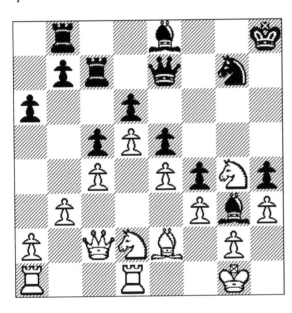

although white is a pawn up and the black king is completely unsheltered by pawns, white is definitely going to lose, after a timely pawn break by black on the queen side, and one of the main reasons for that is the inflexible white king shelter, especially in the form of the g2 pawn, immobilised by the black bishop on g3.

With time, after the queen side break, black will start threatening with mate on the first rank, and that threat, coupled with threats upon other vulnerable objects, will be very difficult to neutralise indeed. Such a threat would have been much less severe,

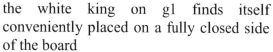

the white king on g1 finds itself conveniently placed on a fully closed side of the board

(as all own and enemy pawns on the king side are blocked, this makes enemy heavy pieces' attacks along the files on that side practically impossible for the time being, with enemy minor pieces' access to that side much more difficult too; this feature is useful with opposite castling, as otherwise both kings should get the bonus)

Value: large bonus, 30cps, only for the mg

Additional information: well, as you see from the diagrammed position, the white king feels safe, even though there are no close own pawns sheltering it. You might think this is stupid, but in chess, every single feature matters.

Frequency: infrequent

Exposed king with blocked center

Definition: king on central e or d file, with the file where it is and the 2 adjacent files all blocked by enemy pawns

the king on d2 represents this condition. The king is on the central d file, and the file where it is, the d file, is closed by the d5/d6 pair of blocked pawns, similarly as the 2 c and e adjacent files, respectively by the c4/c5 and e4/e5 blocked pawn pairs.

Value: bonus, 15cps, just for the mg

Additional information: the bonus is closely related to king safety and is given for the obvious fact, that this configuration makes the king pretty much safe, although it is in the very center of the board. As easily recognised, enemy attacks along the closed central files around the king are close to impossible, so getting access to the king becomes much more problematic. This is a feature that can certainly compensate for the exposed location of the king and help choose lines with other positional assets involved.

212

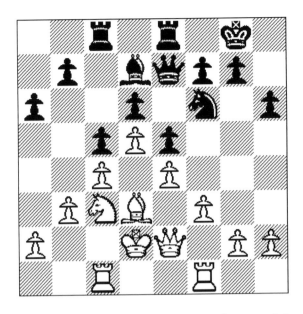

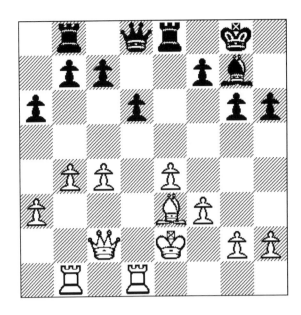

in spite of the abundance of potential attackers, the white king feels quite safe in the center, with files around it closed by pairs of blocked pawns. This might be used to gain valuable positional assets, for example after a2-a4, binding the b7 pawn.

Frequency: infrequent

King in the center sheltered by defended pawn

Definition: king on e or d file, with own defended pawn on the same file on the 3rd, 4th or 5th ranks

Value: small bonus, 7cps, only for the mg

Additional information: the bonus is due for the obvious fact that this improves the king's safety, even if marginally. It is more difficult for the enemy attacking pieces to reach the king, when a defended pawn shelters it from frontal attacks. In order to get to the king, one should first possibly destroy the strong pawn.
This might add nuances to one's king safety, as well as the general evaluation of positional trade-offs.

the e4 strong defended pawn pretty much nicely shelters the white king, in spite of its unenviable position

Frequency: infrequent

King on semi-central file, sheltered by a defended pawn

Definition: king on the c or f file, with own defended pawn on the 3rd rank on the same file

Value: tiny bonus, 4cps, just for the mg

Additional information: the bonus, although microscopic, is due for the sheltering abilities of the pawn with a somewhat exposed king.
Of course, defended pawns are destroyed trickier than non-defended ones.

213

the king on f2 gets the bonus for the f3 defended sheltering pawn.

Indeed, although relatively exposed, and under sufficiently heavy attack by enemy pieces, the white king feels more or less safe.

Frequency: infrequent

Kingside fianchetto

Kingside fianchetto is one of the most important aspects of chess knowledge. Actually, almost all top players throughout the years have preferred openings, both for white and black, including a kingside fianchetto. And that for a reason. Kingside fianchetto offers the player implementing it advantages other opening systems are simply unable to offer. While top humans do understand very well the preponderance of this feature, even the very top of chess engines are largely unaware of its significance. In almost no opening system, if left without a book, engines will choose a development including the kingside fianchetto.

Definition: white bishop on g2, with own king on the h,g or f files, or, alternatively, and purely theoretically, as such cases would only happen very rarely, white bishop on b2, with own king on the a,b or c files.

For black, black bishop on g7, with own king on the h,g or f files, or, alternatively, and again purely theoretically, black bishop on b7, with own king on the a,b or c files.

a kingside fianchetto for white and a non-kingside-fianchetto development for black

kingside fianchetto is also possible on the queen side, though very rarely seen in practice

Value: bonus, 15cps, just for the mg

214

Additional information: it is difficult to overestimate the all-importance of kingside fianchetto. The bonus is due for a couple of reasons:

- the fianchettoed bishop attacks and x-ray-attacks a multitude of objects on the long diagonal, both enemy pieces of different value and enemy pawns
- the fianchettoed bishop, often in concert with own shelter pawns, represents an excellent king-defending feature
- the fianchettoed bishop attacks and x-ray-attacks a number of important central squares, with minor piece control of center being a vital element of the struggle; a fianchettoed bishop on g2 will attack and x-ray-attack the central e4 and d5 squares, while a fianchettoed bishop along the alternative long diagonal, on b2, will attack and x-ray-attack the central d4 and e5 squares
- finally, the fianhettoed bishop does all of the above in a single move, thus providing great efficiency of function

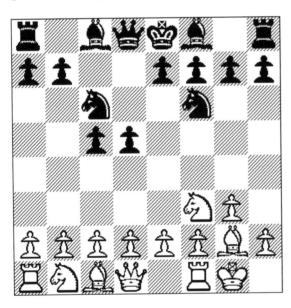

taking even the simplest opening implementation of kingside fianchetto, for example after 1.g3 d5 2.Bg2 Nf6 3.Nf3 c5 4.0-0 Nc6, white already has quite some edge, although even top engines will have very hard time figuring that out, as it takes an amount of time until white's advantages become evident. As is easily seen on the diagram, the bishop on g2 x-ray-attacks

4(!) different enemy objects: the knight on c6, the rook on a8, as well as both pawns on d5 and b7. Currently, there are no immediate tactical threats, but at some point, that will definitely matter. Apart from that, the bishop x-ray-attacks the vital central e4 and d5 squares. Look also at the white king shelter. Can you imagine a better cover for the king? The shelter, apart from pawns, also includes a minor piece in the form of the bishop, which additionally strengthens it, but what is even more important is the excellent harmony of control between the bishop and the shelter pawns on f2,g3 and h2, with the bishop controlling light squares and the pawns dark squares around the shelter, thus ensuring enviable complementarity of defence. There is really no better shelter than this one, all other possible king shelters are only inferior.

A wide range of openings, open and closed, both for black and white, include a kingside fianchetto. It is sufficient to only mention the Catalan, the Reti, the King's Indian Defence and the Gruenfeld, to highlight the importance of this method of development, but the method is also applicable in a long series of other popular openings, like the Sicilian, the English, etc. Actually, as a matter of fact, a kingside fianchetto is feasible in almost any existing opening, regardless of whether theory would recommend that or not. More than that, it is not only feasible, but on most occasions the best line of play.

why would Kasparov and Fischer always prefer the King's Indian Defence? Well, you see that mighty penetrating bishop on g7, that has already, at such an early stage of the game, taken aim at the white knight on c3, the white rook on a1, the white pawns on d4 and b2. Owing to the x-ray control of Bg7 upon the central e5 square, black is able to promptly play e7-e5, even though it does not have sufficient direct control of that square.

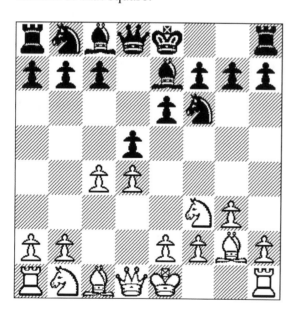

the Catalan, both the open and closed systems of play, for example after 1.d4 e6 2.Nf3 Nf6 3.g3 d5 4.Bg2 Be7 5.c4, is also very favourable for white. In the present case, apart from attacking enemy pieces on the long diagonal, the white bishop on g2,

thanks to the challenge of the c4 pawn upon the d5 square, also greatly helps in undermining the central black d5 pawn. It is difficult to successfully defend that pawn, but relinquishing center control with d5-c4 is even worse.

even in fully closed openings, like for example this English line: 1.c4 e5 2.Nc3 Nf6 3.e4 Nc6 4.g3 Bc5 5.Bg2 0-0 6.Ne2 d6 7.h3 Be6 8.d3 h6 9.0-0 Qd7 10.Kh2, the fianchettoed bishop on g2 plays a major role. Apart from defending the otherwise vulnerable h3 square, it also critically controls the central d5 square along an x-ray, so, black is not able to counter-break with d6-d5 even after first removing the knight on c6 and supporting the break with c7-c6, because white will still have sufficient over-control of d5 in the form of the central bind of the pair of c4 and e4 pawns, the knight on c3 plus, very vitally, the x-raying bishop. Had it not been for the bishop, black could very well have succeeded. Now, white threatens to continue the attack with f2-f4, f4-f5, g3-g4, etc., getting an overwhelming position. Later, white should almost certainly win that, though even top engines will have the greatest of difficulties recognising white's advantage.

In conclusion, kingside fianchetto is easily the most efficient opening technique.

Frequency: very frequent

Trapped rook

Definition: white king on e1,f1 or g1 squares, with white rook on f1,g1 or h1 squares, or, alternatively, on the queen side, white king on e1,d1,c1 or b1, with white rook on d1,c1,b1 or a1, provided that the white rook on the king side has less than 3 available mobile squares, or, if the white rook is on the queen side, it has less than 4 available mobile squares

trapped white rook on the king side; please note, that the rook has just a single available mobile square

trapped white rook on the queen side; this time, the rook has 3 available mobile squares

above, the white rook is already not trapped, as it has 4 available mobile squares. This will allow it to swing via the a3 square to the center of the board or the king side, or at least start sitting in front of the own pawns on the queen side, simultaneously freeing valuable shelter space for the king.

Value: sufficiently large penalty, -70cps, just for the mg

Additional information: this is a major evaluation feature. The penalty is due for the following reasons:
- as the name itself suggests, the rook is trapped, with restricted mobility, much less active and unable to go to the central files of the board, where it will be much better placed, because the own king blocks its route towards the center
- it is difficult to play without a whole heavy piece in the mg, so the side with the trapped rook will usually find itself under dangerous attack, even if it has material superiority
- the king itself, especially if castling rights are lost, will have to stay in the center or close to the center of the board

for quite some while, which bodes nothing well for its safety

- finally, it usually takes a significant amount of time until the king and rook manage to regroup so that the rook is not any more trapped and the king goes to a safer place, and couple of tempos in chess, especially in the mg, are mostly decisive

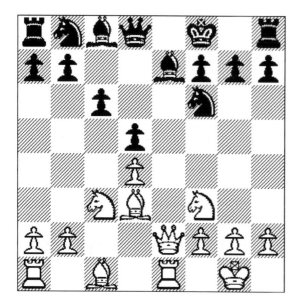

although white plays with a pawn less, it is most certainly winning, mainly because of the trapped black rook on h8. In order to free the rook and get the king to a safer place, black should at least play h7-h6, g7-g6, Be7-d6, Kf8-g7, which is a whole lot of tempos. In the meantime, white will certainly have started mating the opponent.

Frequency: frequent

Temporary prevention of castling

Definition: white king still uncastled kingside, but having castling rights kingside, with any enemy piece attacking the f1 or g1 squares, or, alternatively, on the queen side, white king still uncastled queenside, but having castling rights queenside, with any enemy piece attacking the d1 or c1 squares

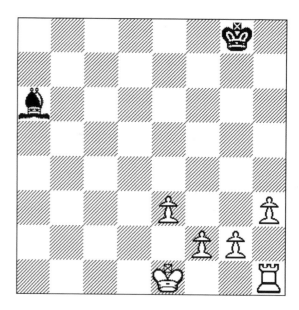

the black bishop on a6 attacks the f1 square between the white king and rook, temporarily preventing kingside castling

the black knight on c3 attacks the d1 square between the white king and rook, temporarily preventing queenside castling

Value: penalty, -20cps, just for the mg

Additional information: the penalty is due for the fact that this feature will deprive the king of the possibility to quickly castle on the relevant side, going to a safer place. Although this is nominally just a temporary situation that will fade away with the removal of the enemy piece thwarting castling or closing the line of

218

attack of a distant enemy slider by dint of interposition of a pawn or piece, it is still usually extremely unwelcome. There is no guarantee the enemy piece preventing castling will be destroyed, or its line of attack closed, and in case the king does not have a good alternative sheltering option, that will mean the king will have to stay in the center of the board for a shorter or longer while, which in the mg is frequently disastrous.

Of course, this is a better situation in comparison to entirely losing castling rights due to a king or rook moves, but still very negative and to be avoided whenever possible.

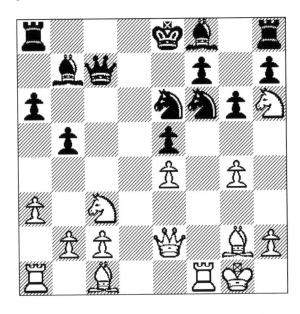

this is from a famous game Nezhmetdinov vs Tal, with Nezhmetdinov playing white. Main reason why black is losing this is the inability of the black king to find a safe haven on one of the wings. Castling queenside is too dangerous, while kingside castling is thwarted by the attack of the knight on h6 upon the g8 square, so the black king has no other choice but to stay in the center. That will be baleful, of course.

Frequency: infrequent

Ability to immediately castle

Definition: king having kingside castling rights, with all squares between the king and the kingside rook free, or, alternatively, on the queen side, king having queenside castling rights, with all squares between the king and the queenside rook free

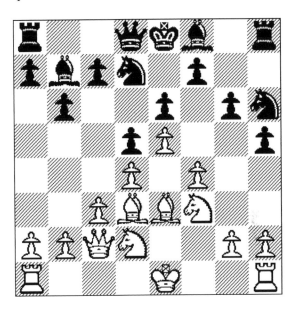

the white king is currently able to immediately castle both kingside and queenside. In distinction, his black counterpart is unable to immediately castle either king- or queenside. This will increase the options for the white king to find a satisfactory shelter, the same not being true for the black king, at least currently.

Value: small bonus, 10cps, just for the mg, for each immediately available castling option

Additional information: the bonus is obviously due for the increased ability of the king to quickly find safe cover in one of the corners of the board.

Although many writers will consider having castling rights as more important, no matter if own pieces currently block such a possibility, I guess simply having castling rights is not sufficient, as it might take quite a bit of time, until the king goes to safety, or even it might be better for the king to stay in the center. With immediate castling possibility, most of above-mentioned concerns are solved.

Frequency: frequent

Chapter VII

General piece activity and coordination

This chapter will include a wide range of evaluation features, pertaining to the realm of piece activity and piece coordination, such as piece and pawn attacks and threats, defence among pieces, positional occupation of vital board lines, specific piece constellations relating to increased positional pressure, etc.

It is difficult to overestimate the importance of such terms. Many of them, primarily attacks and different x-ray attack features, have strong tactical connotations, others, like placing rooks on open files, are of a more positional nature, but all of them have enormous influence on the game.

It really does not make sense to know by heart all the relevant pawn features, and fail in appropriately assessing elements, pertaining to general piece activity, simply because all evaluation elements are part and parcel of the same overarching chess architecture. So, when learning about certain features, do not forget about the rest.

Attacks among pieces

Well, there is really nothing more important than attacks upon enemy pieces, apart from attacking the enemy king shelter, for the very obvious and simple fact that this might lead to material gains. Thus, attacks upon enemy pieces should be very properly assessed.

Engines usually see captures rather easily due to their search, humans, on the other hand, even the very very top, quite often make, even severe, tactical mistakes, because of underestimating a specific threat factor, having to do either with direct or x-ray enemy attacks.

Attacks upon pieces are intrinsically associated with tactics, so that anyone wishing to learn tactics well, should concentrate their attention on existing board piece and pawn attacks, as well as threats. That might not be easy at first, and might even take a long practice until all concepts sink in, but will undoubtedly pay off abundantly, as tactics are extremely important in chess.

Direct attacks upon enemy pawns and pieces

Within our evaluation framework, different piece types directly attacking specific enemy piece types get the following bonus points:

pawn attacks queen: 150cps in the mg, 100cps in the eg

pawn attacks rook: 80cps in the mg, 65cps in the eg

pawn attacks bishop: 60cps in the mg, 45cps in the eg

pawn attacks knight: 60cps in the mg, 45cps in the eg

the white pawn on c5 directly attacks the enemy queen on d6. The queen will have to retreat, otherwise it will be lost.

the white knight on b3 attacks the black pawns on a5 and d4

the black pawn on c6 has just forked the white rook on d5 and the white bishop on b5. Unless concrete tactics exist, one of those will perish. Of course, forks are just double attacks.

knight attacks queen: 110cps in the mg, 75cps in the eg
knight attacks rook: 50cps in the mg, 35cps in the eg
knight attacks bishop: 30cps in the mg, 20cps in the eg
knight attacks pawn: 10cps in the mg, 7cps in the eg

the black knight on c3 attacks the white rook on b1 and the white bishop on e2. Another fork.

bishop attacks queen: 100cps in the mg, 70cps in the eg
bishop attacks rook: 50cps in the mg, 35cps in the eg
bishop attacks knight: 30cps in the mg, 20cps in the eg
bishop attacks pawn: 10cps in the mg, 7cps in the eg

the white bishop on e2 attacks the black pawns on a6 and h5

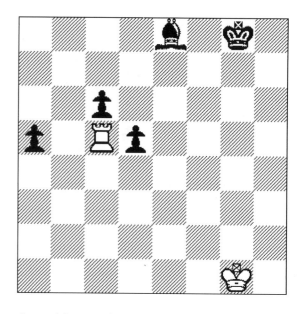

the white rook on c5 attacks the black pawns on a5,c6 and d5

the black bishop on d6 attacks the white queen on a3 and the white knight on f4

rook attacks queen: 90cps in the mg, 60cps in the eg

rook attacks bishop: 30cps in the mg, 20cps in the eg

rook attacks knight: 30cps in the mg, 20cps in the eg

rook attacks pawn: 10cps in the mg, 7cps in the eg

the black rook on d3 attacks the white queen on d1 and the white bishop on g3

queen attacks rook: 50cps in the mg, 35cps in the eg

queen attacks bishop: 30cps in the mg, 20cps in the eg

queen attacks knight: 30cps in the mg, 20cps in the eg

queen attacks pawn: 10cps in the mg, 7cps in the eg

the white queen on f4 attacks the black
rook on d2, the black bishop on f5, and the
black pawn on c7

king attacks queen: 20cps in the mg, 30cps
in the eg
king attacks rook: 50cps in the mg, 65cps
in the eg
king attacks bishop: 30cps in the mg,
40cps in the eg
king attacks knight: 30cps in the mg,
40cps in the eg
king attacks pawn: 5cps in the mg, 20cps
in the eg

Well, in spite of what some readers might
think, the king should also be very actively
involved in attacking and capturing enemy
objects. Quite frequently, this might decide
the outcome of the game.

the white king on g1 attacks the enemy
rook on f2 and bishop on g2 in the mg

The king attacking/capturing properties are
especially useful in the eg, where the king
enjoys less danger and more freedom in
movement. Attacking enemy pawns there,
passers or otherwise, is always a big plus.

the white king on c5 attacks the enemy
pawns on b5 and c6, as well as the enemy
bishop on d5 in the eg. Precisely because
of those abundant attacks, white is able to
capture with the knight both pawns.

Note: of course, it does not quite make
sense to consider attacks upon same type
pieces, for example rook attacking enemy

223

rook, or knight attacking enemy knight, simply because the condition will be mutual and self-scoring

In general, the attacking values more or less follow the material value of the attacked piece, which is just about natural. As a rule, the mg numbers will be somewhat higher, due to abundant tactics in that stage of the game, though with the king things stand opposite: the king deserves bigger numbers in the eg, as it is more active there.

Frequency: *very frequent*

Penalty for pieces attacking an enemy defended pawn

Definition: any own piece attacking an enemy pawn, defended by another enemy pawn

Value: small penalty, specific for the different pieces:
-5cps in the mg, -4cps in the eg, for the knight and bishop
-8cps in the mg, -6cps in the eg, for the queen and rook

Additional information: those penalties aim at subtracting some of the bonus value given for a piece attacking an enemy pawn, making distinction between pawn-defended and not pawn-defended ones.
Of course, this is very reasonable, as pawn-defended enemy pawns are a much less vulnerable target, sometimes to the point that it is even harmful to attack them.

there is certainly a distinction between the white bishop attacking the black h5 and b5 pawns, and the same goes true for the white rook attacking the enemy f4 and b5 pawns. Not pawn-defended pawns are much more vulnerable, of course, the b5 pawn, on the other hand, is almost not a relevant target.

similarly, d6 and f6 black pawns are quite reasonable targets for the white queen and knight, much less so the g5 and e5 pawns

Frequency: *very frequent*

224

Forks

Within our evaluation framework, forks will not be considered separately, as a fork in itself represents nothing more but a double attack upon enemy pieces. As double attacks are sufficiently well seen by the respective bonus points for each attack, the fork automatically receives its bonus.

I do not find any necessity to assign an additional bonus for forks.

Hanging pawns and pieces

Definition: any own piece or pawn, attacked by any enemy piece or pawn, including the king, and not defended by any other own piece or pawn

Value: over-penalty, above the already existing one for direct piece/pawn attacks, valid with the following array:

hanging queen: -30cps in the mg, -20cps in the eg

hanging rook: -20cps, in the mg, -17cps in the eg

hanging bishop: -10cps in the mg, -7cps in the eg

hanging knight: -10cps in the mg, -7cps in the eg

hanging pawn: -3cps in the mg, -2cps in the eg

Additional information: the penalty is given for the obvious fact that such an enemy-attacked and undefended pawn or piece will be easily capturable by the opponent, gaining in material.

As it is not clear under the specific conditions whose turn it is, the penalty is just general and rather small. In case the attacked object's side is not on the move, of course, the numbers might be much bigger, almost the size of the object's material value, as the object will be lost one way or another. With the side with the attacked object on the move, however, the

specific pawn or piece might be easily saved by moving it somewhere else.

the black queen on a5 and the black knight on b2 are both hanging, as attacked by the white bishop and not defended by any own pawn or piece. The black rook on d4, however, is not a hanging one, as, while under enemy attack, it is still defended by the friendly pawn on c5.

the black pawns on a5 and e3 are both hanging, as attacked by the white knight on c4 and not defended by any friendly piece or pawn. The black pawn on d6, on the other hand, is not a hanging one, as being defended by the black bishop on f8.

225

Frequency: frequent

X-ray attacks

X-ray attacks are an extremely important tactical element, widely used by engines and somewhat difficult to grasp for humans of any strength alike.

Definition: attacks of sliding pieces upon enemy pawns and pieces along their ray of action past the first object they encounter

Value: bonus is given with the following array, making distinction between cases when the intermediary object is an enemy or an own piece:

1) enemy piece in between

bishop x-ray-attacking queen: 33cps in the mg, 23cps in the eg
bishop x-ray-attacking rook: 17cps in the mg, 12cps in the eg
bishop x-ray-attacking enemy bishop: 10cps in the mg, 7cps in the eg
bishop x-ray-attacking knight: 10cps in the mg, 7cps in the eg
bishop x-ray-attacking pawn: 3cps in the mg, 2cps in the eg

rook x-ray-attacking queen: 30cps in the mg, 20cps in the eg
rook x-ray-attacking enemy rook: 15cps in the mg, 10cps in the eg
rook x-ray-attacking bishop: 10cps in the mg, 7cps in the eg
rook x-ray-attacking knight: 10cps in the mg, 7cps in the eg
rook x-ray-attacking pawn: 3cps in the mg, 2cps in the eg

queen x-ray-attacking enemy queen: 25cps in the mg, 18cps in the eg
queen x-ray-attacking rook: 17cps in the mg, 12cps in the eg
queen x-ray-attacking bishop: 10cps in the mg, 7cps in the eg

queen x-ray-attacking knight: 10cps in the mg, 7cps in the eg
queen x-ray-attacking pawn: 3cps in the mg, 2cps in the eg

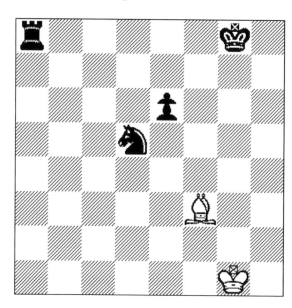

the white bishop on f3 directly attacks the black knight on d5 and x-ray attacks the black rook on a8

the white rook on c1 directly attacks the black bishop on c3 and x-ray-attacks the black knight on c7

the black queen on a6 directly attacks the white rook on c4 and x-ray-attacks the white pawn on e2

2) own piece in between

bishop x-ray-attacking queen: 20cps in the mg, 14cps in the eg
bishop x-ray-attacking rook: 10cps in the mg, 7cps in the eg
bishop x-ray-attacking enemy bishop: 6cps in the mg, 4cps in the eg
bishop x-ray-attacking knight: 6cps in the mg, 4cps in the eg
bishop x-ray-attacking pawn: 2cps in the mg, 1cp in the eg

rook x-ray-attacking queen: 18cps in the mg, 12cps in the eg
rook x-ray-attacking enemy rook: 9cps in the mg, 6cps in the eg
rook x-ray-attacking bishop: 6cps in the mg, 4cps in the eg
rook x-ray-attacking knight: 6cps in the mg, 4cps in the eg
rook x-ray-attacking pawn: 2cps in the mg, 1cp in the eg

queen x-ray-attacking enemy queen: 16cps in the mg, 10cps in the eg
queen x-ray-attacking rook: 10cps in the mg, 7cps in the eg
queen x-ray-attacking bishop: 6cps in the mg, 4cps in the eg

queen x-ray-attacking knight: 6cps in the mg, 4cps in the eg
queen x-ray-attacking pawn: 2cps in the mg, 1cp in the eg

the white bishop on g2 x-ray-attacks the black rook on a8

the white rook on e6 x-ray-attacks the black bishop on a6

the black queen on h6 x-ray-attacks the white knight on c1

Additional information: well, the bonus is due, as the enemy objects under non-direct attack past the first object are really under attack, but not an immediate one. In order for a capture to ensue, a move by one of the sides should be made beforehand. This takes time, sometimes is not feasible at all, and so the attacking values are much smaller than with the regular case of direct attacks. Still, the attacks are completely real.

It certainly makes sense to make a distinction between x-ray attacks upon enemy objects with own and enemy pieces in between, simply because the condition with an enemy piece or pawn in between is much more severe. It offers the possibility to capture one of the attacked objects later, even if the other one is removed from the ray. With an own object in between along the attacking ray of action of the slider, the removal of the enemy piece under x-ray attack simply leaves no enemy pieces capturable. Thus, the first condition is much more tactically relevant.

Frequency: very frequent

X-ray attacks past the second intermediary object

Of course, x-ray attacks also make sense in the case of more distant attacks, when the intermediary objects are more than one. The attacks are still real, but much less significant, for the simple fact that it takes time until a couple of own or enemy pieces are removed until the slider is able to capture the distantly x-ray-attacked piece.

Thus, the bonus values will be very small and in many cases not really matter. Still, when the distantly x-ray-attacked object is an enemy piece of sufficiently high power, such as queen or rook, the x-ray attacks might be quite relevant.

Value: about half of the average bonus for x-ray attacks with a single object in between, when the intermediary objects are 2, no matter if own or enemy ones(it is really difficult to make a distinction here). Thus, an attacked enemy queen will score around 15cps or so, an attacked enemy rook some 10cps, etc.

With more than 2 intermediary objects, the bonus points fall very small, so hardly of big significance, for example an x-ray-attacked enemy queen with 3 objects in between will give only about 8cps or so, with the main scoring rule being dividing by 2 the existing bonus for any further addition of interposed pieces.

On second thought, those are not such small values, after all, 10cps is a pretty good factor with so many interposing objects, bearing in mind other relevant positional factors with similar values and quite evident characteristics. So, it would be nice to still consider also more distant x-ray attacks, unless your head overboils or your engine crashes.

the bishop on g2 attacks the enemy rook on a8 with 2 objects in between, the pawn on d5 and the knight on c6

the rook on b8 x-ray-attacks the white pawn on b2 with 2 objects in between, the white knight on b4 and the black bishop on b5

now, already the intermediary objects are 3, adding the black b7 pawn

the black queen on h8 x-ray-attacks the white knight on a1 with 3 objects in between, the black pawn on e5, the white pawn on c3, and the white bishop on b2. The white bishop on b2, on the other hand, x-ray-attacks the black queen on h8 with just 2 intermediary objects, the white pawn on c3, and the black pawn on e5.

the white rook on d1 x-ray-attacks the black queen on d8 with 6(!) intermediary objects. The same is true for the black d8 queen, attacking the white rook on d1.

Frequency: frequent

Checks

Checks are, of course, direct attacks by pawns and pieces upon the enemy king.

Checks are indeed very important, as checking the king certainly increases the possibility to endanger the enemy king, compromise its safety, and even deliver mate.

It is quite relevant to split the evaluating conditions between safe and unsafe checks, checks given on a square not defended by any enemy pawn or piece, apart from the king, and checks given on a square defended by at least one enemy pawn or piece apart from the king. The reason for this is simple: safe checks leave no other alternative to the king apart from retreating or, with slider checks, possibly interposing a defending piece, while unsafe checks also offer the opportunity to capture the checking piece. Going to a square controlled by an enemy piece is indeed significantly inferior.

Safe checks

Value: bonus, specific for the different checking pieces.

safe queen check: 60cps in the mg, 40cps in the eg
safe rook check: 40cps in the mg, 30cps in the eg
safe knight check: 30cps in the mg, 20cps in the eg
safe bishop check: 15cps in the mg, 10cps in the eg
safe pawn check: 10cps in the mg, 10cps in the eg

safe knight check

230

safe queen check

Frequency: frequent

Unsafe checks

Value: bonus, specific for the different checking pieces.

unsafe queen check: 15cps in the mg, 10cps in the eg
unsafe rook check: 15cps in the mg, 10cps in the eg
unsafe knight check: 20cps in the mg, 10cps in the eg
unsafe bishop check: 8cps in the mg, 6cps in the eg
unsafe pawn check: 5cps in the mg, 5cps in the eg

unsafe rook check

unsafe knight check

unsafe pawn check

Frequency: frequent

Double checks

Double checks, the case when 2 own pieces deliver check to the enemy king at the same time, are very forceful, though a rare guest on the board. They will necessarily arise after a discovered attack/check of a slider upon the enemy king, with the intermediary own piece revealing the check also delivering one.

Within our evaluation framework, double checks will not necessitate any special bonus, for the simple fact that both checks will add up to reflect the mounting effect. I do not see any special ad-hoc value over this addition.

Potential checks

Definition: any possible, but not delivered, check in a position

Value: small bonus, specific for the different pieces.

potential queen check: 10cps in the mg, 5cps in the eg
potential rook check: 8cps in the mg, 4cps in the eg
potential knight check: 15cps in the mg, 7cps in the eg
potential bishop check: 8cps in the mg, 2cps in the eg
potential pawn check: 7cps in the mg, 5cps in the eg

potential rook check on e1, potential bishop check on b5, potential knight checks on f6 and g7

potential queen checks on g5 and c4, potential pawn check on f7

Additional information: well, this is still an important factor and quite tactically relevant, as potential check opportunities will frequently lead to forced sequences, and forced lines are usually detrimental to the potentially-checkable side

Frequency: frequent

Potential discovered checks

Definition: a sliding attacker, bishop, rook or queen, x-ray-attacking the enemy king, with another own piece between the slider and the king

Value: bonus, specific for the different sliders

potential queen discovered checks: 120cps in the mg, 60cps in the eg
potential rook discovered check: 60cps in the mg, 30cps in the eg
potential bishop discovered check: 30cps in the mg, 15cps in the eg

232

potential queen discovered check; Ne7 possible revealing will be double check, too

potential bishop discovered check. One of the possible knight moves, Nc7, threatens to win the black rook on a8.

potential rook discovered check. The bishop on d6 threatens to reveal the checking rook on b6 in a series of possible moves.

potential discovered checks can also have own pawns as intermediary objects, revealing the attacker. This time, the e6-e7 discovered check threatens to win whole queen!

Additional information: potential discovered checks are considered in our framework, because it otherwise does not have standard general bonus for x-ray attacks upon the enemy king with own piece as an intermediary object.

Discovered checks are important in their potentiality, and not in the mere fact of

233

revealing the check, which is a standard check by all means, already provided for. With this specific condition, the turn is very relevant.

As easily seen and imaginable on the diagrams posted, almost any discovered check is extremely dangerous in its nature, simply because the piece, revealing the sliding attacker, will have ample opportunity to attack various enemy objects. As, apart from the attack of the revealing piece, the enemy king will also be checked by the slider, it will have to do a forced move, or a move for interposition or capturing of the slider should be made, thus gaining tempo and giving chance to the revealing attacker to capture on the very next move. Revealed attacks involving double checks are even more forceful, as in this case the enemy king will have as its sole option to try evading.

Queen checks are most dangerous in nature, similarly to the high queen check values, as, apart from the good checking property, this might lead to subsequent queen checks, building a mating net, on occasion with the support of the revealing piece.

The mg bonus is significantly larger, for the very obvious reason that in the mg enemy king safety plays bigger role and there are many more potentially capturable enemy objects.

Frequency: infrequent

Pins

Pins are an extremely important evaluation element, closely related to tactics. As a matter of fact, pins represent a specific kind of x-ray attacks, involving a single intermediary object, the pinned piece, when this object is of lower value than the other own piece at the other end of the pin. The pinner, the sliding attacker, pertains to one side, and both the pinned piece, as well as the piece at the other end of the pin, to the opponent side.

Basically, there are 2 main types of important pins: absolute, king pins, and relative, queen pins. Pins involving other pieces at the opposite end of the pin, like a bishop pinner pinning an enemy knight with enemy rook at the far end of the pin, are mostly completely irrelevant and easily seen by the concrete values for direct and x-ray attack of the pinner.

King pins

Definition: a sliding attacker, bishop, rook or queen, x-ray-attacking an enemy king, with any other enemy piece not directly attacking the slider, or, if doing so, being of higher value than the slider, as an intermediary object

Value: bonus is dispensed in terms of the different pinning pieces as follows:

bishop king pins: 90cps in the mg, 45cps in the eg
rook king pins: 60cps in the mg, 30cps in the eg
queen king pins: 45cps in the mg, 22cps in the eg

a bishop king pin with enemy rook as an intermediary object, the pinned piece

234

a rook king pin with enemy bishop as an intermediary object

a queen king pin with enemy knight as an intermediary object, the pinned piece

As easily seen in all of above examples, the enemy pinned piece completely lacks in mobility, and the enemy king must make at least a single move, until the pin is gone, so the probability for the pinned piece to be lost is very high. That is what the nice bonus is actually dispensed for: good tactical chances to win the pinned piece, as well as increased further tactical possibilities due to its temporary zero mobility.

In some instances, the enemy pinned piece will also attack the pinner of lower power, and still enjoy some mobility, but this will hardly matter, as it will most probably be lost.

well, the black queen can still move along the a8-h1 diagonal, but that does not help a lot

Frequency: frequent

Queen pins

Definition: a sliding attacker, bishop or rook, x-ray-attacking enemy queen, with any enemy piece not attacking the pinner as an intermediary object.
That will exclude enemy bishops for bishop queen pins, and enemy rooks for rook queen pins.

Value: bonus, specific for the different sliders:

bishop queen pin: 40cps in the mg, 20cps in the eg
rook queen pin: 30cps in the mg, 15cps in the eg

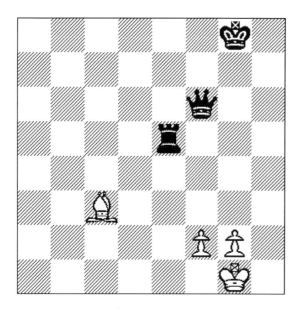

bishop queen pin

rook queen pin, with enemy knight as the pinned object

As easily recognised from above examples, although the enemy pinned piece between the sliding attacker and the queen enjoys some mobility, this is rather subjective, as executing a move will reveal and probably lose the queen. In order to get rid of the pin, the queen should make at least a single move, and this takes time.

That is what the bonus is for: restricted mobility of the pinned piece, with good chances to win it or gain other relevant advantages in the tactical scuffle. Of course, a lot will depend on the side to move.

In relation to absolute, king pins, queen pins are a much milder form of pinning, but still due a significant bonus.

Frequency: frequent

another form of bishop queen pin, with enemy pawn as the pinned object

Skewers

Well, skewers are the case of an x-ray attack, when a sliding attacker of relatively low value, bishop or rook, directly attacks an enemy piece and x-ray-attacks another enemy piece of lower value than the directly attacked piece. Kings are also included in the enemy piece of higher value. For example, one possible

236

constellation is bishop attacking enemy rook and x-ray-attacking enemy knight, another one is rook attacking enemy king and x-ray-attacking enemy queen.

Within our evaluation framework, skewers will not be dealt with separately, for the simple reason that they represent a standard case of x-ray attacks, and all due bonus points are fully seen by the respective direct and x-ray attacks of the sliding attacker, or, alternatively, the respective checks and x-ray attacks.

Pawn defence

Definition: any non-pawn piece defended by an own pawn

Value: bonus, specific for the different pawn-defended pieces

pawn-defended knight: 15cps in the mg, 10cps in the eg
pawn-defended bishop: 10cps in the mg, 7cps in the eg
pawn-defended rook: 5cps in the mg, 3cps in the eg
pawn-defended queen: 3cps in the mg, 2cps in the eg

Note: the bonus will be considered excluding minor piece outposts, as pawn-defended outposts get their separate value

Additional information: pawn defence is an extremely important term, as tactically very relevant. The bonus is obviously due for 2 reasons:
- in case such a piece is under attack by an enemy piece, it is already protected, so this will save time
- even if it is not under enemy attack, such an attack can come at a later stage, so defence is ensured preemptively, which also might matter

Thus, contrary to what some people might believe, pawn defence is always a good thing, and to be encouraged.

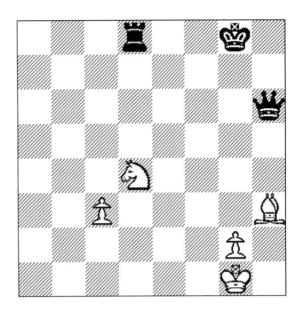

the knight on d4 and the bishop on h3 are under attack, but nothing to fear: they are well-protected by friendly pawns

it is good for pieces of higher power to be pawn-defended, too. This saves time in defence and is tactically relevant.

Additional defence by 2 own pawns is even better, but difficult to measure numerically for the different pieces with no specific conditions attached.

that white knight seems invulnerable, no matter the number of enemy attackers

Frequency: very frequent

Piece defence

Defence among pieces is also quite significant, contrary to what most available engines would think. There are few engines out there that would consider it in their codes, emphasising piece attacks instead, but it is close to impossible to separate attacking enemy pieces from their respective defence. Well-defended pieces feel well even under strong attack, while badly defended ones might suffer tactically even if not immediately attacked.

So, having a good defensive evaluation is a must and more a matter of finding the right values.

Definition: any piece apart from the king and pawns, defended by another own non-pawn and non-king piece

Value: bonus, validated in terms of the different defended pieces and the specific defending ones with the following array:

minor piece defence
minor piece defended by another minor: 15cps in the mg, 10cps in the eg
minor piece defended by rook: 10cps in the mg, 7cps in the eg
minor piece defended by queen: 7cps in the mg, 5cps in the eg

rook defence
rook defended by minor piece: 8cps in the mg, 6cps in the eg
rook defended by queen: 5cps in the mg, 3cps in the eg

queen defence
queen defended by knight: 3cps in the mg, 2cps in the eg
queen defended by rook: 2cps in the mg, 1cp in the eg

the bishop on e1 defends the knight on b4, so the enemy rook attack upon it is not so dangerous

238

the enemy queen attack is not a threat to the white rook on b6, as it is defended by the knight on c4. The white queen on h4 also does not have to bother, as another friendly knight, the one on g2, sufficiently supports it.

the white rook on e4 supports both the white bishop on b4 and the white knight on f4, so the enemy challenge is quite bearable

Frequency: very frequent

Defending pawns

Definition: any pawn defended by any friendly piece apart from the king and another friendly pawn

Value: small, but well-deserved bonus, specified in terms of the different defending pieces

pawn defended by minor piece: 5cps, both for the mg and eg
pawn defended by rook: 3cps, both for the mg and eg

Note: the bonus for pawn defended by queen is obviously so small, that it might be better not to consider it at all

Additional information: some might think defending pawns is not that vital, as they represent just a minuscule material, but that is far from being the case. As pawns are multiple, and the demise of a single one of them without compensation is certainly unwelcome, they should be protected, whenever possible.

As with other kinds of defence, the bonus is due for couple main reasons:
- tactically relevant
- pawns under enemy attack are safe
- even if not under immediate attack, a similar possible attack in the future will only save time

The numbers for the mg and eg are equal, as it is difficult to make a real distinction. It is true that attacks, and consequently respective defences, are more important in the mg, but, on the other hand, in the eg many defended pawns will be passers, which further boosts their value.

the white pawns on a5 and g7 are safe, although under attack by the black rook and king, as defended by the friendly bishop on c3.

It is meaningless to consider the knight defence of the h5 pawn, as it is already very-well protected by the friendly pawn on g4.

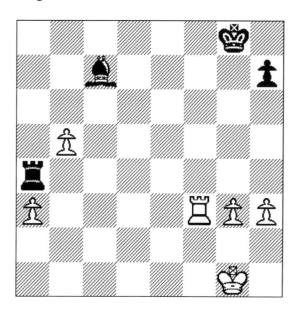

rook protecting the undefended pawns on a3 and g3 is a vital feature, both in the mg and eg

Frequency: very frequent

Minor piece defending passed pawn

Definition: passed pawn, on its 5th, 6th or 7th ranks, defended by a minor

the knight on d3 defends the c5 passed pawn, the bishop on f4 that on h6

Value: bonus, 12cps, both for the mg and eg

Additional information: the bonus is due, because an advanced passed pawn is a valuable asset, and supporting one's valuable assets is always productive.

Even if not currently attacked, they might soon be so.

Note: protected passed pawns might be excluded from the bonus, as they already enjoy the support of an own pawn

Frequency: frequent

Central isolated pawn, defended by minor

Definition: central d4 or e4 isolated pawn, defended by a minor piece, knight or bishop

d4 is such a pawn

Value: bonus, 8cps, both for the mg and eg

Additional information: the bonus is due for the obvious fact, that this is not just a random undefended pawn, but a very important one, under frequent enemy attacks, so protecting it is extremely useful. Minor pieces, of course, will do that best.

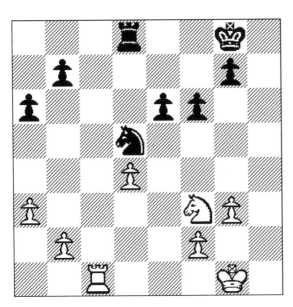

some humans/engines might think that white has much worse, due to its isolated central pawn, but, in actual fact, the position is completely equal. The reason for that is the excellent support, provided

by the knight on f3, making the pawn invulnerable.

A bishop instead of a knight will often also do fine.

Frequency: very frequent

Undefended pieces

Definition: knight, bishop or rook, not defended by any own pawn or piece, including the king

Value: bonus, specific for the different undefended pieces

undefended minor piece(knight or bishop): 15cps in the mg, 10cps in the eg
undefended rook: 10cps in the mg, 7cps in the eg

Additional information: the bonus is due for the obvious reason that such pieces are vulnerable, tactically weak, and can fall prey to enemy attacks, especially queen forks, either immediately, or in a longer forced series of moves.
Thus, it makes sense scoring them, even if there is not a currently available threat.
The mg bonus is a bit larger, as in the mg tactics and forks are much more frequent.

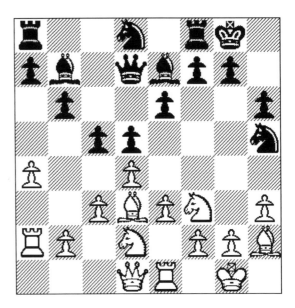

241

white has 2 undefended pieces: the bishop on d3, and the rook on a2. Currently, nothing is visible that might make those pieces suffer, but, with the development of the game, a similar condition might be tactically relevant at any time.

For black, just the knight on h5 is undefended, but, if white is to play, Ne5, combining threats on the enemy queen and knight, already wins the knight.

in the eg, undefended pieces are also an undisputed liability, especially vulnerable to enemy queen checks and forks. Possible Qg4 above threatens to win either the white rook or knight, actually, with the specific board condition, both of them.

Frequency: frequent

Rook on a semi-open file, attacking an enemy pawn-undefended pawn, defended by a minor

the rook on a8 gets the penalty. It is on the semi-open a file, and attacks the white a4 pawn, which is not defended by another pawn, but supported by the bishop on d1.

Value: small penalty, -5cps in the mg, -2cps in the eg

Additional information: the penalty is due for 2 main reasons:
- waste of resources; the strong rook is attacking a weak enemy pawn, that is still invulnerable
- inability of the rook to easily penetrate along the semi-open file

Obviously, this is not quite the place for the rook.

242

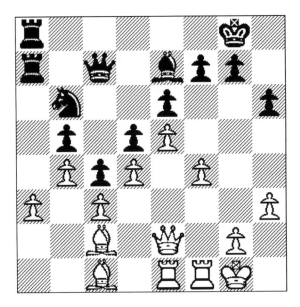

black might think it has achieved a lot by piling up pressure along the semi-open a file, getting sufficient counterplay, with the weak a3 pawn under heavy attack by both black rooks, but in actual fact, black does nothing. The a file is logically closed, black should sacrifice the exchange in order to penetrate, so both black rooks are only wasting their time on the queen side. Of course, white has substantial advantage.

Similar simulations of positional factors, like closed files, are often completely missed by engines.

Frequency: frequent

Threats

Safe pawn push threat

Definition: aligned pawn, with the square in front of it free, and any enemy piece apart from pawn and king positioned 2 ranks higher on adjacent file.
Only in the case of pawns on the 2nd rank, defending pawn, with the squares on the 3rd and 4th ranks in front of it free, and any enemy piece apart from pawn and king positioned on the 5th rank on adjacent file.

bonus goes for the aligned d3 pawn. d3-d4 is a safe pawn push threat upon the black bishop.

bonus goes for the c2 defending pawn. c2-c4 is a safe pawn push threat upon the black queen.

Value: bonus, 15cps, both for the mg and eg

Additional information: the bonus is very-well due for the following reasons:
- there is a potential pawn threat upon an enemy piece
- the threat is tactically relevant

- if executed, the enemy piece will most likely have to retreat, which gains a valuable tempo
- the pawn threat is pretty much guaranteed to succeed, as the square where the pawn will land is defended by another own pawn, either a duo, or a defended one, when the push-threatening pawn is on its 2nd rank

It is difficult to make a distinction between mg and eg values, as, while in the mg gaining tempos and threats might be relatively more important, in the eg on the other hand, such pawn push threats frequently represent important passed pawn advances.

Frequency: *very frequent*

Unsafe pawn push threat

Definition: pawn, that is not aligned, with the square in front of it free, and any enemy piece apart from pawn or king positioned 2 ranks higher on adjacent file.
Only in the case of pawns on the 2nd rank, not defending pawn, with the squares in front of it on the 3rd and 4th ranks free, and any enemy piece apart from pawn or king positioned on the 5th rank on adjacent file.

bonus goes for the b5 pawn that is not aligned. b5-b6 is an unsafe pawn push threat upon the black knight.

bonus goes for the g2 pawn that is not defending. g2-g4 is an unsafe pawn push threat upon the black rook.

Value: bonus, 8cps, both for the mg and eg

Additional information: the bonus is due for the very same reasons as in the case of a safe pawn push threat:
- threat is tactically relevant
- if executed, the attacked piece will likely have to retreat, which gains precious tempo

In distinction to safe pushes, however, the certainty the push will be successful is much smaller, all will depend on the particular friendly and enemy piece and pawn control of the square where the pawn will land, hence the lower values.

Frequency: *very frequent*

Tactical levers

Definition: lever pawn, with enemy piece on the rank behind the enemy lever pawn on adjacent file

244

d4 is a tactical lever for white. It is levering the black e5 pawn, and, on the rank behind the e5 pawn on adjacent file there is an enemy piece, the d6 knight.

b3 is another tactical lever for white, this time, the enemy piece behind the enemy c4 lever pawn is a rook

Value: bonus, 11cps in the mg, 9cps in the eg

Additional information: the bonus is due for the obvious tactical ability of such lever pawns. While both pawns are levers and able to capture, the tactical lever has the additional advantage of attacking an enemy piece upon capturing. As threats usually gain tempos, this might certainly change the course of the game in a range of occasions, so it undoubtedly represents an asset to be counted with.

Frequency: frequent

Tactical pawn threat

Definition: pawn, attacking an enemy piece, with another enemy piece on the rank behind it on adjacent file

b5 is such a pawn. The knight on c6 is attacked, but, apart from that, upon capturing it, the pawn will already attack another enemy piece, the rook on d7.

245

b2 is another such pawn. It attacks the black bishop on c3, and, on the rank behind the bishop on adjacent file, there is another enemy piece, the black queen on b4.

Value: bonus, 20cps in the mg, 15cps in the eg

Additional information: the very-well deserved bonus is obviously for the fact, that such a pawn in combination with the enemy piece configuration is very much tactically relevant. In both instances, upon capturing the enemy piece, the pawn already attacks a second enemy piece. This will certainly be able to gain tempos on many occasions. And gaining tempos, of course, will help in attaining other positional advantages, if not immediately winning material.

Frequency: infrequent

Tactical lever threat

Definition: pawn on the 4th or 5th ranks, with the square in front of it free, one enemy pawn 2 ranks higher on one adjacent file, and another enemy piece 2 ranks higher on another adjacent file

the e4 pawn, together with the knight on d6 and the pawn on f6 represents this condition

one more such condition, this time one rank higher

Value: bonus, 12cps in the mg, 6cps in the eg, for the side with the pawn on the 4th or 5th ranks

Additional information: the advanced pawn is, of course, very much tactically dangerous.
The bonus is given for the following reasons:
- when the pawn moves forward, it will simultaneously attack 2 enemy objects, and, if not captured, will be able to take one of them
- even if the enemy pawn captures it, another own piece can land on the capture square, on an advanced position
- in case the pawn is pushed, and the enemy pawn passes in capturing, under certain conditions, it can advance even further on the very next move

Such advanced pawns are especially dangerous, when central or on the side, where the enemy king is, in the mg. In this case, they might greatly benefit opening lines in the center or, alternatively, breaking open the enemy king shelter.

246

the white pawn on e4 constitutes a tactical lever threat. Upon moving forward one square, on e5, it will simultaneously attack the black knight on f6 and the black pawn on d6. At the same time, on e5, the pawn already builds another tactical lever threat, aiming at the d7 knight and the pawn on f7. As the e5 push will forcefully evict the black knight on f6, gaining tempo, the pawn will be able to execute another pawn push on the very next move, e5-e6, helping to open lines in the center for attack.

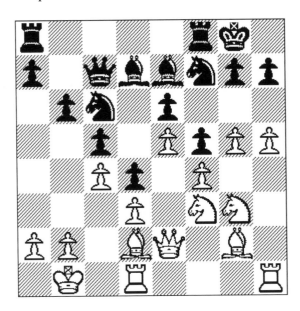

tactical lever threats are even more dangerous, when existing on squares close to the enemy king shelter.

g5 tactical lever threat above is extremely dangerous, with g5-g6 threatening an

immediate destruction of the black pawn shelter.

Frequency: frequent

Knight attack threat upon enemy queen

Definition: knight, attacking a square, from where it will attack the enemy queen, provided that the square is free and not under attack by an enemy pawn

the knight on b2 has an attack threat upon the enemy queen, as upon landing on the c4 square, that is free, and not under attack by an enemy pawn, it will start attacking the queen.

The black knight on f8, on the other hand, although attacking a square, from where it will threaten the white queen, g6, does not get the bonus, as the g6 square is under control of the white pawn on f5.

Value: small bonus, 8cps in the mg, 5cps in the eg

Additional information: this feature is similar to the pawn push threat, but less salient.

The bonus is given for the possibility to gain tempo by threatening the queen, that will almost certainly have to retreat somewhere, with tempos playing an important role, especially in the mg.

This is a much more compelling condition than for example, a bishop or rook threatening to attack the enemy queen on the next move, as, in distinction to those attacks, knight attacks can not be avoided by interposition of a piece.

in the Scandinavian Defence, after 1.e4 d5 2.ed5 Qd5, the black queen falls under the potential attack of the white knight on b1 from the c3 square very early into the opening.

That gives white tempos for development, and that is why the Scandinavian is not a good opening to start with.

Frequency: very frequent

Rook on open file

Definition: rook, with no own and enemy pawns on the file, where it is

the white rook on d1 takes the open d file

Value: bonus, 40cps in the mg, 25cps in the eg

Additional information: this is a very weighty term, no chess handbook will ever miss to mention. The rook on open file prevents enemy pieces from taking active positions along that file and threatens to penetrate all the time deep into the enemy camp.

On the diagrammed position, with everything else being equal, the single placement of the white rook on an open file decides the game. After Rd1-d7, penetrating on the 7th rank, white will win.

Frequency: very frequent

Queen on an open file

Definition: queen, with no own or enemy pawns on the file where it is

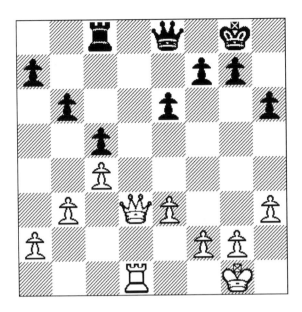

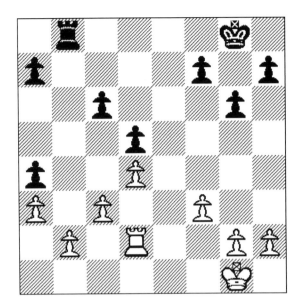

well, this time, apart from the rook, the white queen on d3 is also placed on an open file. Qd3-d7 will similarly decide the game.

Value: small bonus, 10cps in the mg, 5cps in the eg

Additional information: this term is far less weightier than rook on an open file, one of the reasons being that it is frequently much less durable, with queen easily oustable from the file by an enemy rook landing there

Note: it does not really make sense to consider queen plus rook on an open file as a separate feature, as, as easily seen on the diagrammed position, the 2 separate bonuses add to one another in self-elevating the term

Frequency: frequent

Rook on a semi-open file

Definition: rook, with at least one enemy and no own pawns on the file, where it is

the black rook on b8 is placed on the semi-open b file. Although the black pawn structure is severely compromised, the pair of doubled isolated pawns on the a file is more than compensated for by the strong influence of the black rook, simultaneously attacking the b2 pawn. Black enjoys the advantage.

Value: bonus, 25cps in the mg, 10cps in the eg

Additional information: another weighty term. Any evaluation lacking it is simply incomplete and weak. The rook will frequently attack different enemy objects, pawns or pieces, along the semi-open file, with penetration, deep into the enemy camp, also being possible, like, for example, Rb8-b3 thrust on the diagrammed position. At the very least, the possession of a semi-open file will mean the opponent is on the defence.

Frequency: frequent

Queen on a semi-open file

Definition: queen, with at least one enemy pawn and no own pawns on the file, where it is

 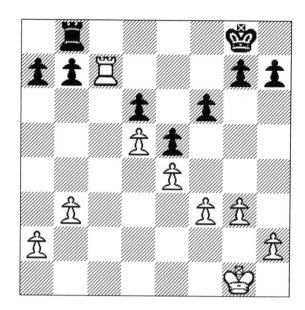

apart from the rook, this time also the black queen on b6 takes up the semi-open b file, ratcheting up pressure

Value: small bonus, 7cps in the mg, 3cps in the eg

Additional information: this is a significantly less important term than rook on a semi-open file, but entirely failing to consider it would be wrong. As seen on the diagrammed position, the pressure from the black queen, though real, is somewhat degraded by the ability of the d2 white rook to effortlessly defend the b2 pawn, even without the support of the white queen. The term also supposes possible penetration into the enemy camp, as with the rook.

Frequency: frequent

Rook on the 7th rank

Definition: rook on any square on the 7th rank

the white rook on c7 enjoys the privilege of occupying the 7th rank

Value: bonus, with average value of 40cps in the mg, 25cps in the eg

Note: within our framework, this is seen by the rook psqt

Additional information: well, an extremely weighty term no handbook will ever fail to pay attention to. Assets are obvious. On the diagrammed position, the c7 rook:
- has penetrated deep into the enemy camp
- directly attacks the black b7 and g7 pawns
- x-ray-attacks the a7 and h7 pawns
- attacks the black king shelter
- restricts the black king to the 8th rank

What else is needed for a term to be influential?

Frequency: frequent

Queen on the 7th rank

well, similarly, queen on the 7th rank, as
c7 is, does deserve some bonus

Value: much smaller than for the rook,
however, this might be seen in terms of
non-redundancy by terms like attack upon
enemy pawns and pieces and attack of the
enemy king shelter. It is also possible to
bonise the queen in psqt.

Additional information: the bonus is
obviously due for the very active,
attacking position of the queen. On the
diagrammed position, the white queen:
- attacks the white rook on b8
- attacks the black king shelter
- attacks the b7 and g7 pawns
- x-ray-attacks other relevant objects and
squares

Frequency: frequent

Doubled rooks on the 7th rank

Note: within our evaluation framework,
this is not considered, as will be more or
less tantamount to adding up the numbers
for the 2 separate rooks. I can't see no
distinction at all.

Doubled rook file control

Definition: 2 rooks, defending each other
on the same file, even if this file is not an
open one

Value: bonus, 15cps, only for the mg

Additional information: this feature is
always useful, and equally so in all
possible constellations. In case the rooks
take an open file, their cumulative value
will be more than double the value of a
single rook on an open file, for the simple
reason that it will be very difficult to
challenge the file upon which the rooks are
placed, unless by an enemy minor,
defended by a pawn. Penetration by the
rooks will also be easier, as the more
advanced rook is already supported.

with everything else being more or less
equal, white enjoys decisive advantage,
due to the overwhelming control upon the
open d file by the self-defended pair of
rooks. No enemy piece can easily take a
place upon that file, the fight for the file
itself is very dreary-looking, for example,
playing immediately Ra8-d8 to attempt
wresting out control is simply impossible,
and not very easy to do, if at all, in the
longer term, and if so, will take some time,
and white even threatens to successfully
sac one rook on d7, gaining superior

position on the 7th rank, with a lot of threats.

In case the rooks were not doubled, most of the above would be not doable, for example, with just a single white rook upon the d open file, the Ra8-d8 challenge by black would be feasible immediately, and the bold Rd7 sally on the 7th rank just a dream.

Placed on a semi-open file, the rooks represent quite an asset, too.

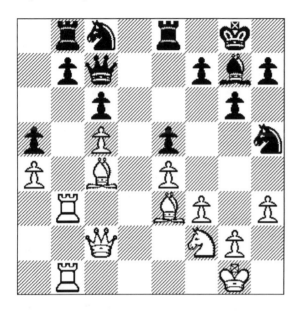

the pair of self-defended white rooks along the semi-open b file are a major asset:
- white threatens with Ba6 to immediately restore the material balance
- a freeing move like b7-b6 is impossible to play, because of the sufficient over-control of the file, more specifically the b6 square
- on occasion, if necessary, white can further increase the pressure along the b file and the black b7 pawn, by switching the queen to b2, or, alternatively, by playing Rb1-b2, followed by Qb1
- very importantly, too, black is all the time on the defence, which really does matter

In case just a single white rook was taking the semi-open b file, most of the above would be impossible:

- Ba6 pseudo-sac would not be quite feasible
- black would be able to successfully choose the freeing b7-b6 move
- lining the queen along the b file to support a single rook in its assault would not really represent a major danger, and even the black position would not look that much defensive, too

Finally, the pair of self-defending rooks are an excellent feature, even if only on a closed file. Who would have thought so? Outwardly, there is nothing to do for the rooks on such a file. But, in reality, the truth is quite the opposite, for:
- the rooks still do defend each other, which on occasion matters
- most importantly, the pair constellation is fit and ready for all of its feats, in case the currently closed file do gets opened, or at least transforms into a semi-open one. As in chess things sometimes change very quickly, and opening a file is frequently quite realistic under many circumstances, having a battery ready to attack is always welcome.

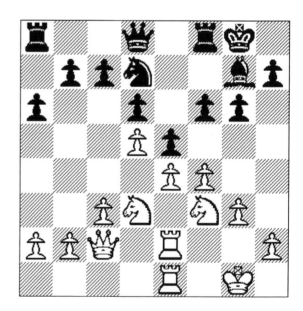

currently, black is able to rather successfully defend the vital e5 square. If, however, at some point it is compelled to relinquish control of that square, under specific tactical circumstances, after, for example, e5-f4 g3-f4, white immediately

252

threatens with an e4-e5 central break, to follow up a bit, after e4-e5 f6-e5 f4-e5 d6-e5 Nf3-e5 Nd7-e5 Nd3-e5 Bg7-e5 Re2-e5, the rooks have already taken up the open e file to great effect. And this mostly happened in a split-second action, after a forced line.

Besides, the current placement of the rooks on different ranks, by definition, does allow them to form the very same self-defending constellation on an alternative file rather quickly, if necessary. For example, on the diagrammed position, white can play Rf2 and Re1-f1, doubling the rooks along the f file, in just 2 moves, the similar manoeuvre, Rd2, followed by Re1-d1, is possible within the same time limits, in case the rooks had not been doubled, usually that would have taken significantly more time.

Thus, a pair of self-defended rooks is a very positive feature on any file.

Frequency: frequent

Royal battery

Definition: pair of rooks and queen on an open file, in the order rook-queen-rook, in terms of more advanced ranks

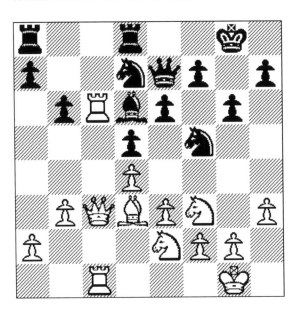

the doubled white rooks and queen along the open c file, with the queen in between both rooks, represent a tremendous asset

Value: bonus, 40cps, just for the mg

Additional information: the bonus is obviously due for the unchallenged control upon the open file.

On the diagrammed position, white is so firmly in control of the open c file, that seemingly nothing can wrest it out, even in the longer term.

Of course, all of the heavy pieces would get a separate bonus for taking the open file, but that is an over-bonus for the specific arrangement with the queen between both rooks, highlighting preponderance.

Other possible constellations of the 3 pieces along the same open file would not be quite so good, for objective reasons. If the queen was first, on most advanced rank, that would signify a probable challenge by an enemy rook along the open file, it would be sufficient for the rook to be supported by any minor piece, or even by another rook. And in case the queen was last in the arrangement, on least advanced rank going behind both rooks, that would on many occasions be tantamount to the inability of effective penetration, as the rooks are a bit clumsy in this specific order. Frequently, for a successful outcome of the assault, you need the queen to switch from the open file to alternative advanced squares and back, and that would not be feasible with the queen so miserably placed on a back rank.

Frequency: infrequent

Continuous rook control

Definition: 2 rooks on the 1st rank next to each other

the white rooks on f1 and g1 represent continuous rook control upon the f and g files

Value: bonus, 15cps, just for the mg

Additional information: the bonus is due for the fact that such rooks would wield a significant direct and x-ray control upon a series of continuous squares along both adjacent files where they are situated. Continuity in control/attack means, that there will be no loose ends, no weak points in the attack/pressure along those files.
For example, on the diagram, white has a devastating position after f2-f4, and one of the reasons for this is the excellent placement of both white rooks on adjacent files. In this way, different pushes, like f4-f5, g3-g4-g5 are easily possible, with black threatened by opening the king side all the time, enemy pieces will have hard time finding postings along the continuous files, and the attack overall will be much more compelling, with the rooks supporting possible activity of other own pieces focusing on the king side and the above-mentioned 2 files all the time.

Above-posted diagram represents a continuous rook control upon 2 adjacent, currently closed, files, but of course, the rooks will only feel quite happy on any other possible combination of file placement, for example on 2 open files, one open and one semi-open file, or one open and one closed file.

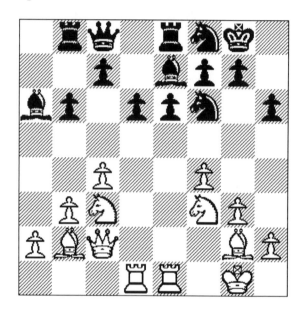

mainly thanks to both white rooks on the semi-open d and e files, and the continuous rook control in the center, white exercises a significant pressure, so much so, that it is better even without a pawn

Frequency: frequent

Rook on the same file as enemy queen

Definition: rook placed on the same file as enemy queen, no matter if the file is closed, open, otherwise, or the number of own and enemy objects, pawns and pieces, between the rook and queen

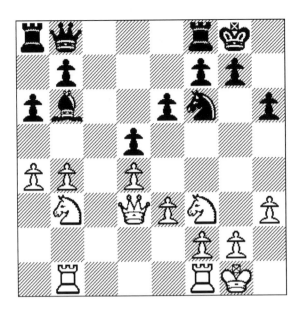

the white rook on b1 is placed on the same file as the black queen on b8, and this bodes nothing well for the queen, as well as the overall game development

Value: bonus, 15cps, just for the mg

Additional information: the bonus is due for 2 main reasons:
- this will help the rook side with gaining positional advantages due to inherent tactical considerations because of the queen-rook opposition
- on occasions, the queen might also fall prey to elaborate tactics, because of the very same opposition motif

For example, on the diagrammed position, white can advantageously open the position on the queen side, after a5, Nc5 and b5, unleashing the b1 white rook. In case the black queen lingers a bit longer on the b file, it might very well also suffer.
Please note, that the opposition is effective, even though there are 4 own and enemy objects between the queen and rook, 2 pawns and 2 minor pieces.

Frequency: frequent

Queen and bishop battery

Definition: bishop attacking own queen

Value: bonus, 18cps in the mg, 7cps in the eg

Additional information: this is a very welcome constellation, indeed. The very-well deserved bonus is due because:
- both pieces simultaneously defend each other
- the configuration ensures thorough control over the diagonal where both pieces are placed. Any enemy piece or pawn will have hard time landing there. This is especially vital in case the battery occupies some important diagonal of bigger square length, emphatically more so if this is one of the 2 longest board diagonals, a1-h8 or h1-a8. Apart from not allowing enemy pieces to land there, the tandem also represents an important form of square control, on occasion targeting the enemy king shelter, too.
- in the very specific case of queen attacking a square of the enemy king shelter, also attacked by the enemy king, and the bishop x-ray-attacking it, this turns into a major attacking formation, threatening quite unpleasant check, and sometimes even mate, with great efficiency attached to it

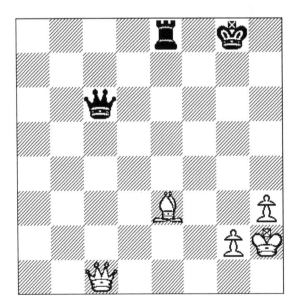

queen and bishop defend each other with little effort. Qc6-c1 is answered by Be3-c1, while Re8-e3, in a real-life situation, could be answered by Qc1-e3, no need to lose tempos on ensuring pieces are supported.

the black queen + bishop battery along the a8-h1 diagonal is extremely powerful. The enemy king shelter is taken aim at, but, apart from that, and most importantly, no white piece can even think of touching that diagonal. Ne4 would lose a pawn, Nf3 is impossible, Bg2 is impossible too. If only a single black piece occupied the long diagonal instead, all of the above-mentioned moves would not lose material. Thus, the prevalence of control upon a specific diagonal is what severely limits opponent choices of piece placements, yielding quite a nice positional plus.

This feature is very similar to a queen + rook battery on an open file.

even though both white attacking pieces are very distantly placed from the enemy king shelter, they do represent a tremendous attacking asset. Qd3-h7 check, and a possible mate, depending on real-life circumstances, is a mighty threat, and the check is feasible, because the batteried white bishop will support on an x-ray the checking queen.

Thus, the tandem guarantees big danger to the enemy king, despite its remoteness. This will allow great efficiency in combining functions and enhanced tactical relevance in the form of forking enemy pieces and the king shelter.

Overall, the term is extremely useful and multi-functional.

Frequency: frequent

Minor outpost stopping enemy rook on an open file

Definition: minor outpost on its 4th, 5th or 6th rank, supported by a pawn, with an enemy rook on the same open file on more advanced square(from the point of view of the minor) attacking it

256

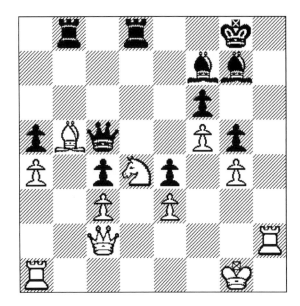

the outposted white bishop on c6, supported by the friendly b5 pawn, stops the enemy rook on the open c file

Value: bonus, 20cps in the mg, 10cps in the eg

Additional information: the bonus is given for the obvious ability of such an outposted minor to prevent enemy rook penetration deep into the own camp along the open file.

On the diagrammed position, the most the black rook can do on the open c file is budge to c7, in case the white bishop was not there, it could have penetrated on c3, c2 or c1.

Of course, the minor is able to do this, because it is defended and strong.

this is a big plus in the mg. While both black rooks on their respective b and d open files are stopped from penetrating by the white outposted minors on b5 and d4, strongly supported by pawns, the white rook on the open h file is very active and pretty much unchallenged, with another white rook and the queen able to soon join it.

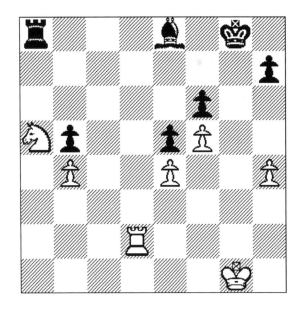

in the eg, the bonus is also due, but less important, as with lower number of pieces in the eg, there are usually sufficient alternative penetration thoroughfares

Frequency: frequent

Minor piece attacking a square on the 8th rank on an open file, simultaneously attacked by an enemy rook

Definition: minor piece, knight or bishop, attacking a square on the 8th rank, that is empty, part of an open file, and simultaneously attacked by an enemy rook on the same 8th rank(its relative 1st rank)

Value: nice bonus, 15cps, just for the mg

Additional information: the bonus is dispensed for the obvious reason, that the minor piece will cut access of the enemy rook to the open file.

This is important, as the penalised side will not be able to quickly take the open file, a significant positional asset, which will allow the opponent to make use of that fact and mobilise one or 2 heavy pieces there. At the very least, this gains some tempos to start developing a more serious initiative.

The bonus is mg-only, as in the eg space advantage, closely related to the term, is far less important, and besides, in the eg there are usually more thoroughfares rooks can utilise to gain freedom.

the white outposted knight cuts the access to the c8 square on the open c file of the black rook on b8.

On the other hand, both white rooks can immediately and without hindrance occupy the open file via the c1 square.

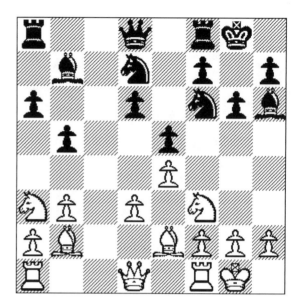

this time, although not outposted and from afar, the black bishop on h6 does the very same with the c1 square, currently inaccessible for both white rooks.

White should try to get rid of that unpleasant condition, by playing Bb2-c1, or, alternatively, interposing a piece along the bishop ray of action, possible after Na3-c2-e3, for example.

Frequency: infrequent

Minor piece attacking a square on the 1st or 2nd ranks on an open file, simultaneously attacked by an enemy rook

Definition: minor piece, knight or bishop, attacking a square on the 1st or 2nd ranks on an open file, simultaneously attacked by an enemy rook on that very same file

Value: small bonus, 8cps, just for the mg

Additional information: the bonus is given for the obvious fact, that such minor, by defending that square, will prevent penetration of the enemy rook on its relative 7th or 8th rank.

The bonus is just mg, as in the eg, with the significantly smaller number of pieces, space advantage loses in importance, and with it, possible penetration.

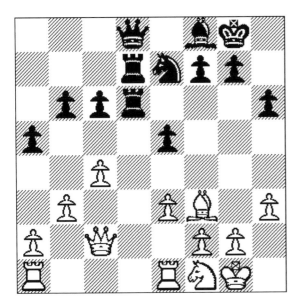

the white knight on f1 prevents possible penetration of the black rook on d6 on d2, a square on the 7th rank for the black rook, the white bishop on f3 does the very same with the d1 square.

Apart from that, the white bishop might help in wresting control of the d line out of black's hands.

Frequency: frequent

Rook supporting a friendly pawn from behind

Definition: rook attacking an own pawn on the same file, with the pawn placed on rank 5 and above

the rook on a1 supports the a6 passer from behind

Value: bonus, 7cps in the mg, 10cps in the eg

Additional information: the bonus is given for 3 main reasons:
- the rook defends the pawn
- the rook will support its advance forward, if the pawn is free
- in all cases, as the pawn will be very much advanced, rank 5 and higher, the rook itself is guaranteed to enjoy good mobility along the file

The condition the pawn should be placed on higher ranks is relevant, because otherwise the rook would not enjoy sufficient mobility and the pawn could easily be blocked close to home, making it more vulnerable than an asset.

Of course, passed pawns will gain in force, when supported in this way, as their advance is even more important, but the supporting rook could defend as well any other pawn.

259

rook supporting the c5 white pawn from behind. This might help with levering on c6 and opening lines for attack.

Frequency: frequent

Preventing enemy minor penetration

Definition: pawn on the 3rd rank, attacking an empty square, also attacked by an enemy minor piece

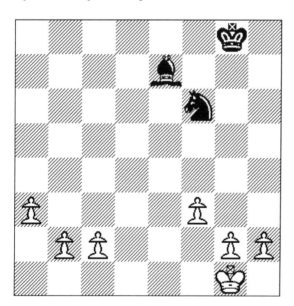

a3 is such a pawn. It attacks the b4 square on the 4th rank, that is free, and simultaneously attacked by the enemy bishop on e7.

f3 is another such pawn. It attacks the e4 and g4 squares, that are both free and simultaneously attacked by the black knight on f6.

Value: small bonus, 5cps, just for the mg

Additional information: the bonus is given for the obvious function of such a pawn of cutting access of enemy minor pieces to the 4th rank, where they already penetrate into the opponent half of the board, becoming quite dangerous.

One might think this is a stupid rule, but, in actual fact, it is difficult to overestimate its importance. The rule is so frequent, and penetration of enemy minor pieces on the 5th rank in the mg is so counter-productive, that such configurations should be created whenever possible. This could completely change whole systems of play.

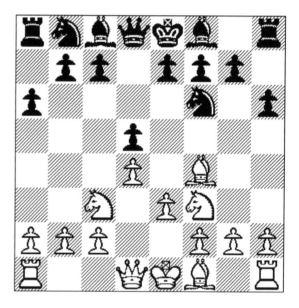

white has substantial development advantage, but, as a matter of fact, only black could be better. Reason? The already developed white minor pieces have no penetration points, so the development lead is pretty much nullified. The h6 pawn controls the g5 square, where neither the bishop on f4, nor the knight on f3 can land. The a6 pawn controls the b5 square, where neither the knight on c3 can land, nor the bishop on f1 deliver tempo-gaining check.

260

On the other hand, black already threatens with a very nasty pin, after Bg4. That is why h2-h3 for white could have been extremely useful.

Such small details sometimes change the whole game!

Frequency: very frequent

Stopping bishops on long diagonals

Definition: bishop on a long diagonal, with 2 enemy pawns on the same diagonal, with one of them defending the other.
Specifically, with white bishop on the h1-a8 long diagonal, black pawns would be found on the e4 and d5, d5 and c6, or c6 and b7 squares; with white bishop on the a1-h8 diagonal, black pawns would take the d4 and e5, e5 and f6, or f6 and g7 squares.

Value: -12cps, only for the mg

Additional information: the penalty is due, simply because this is the best enemy pawn configuration at trying to severely restrict the activity of the bishop along the diagonal. With pawns placed like that, the otherwise extremely efficient bishop x-ray attacks upon enemy objects on the diagonal are almost completely nullified. The long-range bishop power faces the wall of the enemy pawn construction and mostly stops there.

there is certainly big distinction between the power of the white g2 bishop and that of the white b2 bishop. The white g2 bishop develops a tremendous activity along the h1-a8 diagonal, with almost all possible x-ray attacks completely tactically relevant, while his queenside counterpart is fully reined in by the mighty wall of the e5-f6-g7 black pawns, facing it.

The term would be relevant for both kingside and queenside fianchettos.

Theoretically, the feature no doubt deserves great attention, as a very wide range of openings could be treated like that. It is not rare that even top humans will on occasion underestimate its relevance, while, even the top programs, are mostly completely unaware of it.

The relevant construction should be chosen very early in the game, otherwise it might already be too late.

Frequency: frequent

Raking bishops

Definition: pair of bishops on adjacent squares on the same file or rank, provided one of them is on a long diagonal, or a diagonal at least 7 squares long

Bg2 and Bf2 are raking bishops. They are on the same rank next to each other, and one of them is on a long diagonal, Bg2.

Black Be7 and Bd7, on the other hand, although on adjacent squares on the same rank, are not raking bishops, as none of them is on a diagonal at least 7 squares long.

Value: bonus, 10cps in the mg, 5cps in the eg

Additional information: the bonus is given for the continuous control of squares along both diagonals of bigger length, where the bishops are placed.

Continuous control of squares means enemy objects, whether pieces or pawns, will have hard time landing in the whole portion of the board, under attack by the bishops.

As easily seen on the diagrammed position, the pair of white bishops control the adjacent e4,d4,d5 and c5 squares, where enemy pieces will have difficulty appearing.

Such bishops are especially dangerous when attacking the enemy king shelter.

the bishops on b2 and c2 are a tremendous asset

Frequency: infrequent

King restricted on an edge line

Definition: king on edge a or h file, with enemy rook on adjacent file, or king on edge 1st or 8th rank, with enemy rook on adjacent rank, with the rook attacking all 3 squares the king also attacks(just 2, if the king is in a corner), that are empty

the white king is on the edge 1st rank. The black rook attacks all 3 squares the king also attacks, f2,g2 and h2, that are all empty.

Value: penalty, -15cps, both in the mg and eg, for the king

Additional information: the penalty is given for the obvious restricted state of the king.
It is due for the following reasons:
- in the mg, the restricted state might lead to mating situations, involving 2 enemy heavy pieces
- in the eg, such a king will be very much inactive, unable to join in the fight, at least for the time the restriction is perpetuated

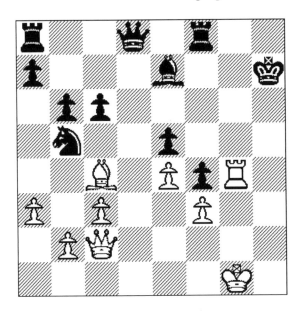

although a rook and a piece down, with its turn to move, white quickly mates the black king, precisely because of its restricted condition on the edge h file

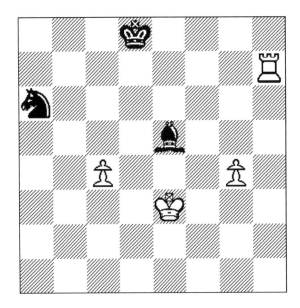

white has excellent winning chances, precisely because of the extremely inactive black king, due to its restriction on the edge 8th rank.
If the black king was more active, somewhere in the center, the game could certainly have ended with a draw.

Frequency: frequent

Pawn support for rook on an open file

Definition: rook on an open file, attacking a square, simultaneously attacked by an own pawn, and not under attack by an enemy pawn

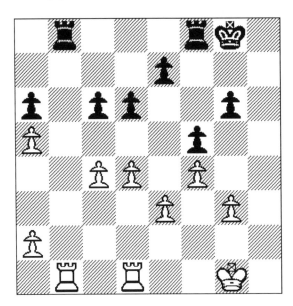

263

Rb1 is such a rook. It is on the open b file, and attacks the b6 and b3 squares, simultaneously attacked by the own pawns on a5 and a2 respectively. Its black counterpart on b8, on the other hand, is not such a rook, as the only square black pawns attack on the open file, b5, is under attack by the white pawn on c4.

Value: small bonus, 5cps in the mg, 2cps in the eg

Additional information: the bonus is due for the simple reason that such condition is very helpful in fighting for the open file. The squares simultaneously attacked by the rook and the own pawn are frequently excellent outpost squares, the rook can use them to penetrate into the enemy camp or, alternatively, to straighten the friendly pawn structure.

Frequency: frequent

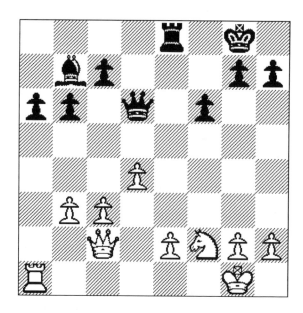

because of the white queen controlling the e4 square, the white e pawn can go there. Otherwise, this would have been impossible.

Frequency: frequent

X-ray square control

X-ray square control will refer to diagonal sliding pieces x-ray-attacking different board squares, with an own pawn between the attacker and the attacked square.

Bishop x-ray-attacking the center

Definition: bishop x-ray-attacking one of the 4 central-most board squares, e4,d4,e5 or d5, with an own pawn between the bishop and the attacked square

Value: bonus, 8cps for the mg, 4cps for the eg

Additional information: the bonus is due, as this helps in controlling the center.

Queen controlling the center

Definition: queen attacking one of the 4 central-most board squares, e4,d4,e5 or d5

Value: minuscule bonus, 3cps, just for the mg

Additional information: such condition is useful in 2 ways:
- the queen can quickly transfer to a center square, and queens feel well on central squares, unless immediately threatened
- the queen can support on such square another own piece taking central position, and especially pawn

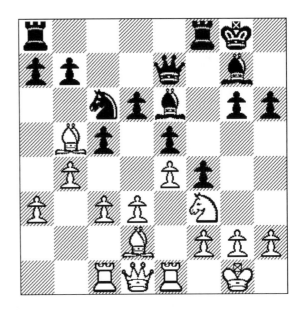

the bishop on c2, x-ray-attacking the e4 square, with the own d3 pawn between the bishop and the attacked square, stops the black e5 pawn from further advancing to e4

This feature can have a big imprint on a range of opening systems.

White can not push the freeing central d3-d4 break, because the black bishop on g7, x-ray-controlling the d4 square, provides one more valuable, as well as the decisive attack upon this square. In case the black bishop did not control that point, white would have played the mentioned break to great effect.

Sometimes, such small details decide the outcome of the fight.

Frequency: frequent

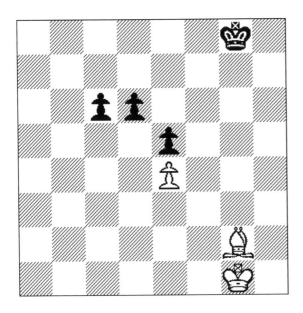

controlling similar squares on the 5th rank is even more important, as this prevents enemy pawns from even reaching the middle of the board, making them backward.

As such pawns would be central, the influence upon the whole game, especially in the mg, will be significant.

Queen x-ray-attacking the center

Definition: queen x-ray-attacking one of the 4 central-most board squares, e4,d4,e5 or d5, with an own pawn between the queen and the attacked square

Value: small bonus, 3cps, just for the mg

Additional information: the bonus is given for the further boost the queen provides in this way to central control.

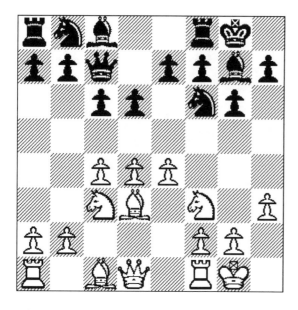

the black queen on c7 x-ray-attacking the vital central e5 square allows black to immediately push e7-e5, with the black pawn taking advantageous central position. In case the queen had not been doing that, the e7-e5 thrust might have been tactically impossible, and in some cases white might have pushed e4-e5 instead.

Frequency: frequent

Bishop x-ray-attacking the square in front of enemy backward pawn

Definition: bishop x-ray-attacking the square in front of enemy backward pawn, with the own backwardmaker between the bishop and the attacked square

Value: bonus, 6cps, both for the mg and eg

Additional information: the bonus is due for the obvious restricting influence upon the enemy backward pawn.
In a way, this makes it even more backward, sometimes even permanently backward, depending on circumstances.

the bishop on e3 x-ray-controlling the b6 square in front of the black b7 backward pawn, with the own c5 backwardmaker pawn on the ray between the bishop and the b6 square, highlights the backwardness of the b7 pawn.

In case the bishop was not attacking the b6 square on an x-ray, with the support of the black knight on d7, black might have gotten rid of the backward pawn after the b7-b6 push.

with opposite colour bishops, such feature might make the enemy pawn permanently backward, as b7 is above, because friendly pieces capable of supporting a freeing push might be lacking

266

Frequency: frequent

Bishop x-ray-attacking the square in front of enemy shelter backward pawn

Definition: bishop x-ray-attacking the square in front of enemy backward pawn, part of the king shelter, on its 2nd rank, with the own backwardmaker on the ray between the bishop and the attacked square

Value: bonus, 12cps, just for the mg

Additional information: the bonus is very well due, as this not only highlights the weakness of the backward pawn, but, as the pawn will constitute part of the enemy shelter, this has immediate consequences upon the king safety, rendering the shelter as a whole more inflexible.

the bishop on b2, x-ray-controlling the f6 square in front of the black f7 shelter pawn, that is backward on its 2nd rank, with the own e5 backwardmaker on the ray between the bishop and the attacked square, makes the black shelter even more inflexible.

In order to defend, black will have sometimes to push f7-f6/f7-f5, and, after the capture of the backward pawn, this will lead to the breakdown of the shelter.

Staying with a backward shelter pawn with this condition is also not an option, as this will give the opponent sufficient time to regroup pieces and start a powerful attack.

Frequency: infrequent

Scaling down of different positions and endings

Scaling down of too closed positions

In case all 8 files are closed with pairs of blocked pawns or pairs of symmetrical twice backward pawns, the positional score(the estimate of all positional advantages) should be adjusted to 0.0/draw, provided that the stronger side leads by less than 200cps(so, if your top engine shows +200cps advantage for one side or lower in such a position, the actual score is of course 0.0/complete draw).

The reason for the 200cps particular value is the fact that, in order for the stronger side attempting to break through, it needs to sacrifice at least a piece for a single enemy pawn.

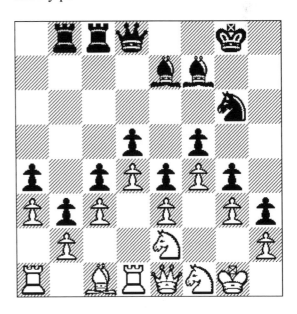

well, one might be inclined to think black has substantial/winning advantage, because of its 6 advanced pawns into the enemy half of the board, but no, this is a

simple draw(which top engines would still
fail to recognise)

sometimes, even a piece more would not
be sufficient to win the game

and one variation with a series of twice
backward pawns(still a draw)

In case not all 8, but only 7 files on the
board are closed by pairs of blocked pawns
or pairs of symmetrical twice backward
pawns, the positional score should be
adjusted to 0.0/draw, provided that its
value is less than 100cps.

still very difficult to break through

Horizontal pawn symmetry

In case all own pawns are opposed by an
enemy pawn, and positional score is lower
than 50cps, it should be adjusted by
halving it.

Horizontal symmetry of all available own
and enemy pawns is simply more drawish
than otherwise, as in such a case there are
no passers that could promote, no potential
passers to create danger, while efficient
breaks are made more difficult by the fact
that the position as a whole is easier to
close.

Reason for the particular 50cps score is an
objective estimate of drawing chances.

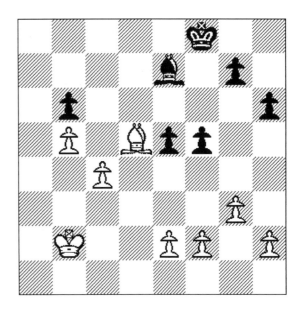

horizontal pawn symmetry is much more drawish than otherwise, of course; in case c5-c4 is played, white might avoid the break by pushing b3-b4, while after f3-f4 break attempt, black could support the e5 pawn with f7-f6, still holding onto the horizontal symmetry

well, this is an easy draw, even though white is a pawn up

Opposite colour bishops

In case one side has only one bishop, and the other side also has a single bishop, with both bishops placed on squares of different colour, the positional score should be adjusted, to one third of its value in the mg, and one half of its value in the eg, provided that the score is lower than 100cps.

The reason is obvious, and frequently easily recognisable by stronger humans, while even top engines sometimes have significant difficulties to understand why similar positions are much more drawish.

With values higher than 100cps advantage, it is difficult to hold such positions in the general case, though there are exceptions, of course.

more pieces in the eg basically change nothing: white does not have an easy time to convert at all

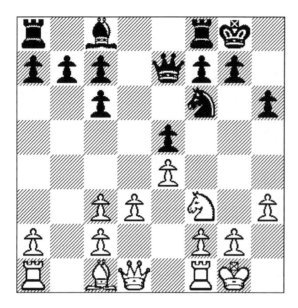

no matter one side might have a bit of an advantage, it is pretty much nullified also in the mg with the presence of lots of pieces

Pairs of bishops endgame

Definition: both sides having one pair of bishops each in the endgame

Value: score could be scaled down by some 20% or so, if lower than 100cps, as such endgames are very drawish

Additional information: the scaling-down of the endgame is necessary, as similar endgames will frequently lead to draws, unless one side has a substantial advantage.

The reason is simple, although not many authors have noted it: in the 2 pairs of bishops you have in a way 2 separate pairs of opposite colour bishops, and, as we all know very well, opposite colour bishops tend to be very drawish in general.

Of course, above condition is not felt very strongly, as the pairs play in tandem, but still, it is quite real.

it is difficult to imagine one side could win, so drawish are such endgames in a pure setting

with more pieces added, such endgames are still very equal

Frequency: infrequent

General endgame scaling

If total non-pawn material(the cumulative value of all own plus all enemy non-pawn pieces) on the board is less than 1/4 of the initial non-pawn material(the material at the start of the game), the positional score

270

should be halved, provided that it is lower than 80cps.

Well, that should see drawish positions with very few pieces, and also some fortresses. The particular 80cps value is due to the fact that 80cps is more or less the drawing margin in the eg.

Scaling with reduced number of pawns in the eg

If one side has a single pawn, and the other side has no pawns at all, the positional score should be adjusted to 7/10 of its value, provided that it is lower than 150cps.

Obviously, such endings are very drawish in view of the almost complete lack of resources(with a single pawn, non-pawn pieces will be few too), so one might scale them down boldly.

well, it is difficult for black to win that(engines would still show significant black advantage)

well, this is an eye-scratching draw

pawns on both wings change nothing; still pretty much a draw

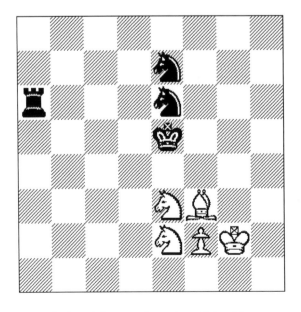

and also this one, in spite of the bigger number of non-pawn pieces

271

If one side has 2 pawns, and the other side one pawn, and there are no passers, or, if one side has 3 pawns, and the other side has 2 pawns, and there are no passers, the positional score should be adjusted to half of its value, provided that it is lower than 100cps.

Reason is obvious: too few material and very difficult or impossible to create passers. Quite probably, the ratio of 3 to 2 pawns will later get to a 2:1 ratio, and then to a single pawn vs no pawns ratio, so drawing chances will always be big.

very easy draw; sometimes, engines, even top ones, would still think the stronger side has good winning chances

straightforward draw too, though some top engines might still think black is winning in terms of positional score

Scaling of rook endgames

Definition: single rook endgame, each side having only one rook, if there are no passers, and the positional score is less than 80cps

Value: the assessment of the position, the positional score, should be scaled down by half

Additional information: single rook endgames, with no passed pawns, and relatively small score, tend to generally be very drawish.

So, it would be nice to actually consider them as such, instead of preferring them in the place of other, objectively much better lines.

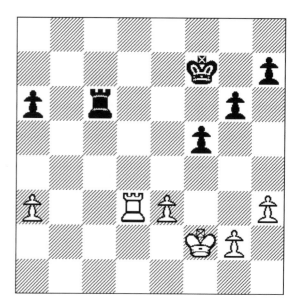

black does not have a way of winning this, in spite of its small positional advantage

nor white this one

this one is unwinnable by the stronger side, too

Frequency: very frequent

Rook vs queen fortress in the endgame

Definition: one side having just one queen, and at most a single pawn, with the other having just one rook, and at least one pawn, if the queen side has no passers, the rook is protected by a pawn on the g or b files on its 2nd rank, the king of the rook side is adjacent to that pawn, the pawn of the queen side is on files h,f,a or c, and the

king of the queen side is not past its 5th rank

the diagram reflects the required conditions. There are no passers for the queen side, the queen side pawn is an h one, the rook is defended by a pawn on the g file on its 2nd rank, adjacent to the king, and the black king has not crossed the 5th rank.

Value: under such circumstances, the score is automatically adjusted to 0cps advantage, draw by fortress

Additional information: well, those are simply theoretically drawn endings.

As easily seen on the diagrammed position, the stronger side can not win, as nothing could be done to break the white positional fortress. The black pawn can not pass beyond its 5th rank, as on h3 it will be captured by the rook, with the support of the g2 pawn, the black king can not penetrate beyond its 5th rank, for the very same reason, the white rook is controlling the entire third row, and it is supported, the white king is in a corner, sheltered by the pawn and rook, while the black queen can not mate the king alone without the help of the friendly king.

So, white just shuffles around with the rook and king, until draw is achieved.

sometimes, more pawns for the stronger side will also lead to draw, but the conditions are too plentiful to enumerate them all. Fortress recognition is a difficult thing, on which thousands pages could be written, so here we will just limit ourselves to this one.

Frequency: infrequent

Alphabetical index of terms

blocked chain

blocked doubled pawn

blocked file

blocked pawn

blocked pawn structure

blocked position

blocked storming pawn

blocker

blocking outpost

blocking pawn

break

C

caged piece

caging

candidate passer

castling

castling rights

center control

centipawn

central attack

central backwardmaker

central bind

central chain

central chain blockade

centralisation

central isolated pawns

central wedge

chain

chain backward pawn

chain pawn see defended pawn

check

clamp

closed center

closed file

closedness

closed position

closed side

closed structure

closure

colour deficiency

compact pawn structure

complementarity

connected passed pawn

connected passer

connected pawn

connecting pawn

continuous control

counter-break

counterplay

cramped position

cramping

D

defended aligned pawn

defended outer central lever

defended pawn

defending aligned pawn

direct attack

distant backward pawn

distant neighbour

double attack

double base pawn see double root pawn

double check

doubled isolated pawn

doubled pawn

doubled rooks

doubled shelter pawn

double pawn push

double root pawn

drawing margin

duo pawn see aligned pawn

durability

E

edge file

edge line

edge storming pawn

horizontal symmetry

I

imbalance

immobile pawn

immobile piece

immobile shelter pawn

immobilisation

immobility

inchoative pointed chain

inflexibility

inflexible pawn

inflexible shelter

intermediary object

interposition

isolated opposed pawn

isolated pawn

isolated shelter pawn

isolated unopposed pawn

J

K

king attack

king cover

king mobility

king pin

king position

king psqt

king safety

king shelter

king side

kingside attack

kingside castling

kingside fianchetto

kingside presence of pieces

king walk

king wing

knight attack threat

knight mobility

knight outpost

knight psqt

kicking

L

lever

levering

lever pawn

lever push

lone queen

long chain

long chain pawn

long diagonal

low mobility

M

mainstay

manoeuvering

mate

material

material imbalance

medium pawn(see long chain pawn)

minor

minor outpost

minor piece

minor piece shelter

minor piece shelter defence

mobile square

mobility

N

non-pawn material

no-pawn-defended bishop outpost

no-pawn-defended knight outpost

no-pawn-defended outpost

no pawn shelter

O

opener

open file

open position

opposed pawn

opposing pawn

opposite castling

opposite colour bishops

outer central lever

outpost

outposted minor

outposted rook

outpost square

overextended pawn(see vertically isolated pawn)

own camp

P

pair of bishops

pair of blocked pawns

pair of knights

pair of rooks

pairs of bishops

passed pawn

passer

passer-maker

pawn advance

pawn break

pawn chain

pawn cover

pawn defence

pawn mobility

pawn psqt

pawn push

pawn shelter

pawn span

pawn storm

pawns on both wings

pawn tension

pawn thrust

penetration

penetration point

permanently backward pawn

permanently trapped piece

permanent outpost

piece activity

piece attack

piece coordination

piece defence

piece value

pin

pinned piece

pinner

pointed chain

positional scaling-down

potential check

potential discovered check

rollercoaster

rook mobility

rook outpost

rook psqt

root pawn

royal battery

S

sac

sacrifice

safe check

safe pawn push threat

same colour pawns

self-trapped bishop

semibackward pawn

semi-backward shelter pawn

semi-central file

semi-central pawn

semi-closed file

semi-open file

semi-outpost

sentinel pawn

shelter attack

shelter pawn

shelter weak spot

side to move

simultaneous attack

single-pawn-defended bishop outpost

single-pawn-defended knight outpost

single-pawn-defended outpost

skewer

slider

sliding piece

space advantage

spearhead

spearhead connected passer

square control

squeeze

squeezed pawn

standard backward pawn

stormer

storming pawn

strong pawn

symmetrical aligned pawn

symmetrical doubled pawn

symmetrical twice backward pawn

T

tactical lever

tactical lever threat

tactical pawn threat

tempo

threat

trappable piece

trapped minor

trapped piece

trapped rook

tripled pawn

triplet

turn

twice aligned pawn

twice backward feature

twice backward opposed pawn

twice backward pawn

twice backward unopposed pawn

twice backward shelter pawn

twice-defended bishop outpost

twice defended knight

twice-defended knight outpost

twice-defended outpost

twice defended pawn

twice defended rook

twice defended storming pawn

U

unadvanced pawn

unattackable object

unbackwarded pawn

unblocked storming pawn

undefended minor piece

undefended pawn

undefended piece

undefended rook

undoubling

unlocking

unopposed backward-maker

unopposed lever

unopposed pawn

unretreatable outpost

unsafe check

unsafe pawn push threat

unstoppable passed pawn

untripling

useless outpost

V

vertically isolated pawn

very distant neighbour

very long chain pawn

W

weak pawn

weak spot

weak spot defence

X

x-ray attack

x-ray control

x-ray shelter attack

Y

Z

zero mobility

zugzwang

Made in the USA
Middletown, DE
28 September 2023

39669568R00161